Unquiet Tropes

In the series ASIAN AMERICAN HISTORY AND CULTURE
edited by David Palumbo-Liu, K. Scott Wong, Linda Trinh Võ,
and Cathy Schlund-Vials. Founding editor, Sucheng Chan;
editor emeritus Michael Omi.

Also in this series:

(Additional titles in this series can be found at the back of this book.)

Unquiet Tropes

Form, Race, and Asian American Literature

ELDA E. TSOU

TEMPLE UNIVERSITY PRESS
Philadelphia • Rome • Tokyo

Temple University Press
Philadelphia, Pennsylvania 19122
www.temple.edu/tempress

Copyright © 2015 by Temple University—Of The Commonwealth
System of Higher Education

Published 2015

LIBRARY OF CONGRESS CATALOGING-IN-PUBLICATION DATA

Tsou, Elda E.
　Unquiet tropes : form, race, and Asian American literature / Elda E. Tsou.
　　pages cm. — (Asian American history and culture)
　Includes bibliographical references and index.
　ISBN 978-1-4399-1124-2 (hardback : alk. paper)
　ISBN 978-1-4399-1125-9 (paperback : alk. paper)
　ISBN 978-1-4399-1126-6 (e-book)
　1. American literature—Asian American authors—History and criticism.
I. Title.
　PS153.A84T78 2015
　810.9'895—dc23

2014039774

♾ The paper used in this publication meets the requirements of the American
National Standard for Information Sciences—Permanence of Paper for Printed
Library Materials, ANSI Z39.48–1992

Printed in the United States of America

9 8 7 6 5 4 3 2 1

THE
AMERICAN
LITERATURES
INITIATIVE

A book in the American Literatures Initiative (ALI), a
collaborative publishing project of NYU Press, Fordham
University Press, Rutgers University Press, Temple University
Press, and the University of Virginia Press. The Initiative is
supported by The Andrew W. Mellon Foundation. For more
information, please visit www.americanliteratures.org.

*To my parents, whose vision, courage, and sacrifice
made it possible for their children to find better futures*

Contents

Acknowledgments

This book would not have come to be without my graduate advisors, who shaped my intellectual life and who guided and chivvied this book's former life as a dissertation. I thank Gayatri Chakravorty Spivak, who showed me by scrupulous example what reading could be and who alternately inspired and scolded me to enlarge my frame of reference beyond Asian America. I thank Gary Y. Okihiro, who mentored me tirelessly and demonstrated what it is to be a scholar and a teacher committed to nurturing the next generation of minds. I thank David L. Eng, who had unflagging faith in me from the start, who took my scholarship seriously and in doing so taught me to do so as well, and who provided indefatigable guidance at every step of the process. My special thanks go to Bob Hanning, who demonstrated how to find the literary in ethnic literature, and to Bob O'Meally, who showed me how to do it all with style.

At St. John's University, I thank Susie Pak, my coeditor, co-organizer, and go-to interlocutor for all things Asian American and beyond. I also thank the members of my department: Steve Sicari, our fearless leader, for supporting me and my work in every way possible; John Lowney, for being a tireless mentor and reader (despite being on Dystopia Blvd.); and Dohra Ahmad, for having more confidence in my project than I did and for advising me to clean house in five minutes. Most of all I thank Amy King, for showing me how to make a book, and Scott Combs, for the phantom traces.

At the University of Illinois, Urbana Champaign, I thank the wonderful people I met and learned from during my post-doctoral fellowship at the Asian American Studies Program: Martin Manalansan, for teaching me about productive tension; Kent Ono, for being my most enthusiastic cheerleader, for being a most patient reader of drafts, and for leading me to unpredictability; Susan Koshy, for her graceful mentorship and for showing me what real criticism should look like; Bob Parker, for sage advice and for challenging me to think more critically about referentiality; Fiona Ngo, for engaging the big ideas; Mimi Nguyen, for hospitality and all-around coolness. Last, but not certainly least, I thank Caroline Yang for being my library buddy, my writing companion, and the very best thing I found in Illinois.

Elsewhere in academia, I am so grateful to Colleen Lye, for being such a rigorous reader and generous interlocutor and especially for her warm and friendly guidance at the eleventh hour, no less. Special thanks go to Jo Park and Min Song, whose early overtures allowed me to refine parts of this project, and my enduring gratitude goes to Daniel Kim, for lively encouragement, for perceptive feedback, and for telling me—despite the very early hour of our panel—that he liked what I was doing with *No-No Boy*. Thanks also go to the members of my New York City writing group: Thuy Linh Tu, Jeffery Santa Ana, James Kim, and Wen Jin, who endured truly ugly versions of this manuscript with great forbearance. Manu Vimalassery, Diana Yoon, and Amy Cabrera Rasmussen have been steadfast interlocutors from grad school onward. I also thank Shannon Wolf, who has always been with me in spirit.

An earlier version of Chapter 3 was originally published by The Johns Hopkins University Press (copyright © 2011 The Johns Hopkins University Press) as Elda E. Tsou, "Catachresis:

Blu's Hanging and the Epistemology of the Given," *Journal of Asian American Studies* 14, no. 2 (2011): 283–303. An earlier version of Chapter 4 originally appeared as Elda E. Tsou, "'This Doesn't Mean What You'll Think': *Native Speaker,* Allegory, Race," *PMLA* 128, no. 3 (2013): 575–89, published by the Modern Language Association of America.

Inestimable thanks go to Janet Francendese, my wonderful editor and ringmaster, whose patience and kindness made this whole process not just bearable but also delightful.

Finally, I thank my family, who have supported me in ways big and small and in between: my mother and father, who encouraged me and prayed for me, despite worrying that being an academic would be much harder than being a doctor, and my sisters, who sent me care packages from all corners of the globe and administered swift and loving kicks in the butt when necessary.

Unquiet Tropes

Introduction: *Aiiieeeee!*
and the Phantom Trope

The award controversy over *Blu's Hanging*, a novel by Lois-Ann Yamanaka, remains one of the most significant and painful debates over the nature of literature in recent memory. In 1998 the Association for Asian American Studies, the professional organization for scholars of Asian American studies, held its annual conference in Honolulu, where it awarded and then rescinded a fiction prize to the novel. In the upheaval that followed, it appeared to some that the future of the organization itself was in jeopardy. Supporters of the award charged its detractors with censorship and denounced them for failing to grasp literary complexity. Critics of the award, on the other hand, protested the novel's portrayal of Filipinos as sexual predators, recurring figures in Yamanaka's work. In the context of Hawaii, where the novel is set, Filipino marginalization is part of a political and economic structure dominated by whites and local Japanese. Stereotypes of Filipinos as sexually deviant thus articulate, in sexualized form, the economic threat of Filipino workers during the plantation era. Given Yamanaka's background as a Hawaiian author of Japanese descent, critics of the award questioned the conspicuous absence of Native Hawaiians in her work and worried that her writing reinforces local Japanese hegemony. Even now, at a distance of some fifteen years, scholars of Asian American literature continue to ponder the award controversy and the issues it raised regarding literature, its status, and its relationship to politics. In hindsight, of course, both sides of the debate found themselves taking up all too familiar positions on either side of the traditional divide between aesthetics and politics. Recent movements in literary studies have challenged the separation of aesthetics from politics by reviving the ideological entanglements of aesthetics and renewing the sociopolitical and historical engagements of form. Returning to the question of reading Asian American literature furthers these discussions.

For political and disciplinary reasons, the scholarly approach to Asian American literature tends to bind the literary tradition quite tightly to the identity formation. Such is the prevalence of this critical tendency that Viet T. Nguyen begins his book on Asian American literature by declaring, "For better or worse, Asian American literary critics have generally approached Asian American literature as being symptomatic of ongoing historical concerns for Asian Americans—to read the literature, then, enables the critic to form political theses about the state of Asian America."[1] Nguyen is describing practices of referential reading that have been essential to constructing an Asian American literary tradition but have been less helpful in clarifying its distinctiveness as literature. The broad sweep of these reading practices tends to obscure how individual literary texts may hint at a different set of concerns or even unsettle their identity to Asian America altogether. For example, the narrative of *Blu's Hanging* seems to confirm the charges of Filipino stereotyping, but a closer look at the novel's figurative activity reveals instead a trenchant critique of those same stereotypes. Referential reading practices have yet another troubling effect. In expecting that Asian American literature is necessarily "about" Asian America—in assuming, that is, that racial signs correspond reliably to racial meanings—do we not reproduce the very racial logic that we contest elsewhere? If we cannot make room for Asian

American literature to mean other than Asian America, do we not acquiesce to the further marginalization of this literature by restricting its scope and reducing its complexity?

The past decade has witnessed a resurgence of scholarly interest in form and aesthetics, which Marjorie Levinson has termed a "new formalism." What differentiates this formalism from previous versions is its commitment to yoking the study of form to history and politics. As Levinson sees it, the new formalism is too heterogeneous to be considered a theory, but two strands may be discerned: an "activist" version, reintroducing questions of form to historical reading, and a "normative" version, returning to Kant to emphasize the disinterested and pleasurable aspects of form (the latter also considered sociopolitical as it involves "norm-setting").[2] Levinson's account does not seek to delineate aesthetic inquiry from varieties of formalism, but for different reasons these approaches and their various commitments sit uneasily with the Asian American texts under consideration here. The new formalism engages predominantly with the early modern and Romantic periods, and such scholarship tends to lack the formidable resources for theorizing race and racial formation that have defined Asian American studies and its sister disciplines. From a slightly different direction, sundry efforts have been made to reclaim the aesthetic, but getting away from its traditional investment in universal categories of value, taste, judgment, truth, and beauty remains difficult. Moreover its reliance on the "disinterested" subject, a vestige of its Enlightenment heritage, cannot help us elucidate the persistent problem of race in Asian American literature. In discussing the "dual quests for freedom and for beauty" in African American literature, Cheryl Wall explains that the pursuit of form in ethnic literatures must be distinguished from the return to the aesthetic in the study of canonical literature. Referring to these mainstream debates, she argues, "Their situation is an inversion of that facing critics of African American literature. From its beginnings in the United States, black writing has been defined as having *only* an ideological importance."[3] Wall's caution is timely, but if African American literature, by her reckoning, has been a forerunner in articulating the study of race with aesthetic or formalist inquiry, such is not the case with Asian American literary criticism, which is a field of more recent vintage.

It is undeniable that a second wave of Asian American literary criticism is making tremendous strides in this direction, but what requires more theorizing is the manner in which some of these studies must perforce resurrect the race-identified author in their investigations of literary behavior. Introducing a recent and influential anthology on Asian American form, Xiaojing Zhou asks us to pay attention to "the ways in which Asian American authors have resisted, subverted, and reshaped hegemonic European American literary genres, as well as the ways in which such interventions demonstrate a much more dynamic and complex relationship between Asian American and traditional European American literature."[4] To be sure, the emphasis on the race-identified author is a means of getting at the formal agency of the literature. Zhou explains, for example, that "a particular literary form . . . is a mode of subject positioning, a means of articulating the writer's resistance or affiliations within the field of literature and in the social spaces."[5] Inadvertently, however, the assertion of formal agency seems to go hand in hand with restoring the race-identified author as the source of literary behavior. There are two important reasons this book takes figurative activity rather than aesthetics or form as its primary point of departure. The first is that these canonical texts upset the typical route to Asian America because they tend to feature authors who insist on their absence from the Asian American text, as Kingston does with *China Men*, or have little relationship to Asian America in the first place—like Yamanaka, who identifies principally as a local Hawaiian author. The second and more compelling reason for the focus on figurative activity is that several of these texts do not conform to the fundamental criterion of the aesthetic because they are far from beautiful. How, for instance, are we to approach a text like John Okada's *No-No Boy* or the infamous preface to the landmark *Aiiieeeee!*

An Anthology of Asian American Writers? Critics have had trouble getting around the "crude realism" of the former and the "vociferousness of the polemic" of the latter.[6] Since these texts are at once aesthetically impoverished and yet intensely rhetorical, since they feature authors who are dead or missing, neither aesthetics nor formalism as presently configured can help us clarify the peculiarly fraught nature of these Asian American texts.[7] It is thus to the classical rhetorical tropes that we must turn to understand the unquiet nature of this literature.

Unquiet Tropes argues for reconceptualizing Asian American literature as a set of rhetorical tropes taking shape around highly specific historical problematics. My five case studies are canonical texts, each of which has been instrumental in representing Asian America: *Aiiieeeee!*, *No-No Boy*, *China Men*, *Blu's Hanging*, and *Native Speaker*. Yet, at the same time, these texts call on ancient rhetorical tropes—antanaclasis, rhetorical question, apophasis, catachresis, and allegory—to work out their concerns with race. In the process they renew and redefine the purview of this older rhetorical language. I call these tropes unquiet for several reasons. These are tropes that call attention to themselves *as* tropes, as turns or deviations from proper meaning or normative usage. They therefore exceed notions of language as referential by flaunting their various affinities for deceit, for error, and for other-speaking. Their rhetorical nature, however, is equally marked by a proclivity for referentiality: antanaclasis, the repetition of a word in a different sense, depends on a clear and obvious reference to the word it seeks to repeat; apophasis, the figure of negation, makes reference to something by telling us what it is not. These tropes are thus defined by a formal tension between their rhetorical inclination toward deviation and their simultaneous insistence on some form of referentiality. Finally these tropes are unquiet because they are not, in the most basic sense, Asian American. Not only are we dealing with linguistic patterns that come from elsewhere, but the historical periods in which the study of rhetoric flourished are thoroughly alien to the concerns of Asian America. That these recognizably rhetorical figures nevertheless appear in Asian American literature indicates a vast and common linguistic heritage, one that far exceeds the parameters of both Asian America and the historical cultures of rhetoric. Far from being timeless or transcendental, though, these tropes figure a specific set of problematics firmly rooted in Asian American history, and because these precipitating historical conditions are *figured*—transformed into figurative language—they are, in the end, indirect and unverifiable.

In alluding to the literariness of these texts, I fall back on an old-fashioned definition of the literary: the surplus of meaning and reference generated by language when it exceeds or deviates from proper usage. Gayatri Chakravorty Spivak sums up this traditional notion when she calls literature "an indefinite structure of possibilities" and directs our attention to the "singular unverifiability of the literary." Against the rational demand of the global marketplace for the other to be verifiable, to be comprehensible to the dominant, she exhorts us to "let literature teach us that there are no certainties, that the process is open, and that it may be altogether salutary that it is so." For Spivak—and Shelley and Sidney, upon whose defense of poetry she draws—literature is that most apt of training grounds for the imagination, the "great inbuilt instrument of othering" that enables the ethical relationship to the other without guarantees.[8] When we close down the possibility for Asian American literature to be anything more than the representation of racial identity, we cannot learn what it can teach us about figuration, about the literary potential for aberration and for multiple or unexpected trajectories. In this book I use *literary* in two senses: in a general fashion, to indicate the qualities of unverifiability associated with the literary, and in a more restricted sense, to designate the formal specificity of literature. I use *figurative* to refer to the special effects—opacity, excess, and errancy—created by language in the context of the literary text; these may include but are not limited to devices, rhetorical figures, patterning, and sequence.

This heightened sensitivity to language has gone by many names, among them, poetics, form, aesthetics, rhetoric, and close reading. In our time the attention to figurative language is typically associated with literary training, but the rhetoricity of language is by no means restricted to literature, which is itself a recent invention. Indeed, rhetoricity is intrinsic to language itself. Paul de Man, for instance, has demonstrated in reading after meticulous reading that philosophical and political treatises are as thoroughly immersed in rhetorical behavior as texts openly acknowledged as literary. While de Man does not hesitate to associate the "rhetorical, figural potentiality of language with literature itself," he does offer a more general definition of the rhetorical when he suggests that "rhetoric radically suspends logic and opens up vertiginous possibilities of referential aberration."[9] With regard to Asian American literature, a racialized literary tradition that continues to exert profound material force on race and racialization, awareness of "referential aberration" becomes all the more important because it invites us to envision alternative trajectories for the racialized sign, trajectories that might bend or swerve, tangle or overlap, or even veer entirely off course. And though I will be arguing for the literariness of Asian American literature, sensitivity to referential aberration does not in any way respect a literary pedigree as scholars of race, gender, and sexuality have long demonstrated similar sensibilities. Robyn Wiegman, for example, begins her genealogy of race and modern vision by asking us to consider race as a set of "corporeal signs that *do not* appear." She would have us understand how the biological definition of race in the nineteenth century gives rise to a curious paradox: "This sphere produced not simply the constancy of race as an unchanging, biological feature, but an inherent and incontrovertible difference of which skin was only the most visible indication."[10] Skin color, then, is the "visible indication" of an interiority that cannot be seen. In another example of referential incongruity, Judith Butler asks us to conceive of gender as corporeal discontinuity: "The construction of coherence conceals the gender discontinuities that run rampant within heterosexual, bisexual, and gay and lesbian contexts in which gender does not necessarily follow from sex, and desire, or sexuality generally, does not seem to follow from gender—indeed, where none of these dimensions of significant corporeality express or reflect one another."[11] In other words, though they may not present themselves as such, theories of race, gender, and sexuality—poststructuralist or not—have suggested a "rhetoricity" to the body-as-sign, and it is this understanding that grants to the sign a potential for new meanings. It is indeed a grim future for Asian American literature if the only path that we can imagine for the sign is an inevitably racialized one, a trajectory that always hits its mark, whose arc is never to be refracted into the "heterogeneity, hybridity, or multiplicity" with which Lisa Lowe has characterized Asian America.

Metaphor for Asian America

It is now a critical commonplace to rehearse the failures of the term *Asian American*. Coined by activists in the 1960s, the term replaced the pejorative *Oriental* to designate a platform for political consciousness and mobilization by calling on the shared history of racialization. Like all identities "Asian American" is a catachresis, a misuse of language, and so, despite persistent attempts to revise, expand, or reformulate it, Asian American scholars have conceded that it is a term we cannot do without.[12] Kandice Chuh thus calls on us to reconceptualize Asian American identity as "a term *in difference from itself*," as "itself deconstruction," and to understand Asian American studies as a "subjectless discourse."[13] Chuh's alignment of Asian American subjectivity with deconstruction is a generative one, but what I find most compelling is an easily overlooked association she makes between Asian America and the rhetorical tradition. The term *Asian American*, she argues, should not be understood as transparent, as simply denoting knowledge about Asian America. Instead, approaching it in Saussurean terms, Chuh wants us to grasp the relationship between the term and what it designates as arbitrary, as consolidated by social systems and relations of power. In her words, the term "*transfers* the properties of the racialized and gendered nation onto bodies—of people, of literatures, of fields of study."[14] As she puts it, "'Asian American' is in this sense a *metaphor* for resistance and racism."[15] Chuh herself does not pursue the bridge between the rhetorical tradition and Asian America, but she does insist on a "literariness" to *Asian American* because the term reflects on, theorizes its own conditions of representation. Following Chuh, I want to pause here at the crossroads of metaphor and race to suggest that there is already a precedent in our field, albeit one not recognized as such, for thinking the literary as figuring and therefore pulling away from identity.

If *Asian American* is a metaphor for Asian American history, what does it mean that an ancient rhetorical trope has such a central relationship to Asian America? Metaphor compares two things, but unlike its kindred term *simile* it insists on more than mere likeness by creating an identity, a resemblance, where none exists, and its work, we might say, involves effacing its own figurative operation. This is why, in part, deconstructive readings of metaphor have assiduously tried to expose what metaphor would have us forget: that its claims to truth, to transcendental meaning, to the unity between language and object are based, as rhetorician Richard Lanham observes, on "changing a word from its literal meaning to one not properly applicable."[16] According to Lanham, *metaphor* means "transference" in the original Greek, and Chuh's language hints at this etymology when she asserts that *Asian American* involves a "transfer" of racial meaning onto bodies and subjects; that is, in assigning race, *Asian American* requires a change in meaning from proper to improper. Chuh's invitation to consider *Asian American* as a metaphor is thus invigorating and disquieting. On the one hand, it reminds us that the relationship between "Asian American" and Asian America is merely rhetorical; this identity is the effect of a figure whose task it is to produce the illusion of identity. On the other hand, if "Asian American" is to succeed as a figure of identity, it must present itself as a "name" for Asian America, that is, as a motivated and natural identity that we must persistently undo to avoid essentializing it. Chuh's handling of metaphor suggests that something changes—enlarges or deviates—in the rhetorical tradition itself when it encounters these Asian American particularities. By designating *Asian American* "a *metaphor* for resistance and racism," her formulation insists that metaphor's emergence in an Asian American context forces it to depart from its customary duties. Now, in the place of identity, it indexes difference (racism), and instead of unity it registers contention and potential deviation (resistance).

Metaphor is a trope from antiquity. It comes to Asian American literature by way of a rhetorical tradition first codified around 500 BCE in Greece. That we find metaphor, and other classical tropes like apophasis and allegory, in Asian American literature suggests at the very least some linguistic and rhetorical basis for multiplying the references for Asian American literature beyond or other than Asian America. These rhetorical figures also remind us of the complicated legacy of Asian America itself, which is an appellation that comes from elsewhere. We know from Edward Said that the "Orient" is an idea invented by the West, a self-consolidating discourse that allowed Europe to rule, know, administer, and represent its colonial other. In the American context the racialized category of "Asian" is superficially imposed on a diverse and heterogeneous group of people whose entry into the United States is precipitated by the European search for Asia. As historian Gary Y. Okihiro avers, "Asians, it must be remembered, did not come to America; Americans went to Asia. . . . And the matter of the 'when and where' of Asian American history is located therein, in Europe's eastward and westward thrusts, engendered, transformative, expansive."[17] If Okihiro is right to posit the historical emergence of Asian America in and through Europe, he gives us warrant to explore, as scholars are doing in new ways today, the vexed and uneven entanglements of these traditions. Josephine Park, for example, demonstrate a direct line of descent between contemporary Asian American writers like Maxine Hong Kingston and poets like Myung Mi Kim and the American Orientalism of Pound and his cohort. Park's book begins by inviting us to "reopen our understanding of the formation of Asian American literature by considering a presently disavowed past. To return to Orientalist literature as an instigator for Asian American literature is to examine anew a political and aesthetic response—one which has long been deemed a case of simple rejection—as a crucial point of contact which defined a literary movement."[18]

In organizing this study of Asian American literature around a set of classical rhetoric tropes, I do not seek a return to historical origins. I observe, as John Bender and David Wellbery have previously, that modern rhetorical inquiry is a different beast altogether from its classical, medieval, and Renaissance predecessors. In its heyday rhetoric was much more than the means by which young men were taught to argue persuasively. As Jenny C. Mann describes it, rhetoric was "the gateway to learning in the postmedieval world, the method through which all other subjects were apprehended."[19] Its demise, according to Bender and Wellbery, was brought about by material shifts accompanying modernization: the new discourse of science arising in the Enlightenment, that period's elevation of an objective language defined by transparency, the onset of print culture, and eventually the Romantic valorization of individual creativity and genius. The past few decades have witnessed a "rebirth" of rhetoric, but Bender and Wellbery encourage us to conceive of its modern reincarnation as a "general rhetoricality," wherein rhetoric no longer designates a special use of language but more fundamental processes of meaning making and subjectivity.[20] In this book I treat the rhetorical figures and their venerable critical resources as shortcuts to understanding certain types of linguistic patterns and devices.[21] I use the term *rhetorical* in a very technical sense to refer to the behavior of these tropes, wherever they are found. In the new formalism of the 2000s, as Levinson indicates, there is exciting Renaissance scholarship adumbrating how "rhetoric speaks culture,"[22] but in historicizing the appearance of these figures to the particularities of Renaissance culture, such studies offer little help in explaining the hows or whys of these figures as they present themselves in Asian American literature. Indeed, I want to suggest that what we have yet to see in the new rhetorical inquiry is a sustained engagement with race, especially as it pertains to whiteness or what passes for it at different historical junctures. Individual critics, of course, have made important interventions—Henry Louis Gates Jr. comes to mind—but if we are to assert, as many scholars do, that Europe's awareness of race begins in earnest with the discovery of the New World, how might rhetorical study benefit from an extended inquiry into race and racialization?[23]

In placing figurative activity at the center of Asian American literature, we can begin to grasp how cautiously, and sometimes suspiciously, these texts view their connection to Asian America. If Asian America has, from the start, been an identity in perpetual danger of unraveling, the existence of Asian American literature is even more precarious because, as Colleen Lye notes, "the problem is that 'Asian American literature' exists largely at the level of the course syllabus, scholarly research monographs, or publishers' catalogues, rather than at the level of an individual text."[24] In other words, the constellation of texts assembled and collated as "Asian American" may speak more to institutional or pedagogical demands than to any natural or intrinsic cohesion among the texts themselves. To provide coherence to individual texts that are often at odds with each other, we have relied on the race-identified author as a way to organize diverse textual material, but this too has problems of its own—for example, the maintenance measures that are periodically undertaken to expand the range of Asian American identity. This is where a recourse to the established patterns of figurative language might prove useful. Jeanne Fahnestock notes that the rhetorical tradition is "remarkably enduring and *trans*lingual" because "devices identified in the Latin *Rhetorica ad Herennium* of 80 BCE can easily be identified in contemporary discourse."[25] From the literary side G. N. Leech observes that "'figures,' in the sense of deviant or foregrounded features of literary language, are observable and classifiable features of texts."[26] Since these figures describe a discrete and long codified set of behaviors, they might be said to constitute concrete examples of Asian American literature as well as instances of rhetorical language being reworked by race. The historical person of the author has never been a particularly reliable barometer for explaining the operations of the literary text. As Robert Dale Parker remarks of Native American literature, the "noisy inefficiency of language and representation" means that "we may lament the way white writers can botch the representation of Indian characters, but it doesn't therefore follow that Indian writers necessarily get it right, or that we can always predict what it might mean to get it right, or that any writer can stick to portraying that writer's own race, gender, sexuality, class, region, cultural disposition, and so on through the curlicue of identities that mean so much to us."[27] There is a place for authorial intention, which shows itself in the "deliberate choices in form, genres, traditions, and conventions" that Sue-Im Lee identifies as evidence of aesthetic activity.[28] When speaking of figurative activity, though, the person or figure of the author is too frail a vehicle for containing the vastness of language and its iterations across the reach of millennia. That these classical rhetorical tropes resurface in Asian American literature suggests that such linguistic patterns do not belong to any single author or individual; they are part of a linguistic inheritance dwarfing any individual's claim to own or originate it. These rhetorical structures may very well be unintended; they are, in this sense, part of the unanticipated and compelling effects of figuration that illuminate the power of the literary text to exceed its historical usage. To give up the person or figure of the author, however, is not to give up the pressing issue of race, as race remains quite forcefully evident not only in the titles of the texts being studied—*Aiiieeeee!*, *China Men*, *No-No Boy*—but in the historical problematics with which these texts wrestle.

Where classical rhetoric differs from its modern descendant, Fahnestock remarks, is that the ancients "did not consider the language a code nor themselves decoders." The purpose of rhetorical instruction lay in passing down a set of practices and techniques, and so "commenting on how others used language effectively or ineffectively was only a means to that end."[29] The opposite must obtain in the study of Asian American literature. Treating these texts as figurative, as requiring a special kind of attention, is urgent because they continue to exert material force on how race is imagined, thought, and lived out. Were we able to approach this literature as highly figured language with unpredictable effects, we might better grasp racialization itself as an ongoing process in which racial meaning is assigned, contested, taken up, and on occasion can stray from its original intent. In tracking this figurative activity we start to glimpse just how deconstructive an attitude these Asian American texts have toward racial interpellation. Each of these canonical texts insists that race may very well miss its mark, stutter, or fail to execute. By staging the gaps, the tensions, and the unverifiable effects of figurative activity, these texts suggest as well that figurative activity, in the service of figuring race, might limn out an unanticipated referentiality. If figurative activity teaches us how literary forms distort their precipitating conditions by twisting or turning them into tropes and figures, perhaps we could learn to think along these lines about race itself.

The referential paradigm has been a powerful way to get at the pernicious effects of race on the subject and on the literary imagination. For one influential model, Rey Chow's "coercive mimeticism," ethnicity functions as what she calls a captivity narrative, "a process (identitarian, existential, cultural, or textual) in which those who are marginal to mainstream Western culture are expected . . . to resemble and replicate the very banal preconceptions that have been appended to them." Chow's particular concern is that the self-referentiality so typical of ethnic representation is far from liberating; such gestures, she argues, are equivalent to accepting one's "otherness," which, more often than not, leads to "the profound sense of self-hatred and impotence among ethnics."[30] The relentless referentiality to which the Asian American subject must answer means not only that she participates unwittingly in her own subjection but that in doing so she cannot be anything other than Asian, reduced to a phenotype. Referential reading practices operate in much the same way; they reduce the distortion effect of literary activity, which may subvert the relation of the text to Asian America or Asian American identity. Chow's general insights notwithstanding, her model founders curiously at the juncture of rhetoricity and Asian America.[31] As she understands it, ethnic studies in the United States "is no longer entirely or at all grounded in language pedagogy," and the Asian American subject is a case in point: "Because so many of them no longer have the claim to ethnic authority through the possession of ethnic languages, Asian Americans are perhaps the paradigmatic case of a coercive mimeticism that physically keeps them in their place . . . in their *genre* of speaking/writing as nothing but *generic* Asian Americans."[32] Chow is too canny not to problematize this presumed linguistic authority, but her preference for the term *ethnicity* (it "avoids replicating the residual biologism that is inerasably embedded in the term 'race'") seems to miss the institutionalized nature of *Asian American* as premised precisely on racial and not ethnic difference.[33] As Lowe observes, "The history of the legislation of the Asian as *alien* and the administration of the Asian American as *citizen* is . . . the genealogy of a distinct 'racial formation' for Asian Americans, defined not primarily in terms of biological racialism but in terms of institutionalized, legal definitions of race and national origin."[34]

In other words, because *Asian American* is so patently an institutionalized discontinuity, because it indexes precisely what Chow is troubled by—the referential aberration of an "Asian" body without a corresponding linguistic authority—the term refuses the illusion of a more "natural" relationship between the body and its interiority. If one of Chow's worries is that the Asian American subject participates unwittingly in her own subjection, Chuh's rhetorical intervention suggests an alternative to this mimetic logic. As a metaphor, *Asian American* involves a transfer of meaning that produces the very relationship in question, but because this transfer is figurative, accomplished by means of a rhetorical figure, it makes room for potential referential aberrations. In fact by referring to metaphor (from *meta*, "beyond, over," and *pherein*, "to carry") as the "figure of transport," one rhetorical treatise recognizes the risks and hazards inherent in the ferrying across of meaning from one term to another.[35] This is why the Asian American texts considered here are so extraordinary. The rhetorical tropes at work offer a way out of Chow's bleak mimeticism by presenting a trajectory that insists on reference and yet somehow skews (or bends) the path between sign and meaning. This figurative activity thus invites us to entertain a model of referentiality that is inconsistent—behaving erratically, with results or effects that we cannot anticipate—without derailing altogether.

For an early if unacknowledged example of this sensibility in Asian American literary criticism, I turn to Sau-ling Cynthia Wong's *Reading Asian American Literature*, a groundbreaking thematic study with a surprising awareness of referential subversion. Her introduction warns us that her "chosen terms of analysis, because of their bias toward 'content,' do not leave much room for investigating *possible tensions* between the thematic import and the stylistic inflections of a work."[36] The notion that "possible tensions" might arise between form and content is not itself new or unusual, but Wong borrows terms from Kingston's *The Woman Warrior* to cast this tension in distinctly Asian American terms: "Certainly a lesson in Extravagance might be subverted by an austere manner of presentation, or a plea for Necessity might be couched in such an Extravagant form that its persuasiveness becomes questionable." According to Wong, Extravagance and Necessity designate Asian American "modes of existence and operation": the former indicates the impulse toward play, freedom, excess; the latter, the pressure of constraint, demand, and conservation.[37] Even as she seeks to construct a coherent Asian American tradition, Wong is acutely aware that the potential tensions at work in the literature present other possibilities for reading, ones in which the text breaks free of its Asian American moorings. By deriving her terms of analysis from a literary text, her project already gestures toward reconceptualizing Asian American literature as a group of texts whose relationship to their originary historical context is no longer easily identifiable, as that relationship has been reworked, *figured*, by literature. I have been suggesting that there is a precedent, if not an outright inclination, for deconstruction already at work in Asian American literature. Wong and Chuh register this tendency; the former by stressing the "possible tensions" between what is said and how it is said and the latter by emphasizing the "literariness" inherent in the term *Asian American*. Taken together they offer powerful inducements to rereading Asian American literature.

For all these reasons I have concentrated on the linguistic patterns found in these texts. If Asian American literature can be imagined as a set of figurative activities that do not ignore or dismiss the question of race, then it suggests a role for Asian American literature in the new formalism. In refusing to deracinate their figurative activity, these Asian American texts demonstrate how modern versions of figurative language are inextricably entangled with claims for racial identity. What we want is a general formalism more persistently attentive to questions of gender, class, sexuality, *and* race, most especially when the occlusion of race has resulted in the invisibility of whiteness. "Theoretically," Hazel Carby reminds us, "we should be arguing that everyone in this social order has been constructed in our political imagination as a racialized subject. In this sense, it is important to think about the invention of the category of whiteness as well as of blackness and, consequently, to make visible what is rendered invisible when viewed as the normative state of existence: specifically the white point in space from which we tend to identify difference."[38] As a persistently racialized category of American literature, Asian American literature can potentially disturb the normative assumptions operating in the deracinated studies of form, rhetoric, and figurative activity by refusing to drop the question of race, even when it appears—in the case of whiteness—not to be there at all.

An Asian American Problematic

Until quite recently Asian American literary criticism had little to do with form. The foundational scholarship upheld the literature as a representation of shared experience and emphasized the uneven material conditions that governed Asian American literary production and reception. At the same time these early scholars exhorted future critics to supplement their own content-driven and thematic approaches with formalist analysis. In the past decade Asian American scholars have begun to do just that. The pathbreaking work of scholars like Lye and Park, along with Steven Yao, Timothy Yu, Dorothy Wang, Joseph Jeon, and Christopher Lee, among others, charts new territory by focusing on textual coherence beyond or disengaged from the identity formation. As a result it is less certain than ever that Asian America is the default analytic framework for the study of Asian American literature. My argument draws its energy from this scholarship, which has expanded the frame of reference for Asian America by exploring its intertextual engagements.[39] This second wave of Asian American literary criticism has busily reconstructed the literary tradition around textual form and function, but in doing so it also understands representation as a problem. As Lye puts it, "In this account, the Asian American text is not one that represents Asian Americans, since there can be none such. Rather the Asian American text is one that is— or can be shown to be—engaged with a problematic of Asian American representation."[40]

The canonical examples in this book wrestle with this problematic in multiple senses of the term. First and foremost, for several of these texts the connection to Asian America is a problem. *No-No Boy*'s rediscovery in the 1970s was a defining moment for Asian American literature, but Asian America as such did not exist when Okada was writing in the 1950s. In a slightly different sense these texts have been problems for Asian America in that many are highly contested sites of representation. The debates over *Blu's Hanging* in the late 1990s, for example, were so contentious that at one point the Association for Asian American Studies was at risk. These incidents suggest that Asian America is a problem for representation, both that it is problematic to represent, being so contested, and that these texts are centrally concerned with the problem of representation. In a second sense these texts are acutely conscious of the problematic of race or racialization. Thematically they present an array of characters involved in various acts of resisting or challenging their interpellation as racial subjects. While they may insist on the importance of race, these texts are less certain, however, about what race means and what circuitous and erratic path its representation may take. They are problematic in a third and more difficult sense: as literary texts, none of them responds to their historical problematic in predictable ways. Indeed, they are nearly counterintuitive in their behavior. To defy the "white racist love" that has caricatured Asian American literature as "aiiieeeee!," the anthology *Aiiieeeee!* repeats it. To defend Japanese American loyalty, *No-No Boy* refuses to represent the reasons behind "yes, yes" and "no, no." To address the historical absence of Chinese Americans, *China Men* makes these subjects disappear. *Blu's Hanging*'s critique of identity politics proceeds by way of racial and sexual stereotypes. *Native Speaker* challenges a discourse of Asian deceit by presenting us with a Korean American protagonist who is both a spy and a traitor.

As literary texts these canonical examples perform a specific kind of work on this historical material by figuring it—turning it into figures or rhetorical patterns. In other words, they give to these historical problematics, ones specific to Asian American history, new and different forms. In foregrounding the imaginative use of language, they announce themselves as literary texts concerned quite fundamentally with processes of figuration. Finally each of these texts takes shape around a specific historical problematic that precipitates the turn to a particular rhetorical trope. *No-No Boy*, for example, is profoundly concerned with the loyalty questionnaire, the mandatory form distributed to Japanese Americans during World War II, but the questionnaire itself never appears in the novel. Instead it is figured in *No-No Boy* as the rhetorical question, a question that pretends to want an answer. In showing us how literary texts take up their historical situations as a problem, a problem that they solve by figurative means, these Asian American texts teach us something about language as it confronts the problem of race. A different way of putting this might be to say that traces of Asian American history live on in these texts, albeit in altered form. If figurative language involves resignifying words by twisting them away from their original meanings, it names a problem that has defined the idea of Asian America. Not only does the term *Asian American* persistently encounter its own referential inadequacy, but the possibility of there being an Asian America at all is predicated on resignification, on "re/signing," in Kent Ono's adroit phrasing, the racial logic that produces this identification in the first place.

Each case study in *Unquiet Tropes* considers a different scenario in which literary representation responds to a specific political condition. These conditions—defiance, coercion, necessity, error, and deceit—designate the politics of production and reception surrounding the text. The chapters follow a rough chronological order, beginning in 1957 with *No-No Boy* and ending in 1995 with *Native Speaker*. They are better approached, however, as ascending in degree of complexity according to their governing rhetorical tropes. The formal tensions unique to each rhetorical trope constitute a part of the figurative resources that these texts draw on in responding to and thinking through these political conditions. The first two chapters deal with very straightforward tropes: the rhetorical question and apophasis are easily recognizable; they pose no puzzle for the reader. Chapters 3 and 4, however, are a different story, as their tropes involve deception and disguise: catachresis must use the wrong term because no other will do; allegory is even trickier as it says one thing to mean something else.

In Chapter 1 I examine *No-No Boy* as the response to coercion. The novel investigates a whole range of activities organized around acts of questioning, answering, and misspeaking, and it turns to the rhetorical question to suggest that racialized speech acts can be nothing more than "rhetorical." The novel's title refers to one of two possible responses to a loyalty questionnaire seeking to establish the allegiance of Japanese Americans interned in concentration camps during World War II. Those who answered "yes, yes" were considered loyal; those responding "no, no" (nono boys) were viewed as traitors. Given the coercion to represent oneself exerted by this interrogative scenario, why does the novel persistently stage the refusal to represent Japanese American intentions? The novel's preface, for example, presents a conversation between a Japanese American soldier and a sympathetic white lieutenant who wants to know why his companion enlisted. Their exchange, in which the racialized subject is staged as refusing to answer, is the novel's response to a classical philosophical scenario of deracinated self-representation. This chapter joins a recent conversation on Asian American aesthetics by suggesting that the tension between *No-No Boy*'s aesthetic crudeness and its complex figurative activity demands rhetoric, not aesthetics.

In the second chapter I consider Kingston's *China Men* as the response to political obligation or necessity. Chinese American history has been deeply shaped by exclusion: a series of immigration laws enacted in the nineteenth century prohibited the entry of women and male workers. Meanwhile another set of laws regulated Chinese sexuality, consigning male workers to live in "bachelor societies" until the mid-twentieth century. *China Men* grapples with its obligation to represent the subject excluded from history, and it acknowledges quite explicitly its desire to fill in the lacunae of American history. Why, then, does it pursue this task by calling on apophasis, the figure of negation or denial, to disappear its subjects from the frame of representation?

In chapter 3 I turn to *Blu's Hanging* to explore literary representation under conditions of error. I explore how the novel turns to catachresis, the figure of abuse, to present identity under multiple colonialisms as a necessary misrecognition, a misuse of language. Conversations about *Blu's Hanging* tend to be overshadowed by the award controversy and the stereotyping of Uncle Paulo, the controversial Filipino character who molests his adolescent nieces and rapes one of the main characters. As a result little attention has been paid to how the novel offers a serious critique of identity politics through its figurative activity. If Uncle Paulo is the representation of a Filipino subject, why does the novel tell us that he fails to "look" Filipino, and why does it repeatedly present him playing the role of a Filipino? And if *Blu's Hanging* is a female coming-of-age story, why does the novel stage the narrator's entry into womanhood as a mistake? Catachresis is a trope with its own formal tension; it is the wrong word for something, yet no other word will do. For the imaginative landscape of the novel, catachresis figures that which cannot be represented—an alliance between the narrative trajectories designated by Ivah and Uncle Paulo—and thus suggests a kind of misrecognition inherent in literary form itself.

In the final chapter I consider *Native Speaker*, a novel about a Korean American spy and traitor, to examine the literary response to the discourse of Asian deceit. Most readings of the novel have focused on its cynical portrayal of race: the protagonist has been hired for his ability to play the role of a Korean American. Yet there is far more at stake in the novel, as it turns to allegory, the figure of other-speaking, to suggest a much larger argument about our desire for transparency and for referentiality. Why does the novel challenge the stereotype of Asians as deceitful or treacherous by offering us a narrator who uses referential language so exactly that he manages to speak allegorically? In calling on allegory's formal tension as the figure that says one thing but means something else, the novel brings together referential language, whiteness, and native speaking to suggest that each of these is a figurative mode of representation concealing its own rhetoricity, and in doing so offers a far-reaching critique of signs pretending to be a "white" language.

Rebounding *Aiiieeeee!*

I want to turn now to *Aiiieeeee!*'s preface to explore how the early texts of the Asian American literary tradition can lack aesthetic richness *and* be rhetorically sophisticated. Before I begin, however, it is important to point out that the preface is not strictly literary. It does not announce itself as literature, and yet we can discern in it the concrete patterns of figurative activity. From this, it follows that it might be our own reading practices, in combination with the traditional standards of aesthetics, that are partially responsible for reducing the complexity of Asian American writing. The four editors of the anthology—Frank Chin, Lawson Inada, Jeffery Chan, and Shawn Wong—were writers dedicated to what they called the "living tradition of Asian-American action and thought."[41] The anthology's subsequent status as one of the most troubled and troubling texts in the Asian American canon is largely due to its strident identity politics. Asian American identity, the preface declares, is "Filipino-, Chinese-, and Japanese-Americans, American born and raised."[42] Feminist and queer critics have been concerned that in describing Asian American identity as masculine and heroic, the preface rearticulates, as David L. Eng suggests, "a dominant system of compulsory heterosexuality with all its attendant misogyny and homophobia."[43] Other critics, noting the cultural nationalist stance the preface is known for, point to its static view of culture and its dismissal of foreign-born Asians. Whatever its many faults, *Aiiieeeee!*'s importance to the Asian American literary tradition cannot be overstated, as its delineation of a self-determined and "authentic" Asian American culture sets the terms of debate for decades to come.

Critics like Mark Chiang, David Leiwei Li, and Daniel Kim have reframed our understanding of *Aiiieeeee!* by demonstrating that its prefatory material should be understood as marking out a position on aesthetics rather than identity politics. Jinqi Ling further observes that the essentialist claims in *Aiiieeeee!*

are rhetorical and should not be considered as foregone political conclusions. In joining this extant conversation I want to show how the rhetorical activity of the preface undermines its own overt proclamations for an essentialist identity politics. The first difficulty in approaching the preface is its language, which, despite its polemical exuberance, is not intended as "literary." The second difficulty is that there is no equivalent term in the classical rhetorical tradition for describing the kind of figurative activity appearing in the preface. This lacuna is an Asian American point of entry into the traditional concerns of rhetoric and form.

The historical problematic that animates *Aiiieeeee!* involves defiance through repetition. The editors reject the "white racist love," the institutionalized Orientalism, that interpellates Asians as foreign and marginalizes the literature from the established American canon. Thus the preface declares, "Seven generations of suppression under legislative racism and euphemized white racist love have left today's Asian Americans in a state of self-contempt, self-rejection, and disintegration" (xii). It goes on to inform us that "aiiieeeee!" is a racist slur invented by the "pushers of white American culture" who "pictured the yellow man as something that when wounded, sad, or angry, or swearing, or wondering whined, shouted, or screamed 'aiiieeeee!'" (xii). The next sentence reclaims "aiiieeeee!" as the "voice" of Asian America: "Asian America, so long ignored and forcibly excluded from creative participation in American culture, is wounded, sad, angry, swearing, and wondering, and this is his AIIIEEEEE!!! It is *more than* a whine, shout, or scream. It is fifty years of our whole voice" (xii, my emphasis). If the editors seek to defy the Orientalism of "aiiieeeee!," why do they claim it as the name of the anthology? When the preface portrays "AIIIEEEEE!!!" as *"more than* a whine, shout, or scream," it suggests, I argue, that this "more than" has something to do with the nature of language itself. The "more than" of "AIIIEEEEE!!!" exceeds its original referent—"aiiieeeee!," the Orientalized speech of the yellow man—and sketches out an arc that is more than referential, as it both refers to *and multiplies* its original referent. According to the preface, this "AIIIEEEEE!!!" is a synecdoche, the rhetorical trope substituting part for whole, because it stands in for the "whole voice" of Asian America, just as the anthology stands in for the entirety of Asian American writing. This kind of move is quite typical of Asian American literary criticism, but when Lye suggestively characterizes it as a form of "synecdochic" reading, she makes it possible for us to imagine such practices, despite their referential treatment of literature, as constituting an unexpected form of *rhetorical* reading.[44]

Kim reads the "more than" designated by "AIIIEEEEE!!!" as a kind of "repetition with a difference." He aligns its rhetorical energy with an African American tradition of "guerilla/gorilla warfare" elucidated by scholars like Henry Louis Gates Jr. and Houston A. Baker. Kim is one of the few critics to consider the significance of the different versions of "aiiieeeee!": in lowercase "aiiieeeee!" refers to the voice of Asia as imagined by a white racist culture; in capital letters "AIIIEEEEE!!!" refers to the resignified voice of Asian America. "In upper case," Kim observes, "AIIIEEEEE! apparently signifies something else." The passage between the two, he argues, is an act of "willful aping" involving masculine aggression. For him, this move constitutes a kind of "repetition with a difference," a signature deconstructive move derived from Derrida's reading of the sign as constituted by *différance*, a process of differentiation involving the perpetual differing and deferring of meaning.[45] "Iterability," a related Derridean term, helps us parse the complex trajectories of "aiiieeeee!" here. By iterability, Derrida refers to the sign's emergence through rupture, the fact that it can be "*cited*, put between quotation marks; in so doing it can break with every given context, engendering an infinity of new contexts in a manner which is absolutely illimitable." He goes on to suggest that "*iter*, again, probably comes from *itara, other* in Sanskrit, and everything that follows can be read as the working out of the logic that ties repetition to alterity."[46] Iterability's capacity for identity and difference can be traced to its etymology, which rearticulates, unquietly, "Asia" (Sanskrit, the ancient language of India) as the language of the "West" (Latin, once the lingua franca of Europe). In other words, the possibility of the sign, its ability to be (repeated) derives from this lineage of "otherness." I want to build on Kim's reading to tease out what Asian American literature might possibly bring to deconstruction. In the case of *Aiiieeeee!*'s preface, what seems to call out most loudly for deconstruction is that *Aiiieeeee!*, both the anthology and the voice of Asian American literature, depends on and repeats an old racist logic, "aiiieeeee." Indeed this repetition reflects the organizing principle of the field, as Asian American studies attempts, on a grander level, to take a racialized relationship—"Asian" bodies designating "Asia"—as the platform for self-determination. As a category, then, Asian America seems to call on the same logic that it seeks to overcome. Even as it redirects the punishing force of this logic, it cannot but repeat—differently, for certain, but repeat nevertheless—its original referent in some form.

As previously mentioned, the preface features multiple iterations of "aiiieeeee!" There is the original racist slur, "aiiieeeee!" (xii); the voice of Asian America, "AIIIEEEEE!!!" (xii); and the recovered writings of seven generations, "Aiiieeeee!!" (xxii). Of course there is also *Aiiieeeee!*, the title of the anthology itself. I am less interested in these typographical differences than in what these repetitions are doing to the idea of reference when the preface sends the term "aiiieeeee!" volleying between its variants. As speech these different trajectories are quite easily confused; after all, they sound identical. In and as writing, however, the crucial differences between a racist past and a racialized agency can emerge. The various iterations of "aiiieeeee!" in the preface seem to accommodate a very different notion of the referential. For the resignification of "aiiieeeee!" to be apparent to the reader, it is absolutely essential that these "willful apings," as Kim calls them, refer clearly and distinctly to the original. Yet without giving up altogether on the importance of the referential, these iterations also somehow suggest that their trajectories, *even in the act of reference*, end up somewhere unexpected.

Through its iterations "aiiieeeee!" bends the arc of reference to the racist past, but because its repetitions do not relinquish their reference to the first "aiiieeeee!," they demand a reconceptualization of the referential. It is training in figurative activity, I will argue, that can teach us how to *read* these repetitions.

As James Kim has observed, "aiiieeeee!" is not really a word at all, but a "noise."⁴⁷ What does "aiiieeeee!" mean? Strictly speaking, it "means" nothing. Insofar as the iterations "AIIIEEEEE!!!," "Aiiieeeee!!," and *Aiiieeeee!* also refer to this original "noise," they too do not "signify." Indeed not only is "aiiieeeee!" a term missing a proper referent (it is a caricature), but we cannot even understand as original its first appearance in the preface because that "aiiieeeee!" is already a repetition. In other words, "aiiieeeee!" as it appears in the preface is *nothing but resignification*. This does not stop it or its iterations, however, from producing a certain kind of surplus, but rather than denoting an excess of meaning, they designate the surplus of reference. Repetition is a basic principle of rhetoric, and the classical rhetorical tradition can tell us much about the kinds of repetition employed to achieve "emphasis, beauty, or drama" or to create other rhetorical effects but there is little that it can tell us about the type of repetition we find in *Aiiieeeee!*⁴⁸ It is less a matter of the act of repetition, about which the rhetorical tradition has much to say, and more an issue with the kind of repetition occurring here because "aiiieeeee!" does not involve the multiplication of sense but of reference.

To what do these various forms of "aiiieeeee!" refer? The first "aiiieeeee!" indexes, as the editors put it, "legislative racism and euphemized white racist love" (xii). Its subsequent iterations, however, are supposed to designate different entities. The second repetition of "AIIIEEEEE!!!" refers to the first "aiiieeeee!" (the racist caricature of the "yellow man"), but since the preface insists that it is "*his* AIIIEEEEE!!!" (my emphasis), this iteration also refers to a male and masculine voice, and it is this gendered "AIIIEEEEE!!!" that is to be equated to Asian America as a whole, or "fifty years of our whole voice." The third iteration,

"Aiiieeeee!!" (xxii), appears at the very end of the preface and again makes reference to the original slur, but it alludes as well to the previous "AIIIEEEEE!!!" (the gendered voice of Asian America) and also to the anthology itself: "But from the few decades of writing we have recovered from seven generations, it is clear that we have a lot of elegant, angry, and bitter life to show. We know how to show it. We are showing off. If the reader is shocked, it is due to his own ignorance of Asian-America. We're not here new. Aiiieeeee!!" (xxii). By its final iteration, this "noise" now refers to the original racist slur, the voice of Asian America (gendered male), and seven generations of Asian American writing, not to mention the anthology, which does not make an explicit appearance but is obliquely referenced in the third paragraph of the preface: "Our anthology is exclusively Asian-American" (xi). In a way that is unverifiable (there is no empirical proof except the words on the page), these iterations, as well as the pages of *Aiiieeeee!* itself, work to disperse the unidirectional force of the original racist slur by multiplying it. These repetitions do not forget the first "aiiieeeee!," to which they continue to refer. At the same time, however, by its very multiplication, the concentrated force of the original "aiiieeeee!" designating the oppression, marginalization, and silencing of Asian American voices is, if not diminished, at least confused. If we were to ask again, at the end of the preface, to what these iterations of "aiiieeeee!" refer, the answer would certainly be more complicated and far less certain.

I have been reading the various iterations of "aiiieeeee!" as instructive of the kind of figurative activity we find in Asian American writing. In pondering the vexed referential trajectories of these repetitions, such an inquiry unsettles the traditional boundaries between Asian American literature and rhetoric, even as it connects them by means of these concrete rhetorical activities. The referential trajectory of "aiiieeeee!" suggests a different model for referentiality, one that registers both the strictures on and the deviations from the referential. In presenting a multiple path for the racialized sign, *Aiiieeeee!* demands nimbler and more

complex approaches to reference. The trajectories of "aiiieeeee!,"
as I have been arguing, multiply reference for Asian American
literature, but they also perform this task for the classical rhetorical tradition. As mentioned earlier, there is no exact equivalent
in the rhetorical tradition for the figurative activity enacted by
the Asian American repetitions of "aiiieeeee!" Its closest counterpart is "Rebound," the name that Renaissance rhetorician George
Puttenham gave to antanaclasis, the "repetition of a word whose
meaning changes in the second instance."[49] "Rebound" appears
in the third book of *The Art of English Poesy*, where Puttenham
writes, "Ye have another figure which by his nature we may call
the Rebound, alluding to the tennis ball which, being smitten with
the racket, rebounds back again, and where the last figure before
played with two words somewhat like, this playeth with one word
written all alike but carrying divers senses."[50] Puttenham's term
expands on antanaclasis, which means, in the original Greek,
"reflection" or "bending back."[51] "Rebound" implies the idea of
repetition, of returning the serve, so to speak, but it also suggests
the potential skewing of the return volley as it travels back to its
origin. We can think of "Aiiieeeee!!" (and "AIIIEEEEE!!!" and
Aiiieeeee!) as "rebounding" the original referent, "aiiieeeee!" the
racist slur.[52] In warping the trajectory of the referential, without
giving up the idea of the referential entirely, *Aiiieeeee!* as Rebound
offers us a route into reconceptualizing the referential in Asian
American literature.

What is most remarkable about Puttenham's *Art*, however,
is its "Englishing," as its editors call it, of the Greek and Latin
names for the rhetorical figures.[53] Puttenham is part of a larger
vernacular movement in which early modern writers sought to
translate the classical rhetorical tradition, in Mann's phrase,
into "particularly *English* figures of speech."[54] Because the
humanist education of the Renaissance inculcated a powerful
reverence for the cultural authority of the classical world, these
English rhetoric manuals betray acute anxieties about adapting
this classical tradition, as is evident in Puttenham's defensive-
ness when he claims that his "Englishings" are superior to their

classical antecedents. Mann explains, "Although we now tend to think of rhetorical techniques as applicable across language cultures—after all, the Romans themselves adapted them from Greek—early modern English writers worried that their 'barren' and 'barbarous' tongue lacked the substance to supply the demands of the ancient art of rhetoric."[55] Given this particular context, these Renaissance attempts to make the classical tradition of rhetoric "speak English," as the author of one such manual declares, are not so far removed from the struggles animating the *Aiiieeeee!* editors, who occupy, mutatis mutandis, a similarly anxious and defensive position vis-à-vis the canon of American literature.[56] As the preface indignantly declares, for example, "American culture, protecting the sanctity of its whiteness, still patronizes us as foreigners and refuses to recognize Asian American literature as 'American' literature" (xiii). Puttenham's project of "Englishing" the classical rhetorical tradition is a nationalizing model that anticipates the cultural nationalist claims made by *Aiiieeeee!* on behalf of Asian American literature. In this sense Puttenham's move suggests a rhetorical bridge between these two worlds. The various iterations of "aiiieeeee!" in the preface elucidate the kind of figurative activity we find in Asian American writing. The vexed referential trajectory of these repetitions propose a different model for referentiality as the repetitions of "aiiieeeee!" figure a different, unpredictable path for the racialized sign. Insofar as Rebound suggests that reference can be unpredictable while remaining referential, it helps us understand the figurative movement occurring in *Aiiieeeee!*, but because it, like the rest of the rhetorical figures involved with repetition, is designed to indicate a change in meaning, it does not perfectly describe what is happening with "aiiieeeee!" and its repetitions. Despite its ancient and venerable status, the rhetorical tradition is far from infallible or complete. How then might *Aiiieeeee!* supplement the rhetorical tradition as we know it today? What different sorts of questions might arise were we to consider "aiiieeeee!" as a particular kind of repetition involving the racializing of reference?

My reading of *Aiiieeeee!* has tried to brush against the critical grain. In returning us to its figurative activity, I hope to better glimpse the questions we should be asking of Asian American literature and to understand more acutely how it can disturb the classical and canonical traditions with which it argues. In complicating these various activities, *Aiiieeeee!* gives us a vexed and vexing, troubled and troubling inheritance of language and race as historically specific articulations of relations of power. The figurative activity characterizing "aiiieeeee!" is significant because "aiiieeeee!" repeats, but it also multiplies. In other words, it gives us both mimesis and something else.[57] Unlike the typical fate of rhetorical activity or formal behavior, "aiiieeeee!" and its variations are profoundly attuned to historical relations of power concretized as race. By failing to investigate the rhetoricity of Asian American writing, we only diminish our own critical resources. If we can think of *Aiiieeeee!* as an object lesson on reading Asian American writing, what it can offer us is a way to read as literary—as figurative and unverifiable—the very moves that appear most referential or commonsensical. A reading strategy like this would treat the "evident" as a literary effect and claims to referentiality as literary techniques. In this way Asian American literature becomes far more than the representation of political or historical concerns. Instead it becomes a way of thinking about the complicated intersections of figurative activity and race.

Spivak's notion of "deconstructive homeopathy," what she defines as a "deconstructing of identity by identities," offers another way to think about the complex trajectories initiated by "aiiieeeee!" She proposes that when one is able to imagine oneself "as an example of certain kinds of historical, psychosexual narratives that one must in fact use," what happens is "a deidentification of oneself, a claiming of an identity from a text that comes from somewhere else."[58] In this particular instance Spivak is discussing gender, but her reminder that identity—whether gendered, sexual, or racial—is a script from elsewhere is eminently appropriate for what is happening in *Aiiieeeee!* It is quite clear that "aiiieeeee!" is a "text" from elsewhere: it designates a form of Orientalism whose origins reach as far back as the ancient Greeks and whose work in the nineteenth, twentieth, and twenty-first centuries is to interpellate Asian-origin individuals *as* Asian or Oriental. Yet the complex multiplication of "aiiieeeee!" and its repositioning in the preface as an affirmative form of identity politics suggest that Asian American identity, much like "aiiieeeee!" itself, is most productively imagined as a kind of homeopathy—in short, as the poison whose judicious application functions like medicine.[59]

If I have managed to persuade you that there is an unnamed trope at work in *Aiiieeeee!*, a phantom trope for a term that is missing a referent, the rest of the examples that I explore in this book are comparatively straightforward, but they are, each of them, cast in the shadow of this originary phantom trope. Aiiieeeee!

1 / Rhetorical Question: *No-No Boy* and Coercion

John Okada's *No-No Boy* was poorly received when it was first published in 1957 and remained obscure for nearly two decades before it was rediscovered by the editors of *Aiiieeeee! An Anthology of Asian American Writers*. Since its reprinting in 1976, the novel has become a cornerstone of the Asian American canon, but despite this status there is a conspicuous lack of scholarly commentary on *No-No Boy*'s formal or figurative qualities. Why this is so can in part be attributed to the critical momentum established by its initial reception, which valorized the novel for its unflinching portrait of Japanese America; another reason may be the prevailing tendency in Asian American literary criticism to privilege sociopolitical approaches to literature. I suspect, though, that the major reason for the lack of formal attention may be *No-No Boy* itself, which is a remarkably simple if not outright crude text. Even as its unrelenting realism made many of its early reviewers uncomfortable, much of its ability to move and disturb us today is due to the power of its raw and direct language. The novel's apparent simplicity, however, is deceptively at odds with the complexity of its figurative activity. From its opening preface to its haunting conclusion, *No-No Boy* persistently stages and thwarts the desire to represent Japanese American intentions, "to put it into words."[1] Given the racial hysteria surrounding the perceived inscrutability of Japanese American intentions both in the postwar period of the novel's setting and in the cold war era of its writing, why does *No-No Boy* stage, again and again, the compulsion to represent and the refusal to do so?

No-No Boy is set in Seattle after the end of World War II. Ichiro Yamada, the no-no boy of the title, is wracked with anger and despair. In the wake of his internment and imprisonment, he struggles to regain a sense of meaning for himself and for America. His nuclear family, a microcosm of the deeply fragmented Japanese American community, is similarly dysfunctional: Ma is a Japanese zealot who goes mad and commits suicide, Pa is emasculated, and younger brother Taro escapes to join the army before graduating high school. Whereas Ichiro understands his "no, no" as a matter of misplaced loyalty to his mother, the novel indicates that far more is at stake: the no-no boy intends to say yes, but the consequence of his racialization (and gendering) is such that he cannot say what he means. As a result the novel sends him on a quest, and in his encounters with Kenji, the sympathetic veteran who befriends him, with Emi, a nisei woman who becomes his lover, and a motley assortment of no-no boys, angry veterans, and benevolent white men, Ichiro's task is to learn to "put it into words."

As an aesthetic object, *No-No Boy* is deeply flawed, but critics have mostly bypassed the issue of its aesthetics. The few critics who do acknowledge its shortcomings—Elaine Kim concedes that the "characters are not fully developed"; Lisa Lowe comments on its "long, run-on sentences"; William Yeh describes it as "occasionally didactic and melodramatic" and Gayle K. Fujita Sato as "one-dimensional"—tend, for the most part, to recuperate these qualities as achieving their intended effects or as evidence of the novel's subversive style.[2] For Mark Chiang, *No-No Boy*'s "crude realism" demonstrates the unity of the field's aesthetic and political agendas at its moment of formation; he is

concerned that the institutionalization of Asian American studies increasingly participates in distancing its aesthetics from its
politics, as exemplified by the sea change that has replaced *No-
No Boy* with the high modernism of Theresa Hak Kyung Cha's
Dictée. Chiang concludes, "Against the realist aesthetics of earlier Asian American writing, recent Asian American literature
achieves its subversive effects through complex and elaborate
formal structures," yet such a conclusion seems not to take into
account the shape of our reading practices as potentially limit-
ing factors on the complexity of these texts.[3] The aesthetic has
long been a default category for understanding literariness, but
a text like *No-No Boy* is confounding precisely because, while
its aesthetics are simple to the point of crudeness, its figurative
activity is unexpectedly dense and complicated.

It is this figurative activity, operating in tension with the
novel's form, that demands of us not aesthetics but rhetoric. By
rhetoric I do not mean a return to classical rhetoric, which is a
robust and comprehensive discourse involving the art of persuasion in all its forms, but a more modest investigation into the
highly figured language that we find in *No-No Boy.* These are
patterns best explained by the rhetorical tradition, which classified, codified, and studied these phenomena as elements of style,
one part of which we recognize today as the figures of speech.
While rhetoric has passed out of style, its influence remains, as
G. N. Leech, writing in the heyday of structuralism, concedes
in a discussion of metaphor and antithesis: "Rhetoric . . . has
provided us with most of our terminology for talking about
these features."[4] In *No-No Boy* these patterns—what I am calling
figurative activity—are the means by which the novel "thinks"
in its own irreducible way and in its own particular terms about
its thematic and historical concerns. Figurative activity "theorizes"; that is, it reflects on its own operations and in so doing
questions or problematizes the premises we take for granted.
In this way it functions like theory, which, in Jonathan Culler's
estimation, functions as a set of texts "that succeed in challenging and reorienting thinking."[5] Kandice Chuh has made a case

for Asian American literature as distinctly "theoretical," arguing that the term *Asian American* reflects on its own representation by "call[ing] attention to the workings of language, to its structures and functions."[6]

The specific task of this chapter is to consider literary representation under the condition of coercion, an especially fraught condition because literature itself is so often understood, in its aspect as fiction, as the liberty or freedom to say anything. Indeed critic Russell Berman goes so far as to identify literature with the idea of democracy itself.[7] For these reasons *No-No Boy*'s response to the political condition of coercion offers a valuable case study in how the literary text responds, in distinctly literary ways, to such circumstances. The freedom to say anything is sharply criticized by *No-No Boy*, which stages a deep structural tension between the capacity for literature to say anything and the political coercion under which Japanese American literary representation is made to take place. This structural tension is articulated by the novel's governing trope, the rhetorical question, which serves as the formal means by which *No-No Boy* wrestles with its historical problematic, the interrogative apparatus of the Japanese American loyalty questionnaire. *No-No Boy* uses the formal tension of the rhetorical question to investigate a whole range of activities grouped under the category of coercive representation and the ruse of consent that is implied by these acts of intending, questioning, responding, and refusing to speak.

It is precisely because *No-No Boy* has been so relentlessly politicized that we must reconsider its apparent referential transparency and attend instead to its complex figurative activity. Figurative language by definition says one thing and means something more. And yet, given *No-No Boy*'s acute awareness of the catastrophic consequences that ensue when signs fail to be referential, it rather remarkably insists on the figurative potential of the sign. By racializing this rhetorical excess *No-No Boy* suggests a different way to engage the divide traditionally imposed between aesthetics and politics. It is this figurative activity that figures, translates into a rhetorical figure, *No-No Boy*'s historical problematic, and it is this figurative activity that challenges us to think more complexly about racialization itself. *No-No Boy*'s figurative activity offers a critical intervention in two different directions. On the one hand, it demonstrates the limits of referential reading practices unable to come to terms with the inevitable tensions that follow when signs *look* the same but designate radically divergent meanings. On the other, it supplements the new formalism, which has pursued the rearticulation of literary with sociopolitical and historical forms but omitted a sustained consideration of race. *No-No Boy* prompts referential reading practices to be wary of contributing to the separation of politics from aesthetics and reminds the new formalism that it must also reflect on its own deracination.

The novel's central place in the Asian American canon has much to do with the narrative surrounding its moment of recovery. It is arguably the first Japanese American novel, and yet it, and its author, languished in obscurity until they were recuperated by Asian American writers in search of a literary tradition. The novel's first publisher, Charles Tuttle, expressed surprise when its expected readership, the Japanese American community, rejected it for its painful portrait of postwar life. Mainstream critics at the time found fault with its language and syntax, while Japanese American critics considered it valuable as "social history" but otherwise of little literary value.[8] Jinqi Ling argues that "the novel's poor sales suggest that the ambiguous Ichiro created by Okada failed to provide a comfortable ideological stance or clear narrative guidance for the majority of readers of his novel, who . . . were accustomed to autobiographical representations of Asian American life that did not explicitly challenge assimilationist positions."[9] A decade and a half later, in the charged ideological climate of the 1970s, *No-No Boy*'s defiant tone of racial discontent would resonate with the masculinist editors of *Aiiieeeee!*, who saw in the novel's eponymous character a model for their own relationship to the literary establishment. The critical narrative subsequently constructed around the novel's neglect and eventual recovery reflects a larger narrative of Asian American identity and literature as heroic acts of resistance and agency.[10]

Literary criticism on the novel has generated a deep archive of historical and sociopolitical knowledge about the Japanese American experience, but there has been little discussion of its formal specificity.[11] This lack of formal attention is so pronounced that Ling, in one of the first sustained formalist treatments of the novel, concludes that its scholarship is defined by "a partial but continued suspension of critical consciousness about analyzing *No-No Boy* as a work of fiction."[12] Two exceptions to this are Ling himself and Lowe, but while these scholars consider the novel's form, they do not specifically pursue its figurative activity. Today Asian American literary study is undergoing something like a formal turn as scholars increasingly engage with questions of form and aesthetics. Even so, *No-No Boy* has yet to benefit from this renewed focus on literariness. This chapter takes up Ling's invitation to investigate the work of literature, and it does so by focusing on the novel's figurative activity as the means by which it both figures a historical problematic and thinks about the activity of representing that problematic.

Coercion

Most definitions of the rhetorical question understand it as "any question asked for a purpose other than to obtain the information the question asks."[13] The technical term for this figure is *erotesis* (from Greek, "questioning"). Like the other tropes we will encounter in the book, the rhetorical question is an unquiet figure; it may take the grammatical form of an interrogative, but it is, in its rhetorical capacity, at odds with this form. For this reason the rhetorical question constitutes a uniquely appropriate figure for the loyalty questionnaire, which, in its format and context, also involved a ruse of agency. *No-No Boy* calls on the rhetorical question to present a cast of Japanese American characters who say no when they mean yes or who refuse to say anything at all. In articulating this classical rhetorical figure with Japanese American internment, the novel delineates a type of racialized speech act that demands we acknowledge the normative subject of questioning as deracinated.

No-No Boy is a literary response to conditions of coercion, and its immediate historical problematic is the loyalty questionnaire. In the context of Japanese internment, the questionnaire was one of several instances of coercion masquerading as apparent consent. It comes about in January 1943, when the War Department decided to create a voluntary combat unit comprising nisei, second-generation Japanese Americans, a decision that reversed a previous ban on their military service. The questionnaire was initially intended to help the army ascertain the loyalties of these volunteers. However, the War Relocation Authority (WRA), the civilian agency in charge of the camps, decided to use the questionnaire as a sorting mechanism to help separate "loyals" from "disloyals" and to process the former more quickly out of camp. As a result the WRA made "registration," as the questionnaire was called, mandatory for all internees over the age of seventeen. The key loyalty questions were numbers 27, which asked for military service as proof of loyalty, and 28, which asked the respondent to swear an oath of allegiance to the United States and forswear allegiance to the Japanese emperor. Those who answered yes were identified as loyal, those answering no (no-no boys) as disloyal. In the context of World War II, the questionnaire is certainly a rather benign form of state violence; my point here is how this coercion is obscured by the voluntary format of the questionnaire. Under the guise of soliciting its responses, the questionnaire became a disciplinary mechanism producing what appeared to be self-determined performances from subjects who seemed to represent and speak for themselves. This situation, this precipitating historical problematic, is what the novel grapples with in figurative form as the trope of the rhetorical question.

Internment, as historian Mae Ngai observes, "rested on a foundation of simple racism—'a Jap is a Jap.'"[14] This racism was "simple" insofar as it presumed a referential relationship between the "Jap" body and its corresponding "Jap" intentions.[15] Yet the very fact of internment itself, and the array of diagnostic instruments it generated—the voluntary combat unit, the questionnaire, repatriation—should be regarded as indicative of a greater crisis involving the ultimate inscrutability of Japanese intentions. Indeed the authority of the questionnaire to function reliably as a form for representing Japanese American intentions was immediately called into question.[16] The initial wording of questions 27 and 28, for example, caused tremendous confusion and had to be revised. Furthermore despite the apparent clarity of format, none of the responses to the questionnaire—whether yes, no, qualified, or blank—was a straightforward declaration of loyalty or disloyalty. As historians of internment have pointed out, those responding no did so for multiple reasons, few of them having to do with disloyalty.[17] Some answered no to keep their families intact, others to protest their unconstitutional treatment, and still others to avoid resettlement. Ngai's discussion of yes answers draws similar conclusions: "Those who answered 'yes' represented a range of motivation and belief. While many undoubtedly welcomed the opportunity to state their loyalty to the United States, others trod the path of least resistance and hoped that a 'yes' answer would shield them from further accusations of disloyalty."[18] In other words, despite the administrative expectations placed on these responses, yes and no could no longer be relied on as referential signs conveying, without interference or distortion, the intentions of their subjects.

Indeed, the context of internment transformed yes and no into loyalty oaths, into speech acts. No longer referential statements, they became what philosopher J. L. Austin calls "performatives," a class of language "in which to *say* something is to *do* something; or, in which *by* saying or *in* saying something we are doing something."[19] Since performatives "do" something rather than merely report on an existing reality, they cannot be evaluated, Austin argues, by the usual standards of referential language. Because they bring something into being, performatives constitute an exception to the usual philosophical attitude regarding language, which approaches it as a set of referential statements adequately evaluated as truths or falsehoods. Given the specific exigencies of Japanese internment, the loyalty questionnaire becomes a referential crisis, one that challenges the status and role of writing—and of the sign more generally—in relation to the intending subject and to meaning. It is this scenario, so fundamental to Western philosophy, that *No-No Boy* challenges in its preface. Although the questionnaire itself does not appear in *No-No Boy*, the novel makes continued reference to it by staging repeated scenarios of interrogation and declarations of identity. Its treatment of these interrogative scenarios, though, offers a very different conclusion than that of Ngai, who writes of the questionnaire that government "officials failed to recognize the perverse meanings that loyalty and disloyalty had acquired through registration and segregation."[20] If Ngai suggests that the referential aberrations of yes and no were inadvertent, for *No-No Boy* a complex structure of subjectivity, agency, and referentiality lies behind these "perverse meanings," further complicated by the intersection with race, gender, and nation. What historical analysis can recognize only as "perverse meanings," the novel demonstrates to be part of the fundamentally figurative or rhetorical nature of the sign.

The particular configuration of figurative activity assembled by the texts I consider here is specific to each, but the tropes that organize this activity are not so unique. That a rhetorical figure from classical antiquity appears in a canonical Asian American text pushes against the critical tendency to treat these texts as speaking primarily to other Asian American texts. It also suggests that Asian American literature has all along been engaging issues of representation at a level of complexity and sophistication conventionally reserved for canonical literature. In tracking the rhetorical question through *No-No Boy*, I will borrow promiscuously from both the classical and the Asian American traditions; this audacity, however, is sanctioned by the novel itself, which makes an identical move in its preface. In our so-called postracial moment, when a color-blind discourse is obscuring the exponential increase of racial stratification and ethnic segregation, it seems incredibly urgent to demonstrate how a text like *No-No Boy* is not only engaged in a forceful conversation with these classical forms but redeploying them to criticize the process of racialization itself.

Ratiocinatio: "I Got Reasons"

I want to begin my discussion of *No-No Boy* by looking at its preface, whose literariness critics have yet to consider. The preface is composed of several vignettes that collectively recount the dehumanization of the Japanese after the bombing of Pearl Harbor. The final and longest vignette stages a conversation between a Japanese American soldier and a white lieutenant. In their exchange, the lieutenant learns for the first time about internment, and when he inquires about his companion's decision to enlist, the only response he receives is the cryptic phrase, "I got reasons." The phrase is repeated three times, and with each repetition the tension increases between the white lieutenant's desire to know and the Japanese American soldier's refusal to say. Given the historical pressure for Japanese American speech acts to be intelligible, why does the vignette withhold these "reasons"? At the diegetic level the lieutenant never finds out what these reasons are, and by refusing to enlighten him, *No-No Boy* turns his questions into rhetorical ones, intimating to the reader at least that figurative opacity might have something to do with race itself. Indeed in this vignette the lieutenant is persistently deracinated, just as the Japanese American soldier is persistently racialized. In staging a dialogue about reason between the deracinated subject and his racialized counterpart, *No-No Boy* insists on marking the deracination of the rational subject, the abstract individual that has played so prominent a role in Western philosophy from the Enlightenment onward.

More ambitiously, in refusing to represent these Japanese American reasons, the novel contests a specific notion of interpretation, involving a particular scenario of communication that has governed, as Derrida claims, "the entire history of philosophy as such." It is a scenario that depends on the sign as essentially mimetic. Insofar as the sign functions as a transparent form of communication, it conveys the thoughts and intentions—the consciousness or presence—of the intending subject to absent others. For Derrida, this schema of representation "presupposes the simplicity of the origin, the continuity of all derivation, of all production, of all analysis, and the homogeneity of all dimensions."[21] Needless to say, a similar understanding of representation directs our approach to the Asian American or ethnic text as continuous with or homogeneous to the person of the race-identified author. *No-No Boy* questions this scenario on two levels. First, it demonstrates that this scenario, far from being universal, best characterizes a very specific subject, one that Denise Ferreira da Silva characterizes as the "self-described (abstract) universal."[22] Second, despite the tremendous historical pressure on Japanese American signs to be referential and for Japanese American intentions to be made transparent, *No-No Boy* insists on their referential opacity, using, in the vignette, the form of the rhetorical question to withhold any easy sense of referentiality.

Where the rhetorical question is most relevant to the racial concerns of *No-No Boy* lies in the lack of formal differentiation between rhetorical and grammatical questions. As Juhani Rudanko points out, "there is no distinction between ordinary and rhetorical questions as regards their form."[23] To distinguish them the reader or listener must rely on context. *No-No Boy* explores this visual predicament in the preface by pondering the institutional anxiety regarding bodies that may *look* the same but harbor different loyalties. The formal confusion between referential and figurative language here implies more basic questions about the reliability of the seen in relation to the known, and it is a predicament that *No-No Boy* connects directly to the visual anxiety of race. General John DeWitt famously averred that "all Japanese look alike," but why this is so is explained by a Justice Department official: "Unlike individuals of German and

Italian ancestry . . . who could be individually recognized and kept under watch . . . the Occidental eye cannot rapidly distinguish one Japanese resident from another."[24] To be identifiable as Japanese during World War II was, by definition, to be "visible" solely as a *form*, a racial type. As historian Sucheng Chan puts it, "According to this logic, because of Euro-American failings, it might be necessary to evacuate en masse persons of Japanese ancestry."[25] Consequently administrative measures like registration, the questionnaire, and the nisei combat unit were disciplinary instruments that could help the "Occidental eye" manage the differences it could not see by making them visually apparent.

It is significant that the exchange between the two soldiers in *No-No Boy*'s preface takes the form of the rhetorical question. Like the figure itself, their conversation too involves a certain rhetorical sleight of hand. The first time the phrase "I got reasons" occurs, it is in response to the lieutenant's declaration, "If they'd done that to me, I wouldn't be sitting in the belly of a broken-down B-24 going back to Guam from a reconnaissance mission to Japan" (xi). The response—"'I got reasons,' said the Japanese American soldier soberly" (xi)—states the existence of these reasons but does not disclose them. The white lieutenant's response is to swear, "They could kiss my ass," but the Japanese American soldier's answer is the same. Finally, confronted by reasons that elude him, the white lieutenant asks, "What the hell are we fighting for?" and again receives the enigmatic response. The lieutenant's state of confusion is deftly explained by the rhetorical question, which, in the words of one contemporary rhetorical handbook, "implies its own answer. In other cases, the speaker expects that no good answer is possible."[26] It is certainly the case that no good or reasonable answers are offered to the lieutenant, but Jonathan Kertzer hints at the greater epistemological implications behind the novel's refusal to answer the good lieutenant's questions. Typically speaking, he explains, questions suggest "an opening that in some way seeks to be closed," while answers are "a form of closure." Together the two present "a dialectic of question and answer, need and satisfaction, beginning and end, vacancy and plenitude." Rhetorical questions, he remarks, "play with the conditions of questioning."[27] We might say that the usual dialectic of questioning is refused by *No-No Boy*. The vignette does not allow the Japanese American soldier's response to close the openings set in motion by the lieutenant. In fact, given the lieutenant's curiosity about his companion's background, it is significant that the vignette does not volunteer similar details about the lieutenant other than his Nebraska origins. The burden to explain one's reasons and to educate the other falls on the Japanese American subject, and by refusing to satisfy the lieutenant's curiosity, *No-No Boy* challenges the racialization of reason itself. To use Kertzer's language, the lieutenant's questions have been transformed into questions without answers, beginnings without ends—a subtle criticism of the loyalty scenario.

The appearance of the rhetorical question in *No-No Boy*'s preface considerably broadens the novel's range of reference. As we shall see, its subject matter here is the abstract subject of reason itself, and the racialization of human reason as Japanese reasons. Since it is reason that is at stake here, the vignette turns to a kind of rhetorical question called *ratiocinatio* (from Latin *ratio*, "reason"), defined as "reasoning (typically with oneself) by asking questions."[28] Richard Lanham translates the term as "calm reasoning" or "reasoning by asking questions."[29] The subject of *ratiocinatio*, however, is not the Japanese American soldier, as we might presume, but the white lieutenant. This is a strange reversal, as one might expect a novel like *No-No Boy* to be primarily concerned with the male nisei subject. Why might this be? Let us follow the etymology of *ratiocinatio* as our way into this passage. From Plato onward Western philosophy has elevated reason or the mind over the body or matter and defined the human subject as a rational being. Elizabeth Grosz observes, "It could be argued that philosophy as we know it has established itself as a form of knowing, a form of rationality, only through the disavowal of the body, specifically the male body, and the corresponding elevation of mind as a disembodied term."[30] If this rational subject is a masculine being, *No-No Boy* shows us that it is also a deracinated one, that is, what David Lloyd, glossing Kant, describes as the "Subject without properties." Lloyd proposes that "the Subject without properties is the philosophical figure for what becomes, with increasing literalness through the nineteenth century, the global ubiquity of the white European."[31]

When *ratiocinatio* appears in *No-No Boy*'s preface, it suggests the larger philosophical stakes implicit in the form of the loyalty questionnaire because *ratiocinatio*—"asking ourselves the reasons for our statements," in Lanham's definition—is a figure that seems, once again, to turn to the self and its consciousness as the origin of reason and meaning. In "Signature Event Context," Derrida shows us how the sign, contrary to the desire of metaphysics, does not in fact communicate or extend the author's consciousness and presence. Instead, defined by its iterability, the sign is constituted by the structural possibility of its rupture from any given context, which is what enables it to be repeated—cited—in a potentially infinite number of contexts. As Derrida puts it, "This essential drift [*dérive*] bearing on writing as an iterative structure, cut off . . . from *consciousness* as the ultimate authority . . . is precisely what Plato condemns in the *Phaedrus*." The sign, he argues, functions in the "non-presence of my intention of saying something meaningful [*mon vouloir-dire, mon intention-de-signification*]." The French verb *vouloir-dire* means, simply, "to mean," but when we separate its compound infinitives (*vouloir*, "to want," and *dire*, "to say"), we get closer to Derrida's point, which is that my intention or consciousness, my wanting-to-say appears inextricably bound up with my meaning (*mon vouloir-dire*), and it is this idiomatic quirk of French that enables us to glimpse how the illusion of referential transparency occurs in the very language we have for "meaning."[32]

If referential transparency, or the illusion thereof, is what is at stake in *No-No Boy* and its immediate historical situation, *ratiocinatio* is the means by which the vignette shifts the burden of rhetorical opacity away from the Japanese American soldier, who must declare himself as Japanese by saying yes or no, and toward the deracination of his white companion and the political conditions under which he is not called upon to explain *his* reasons. As Robyn Wiegman suggests, "Modern citizenship functions as a disproportionate system in which the universalism ascribed to certain bodies (white, male, propertied) is protected and subtended by the infinite particularity assigned to others (black, female, unpropertied). . . . This system is itself contingent on certain visual relations, where only those particularities associated with the Other are, quite literally, *seen*."[33] No personal names are given in the vignette, and both soldiers are understood to be racial types, but even given this degree of generality, the nisei soldier is, without exception, repeatedly racialized: he is either "a good Japanese-American" (x), "the Japanese-American who was an American soldier" (x), or, most often, "the Japanese-American soldier" (x, xi). The lieutenant, on the other hand, is described twice as "a blond giant from Nebraska" (x) and then referred to as either "the lieutenant from Nebraska" (x, xi) or just "the lieutenant" (xi). In stark contrast to his companion, the vignette refuses to racialize the lieutenant. His description is consistently deracinated, that is, evacuated of any racial or ethnic meaning. "Blond" is all that remains of the trace of whiteness. The vignette may acknowledge the apparent invisibility of whiteness by refusing to racialize the lieutenant, but because it places him in direct conversation with his Japanese American comrade, it makes the point that the lieutenant's status as unmarked, as the universal depends on his differentiation from a racialized other (an other who is raced against the subject self-described as without properties).

For a historical instance of this reasoning, we may look to Earl Warren, then attorney general of California, who endorsed internment by declaring, "We believe that when we are dealing with the Caucasian race we have methods that will test the loyalty of them. . . . But when we deal with the Japanese we are in an entirely different field and cannot form any opinion that we believe to be sound."[34] As Ngai points out, Warren conveniently forgets that German nationals were interned during World War I and that the individual screenings of Italian and German nationals during World War II was the direct result of decisions made by the federal government to avoid its earlier mistakes: "Earl Warren's assumptions about the loyalty of 'Caucasians' elided the history of war-induced assimilation and the constructedness of Euro-Americans' ethno-racial identities."[35] In other words, whiteness too is a historically specific racial formation. Its roots lie in Enlightenment philosophy and in theories of abstract liberalism, but the presumption of its invisibility, at least in the United States, has more to do with the enduring power of socioeconomic and political formations to normalize whiteness than any intrinsic quality it possesses of being transparent. Richard Dyer warns against equating whiteness to being nonraced when he observes, "As long as race is something only applied to non-white peoples, as long as white people are not racially seen and named, they/we function as a human norm. . . . There is no more powerful position that that of being 'just' human. The claim to power is the claim to speak for the commonality of humanity."[36] In an important correction to Dyer, Sara Ahmed reminds us, as *No-No Boy* does in its vignette, that "of course whiteness is only invisible for those who inhabit it. For those who don't, it is hard not to see whiteness; it even seems everywhere." Ahmed concludes that a critique of whiteness from the point of view of nonwhites must proceed differently: "It would be about making what can already be seen, visible in a different way."[37] If internment and the loyalty questionnaire were instruments whose purpose was to make visible the racialized reasons lurking inside the Japanese American subject, they simultaneously functioned to obscure the *deracination* of German and Italian reasons.

In the face of political realities like registration, the loyalty questionnaire, and the voluntary combat unit, each of which functioned, in different ways, to compel the subject identifiable as Japanese to represent his reasons, *No-No Boy* nevertheless insists on the sign's rhetorical possibilities. Its reluctance to represent these Japanese American reasons is all the more extraordinary given the various pressures from the War Department and the Japanese American Citizens League (JACL) to generate, in Michi Weglyn's phrase, "proof, proof, and more proof" of Japanese intentions.[38] That the form of this proof invokes the abstract subject of classic liberalism seems largely lost on either side of the barbed-wire fence. As Ngai explains, some members of the War Department came to believe that a voluntary all-nisei combat unit would serve as "counter propaganda" against Japanese charges of a "racial war."[39] Colonel William Scobey, for example, is blithely unaware of the irony here when he declares that the "advantage of the voluntary program to the Japanese Americans cannot be overemphasized. They must realize that a voluntary combat team constitutes a symbol of their loyalty which can be displayed to the American public and to those who oppose the Japanese Americans."[40] From the Japanese American side, Mike Masaoka, secretary of the collaborationist JACL, had lobbied for the nisei "right," as American citizens, to prove their loyalty: "We had to have a demonstration in blood."[41] *No-No Boy*'s preface picks up on this fiction of agency, intrinsic to abstract personhood, when it begins the vignette by telling us that its protagonist is "a good Japanese-American who had *volunteered* for the army" (x, my emphasis). In the guise of the rhetorical question, the loyalty questionnaire as it appears in this little vignette elucidates how *No-No Boy* is, at the level of its figurative activity, tackling issues that have been central to the history of philosophy as well as classical liberalism.

It is against this backdrop of "visible" proof—whether in blood or in words—that *No-No Boy*'s reticence to reveal Japanese American reasons becomes so significant. The vignette maintains its refusal to represent to the level of its punctuation. When the vignette begins, the Japanese American soldier is trying to explain to the white lieutenant why his parents are in Wyoming even though they are not, as the lieutenant initially assumed, farmers. "What's that mean?" asks the lieutenant, and the Japanese American soldier replies,

> "Well, it's this way. . . ." And then the Japanese-American whose folks were still Japanese-Japanese, or else they would not be in a camp with barbed wire and watchtowers with soldiers holding rifles, told the blond giant from Nebraska about the removal of the Japanese from the Coast, which was called the evacuation, and about the concentration camps, which were called relocation centers. (x–xi, original ellipsis)

At first the vignette puts the Japanese American soldier in the position of narrator: "Well, it's this way . . . ," he begins to explain, but the passage immediately switches to impersonal narration to finish recounting these events. With this little switch the vignette stages how the thoughts of the Japanese American soldier are represented *for* him: he does not represent or tell his own thoughts. The rest of the vignette, as we have seen, continues to stage the difficulty of representing Japanese American reasons, which suggests, as I have argued, a genuine inquiry into whether Japanese American interiority can be represented at all under these historical conditions. By inserting an ellipsis, a mark indicating that something has been left out, in the place of what would have been the narrative of the Japanese American soldier, the preface signals its refusal to represent Japanese American reasons. Such reasons, it insists, can be figured only elliptically, by means of a sign pointing to something absent or excluded.

Returning to the diegetic level of the vignette, *No-No Boy* denies the white lieutenant's desire to know his companion's reasons for enlisting and thwarts the desire of even this most sympathetic of characters to access Japanese American reasons. Frustrated by the lack of answers, the anguished white lieutenant demands, one final time, "What the hell are we fighting for?" (xi). Paul de Man's well-known reading of the rhetorical question helps us understand what is at stake here when the novel transforms the lieutenant's interrogative questions into rhetorical ones. In deconstructing "What's the difference?," the question that an irritable Archie Bunker asks his wife, de Man argues, "The grammatical model of the question becomes rhetorical . . . when it is impossible to decide by grammatical or other linguistic devices which of the two meanings (that can be entirely incompatible) prevails." He goes on to explain just why Bunker finds this prospect so troubling: "The very anger he displays is indicative of more than impatience; it reveals his despair when confronted with a structure of linguistic meaning that he cannot control and that holds the discouraging prospect of an infinity of similar future confusions, all of them potentially catastrophic in their consequences."[42] Archie Bunker's despair in the face of a linguistic predicament over which he has no control is one that the agitated lieutenant shares, but for the Japanese American soldier the possibility of a language perpetually slipping away from his ability to intend or mean is even more hazardous. Why, then, does the vignette make him risk a rhetorical structure that he cannot control and whose impact on him is already materially evident by the uniform he wears and his demonstration "in blood"?

No-No Boy gives us no direct answers; instead it does something distinctively literary. It employs the device of a story within a story, using this unverifiable means to tell us something about Japanese American reasons. By means of this device, the novel offers the reader a partial glimpse of these reasons through the narrated thoughts occurring directly after the second and third repetitions of the soldier's enigmatic phrase. The second time the phrase appears, we are told, "'I got reasons,' said the Japanese-American soldier soberly, and he was thinking about a lot of things but mostly about his friend who didn't volunteer for the army because his father had been picked up in the second screening and was in a different camp from the one he and his mother and two sisters were in" (xi). In the short paragraph that follows, we discover that the friend, a no-no boy, has been imprisoned because his request for his family to be reunited in exchange for his military service has been denied. After the third and final repetition of the phrase, we find another allusion to the soldier's no-no friend: "'I got reasons,' said the Japanese-American soldier soberly and thought some more about his friend who was in another kind of uniform because they wouldn't let his father go to the same camp with his mother and sisters" (xi). Through the use of this little fiction within a fiction, *No-No Boy* allows for the ethical possibility that signs appearing to be referential may not only signify otherwise but may in fact articulate aberrant and different trajectories that cannot find expression in the limited racial framework of World War II. Within the vignette, for example, the white lieutenant is genuinely moved by his companion's story and identifies with him, even though the former's curiosity about his companion is never satisfied. In staging these Japanese American reasons as a story, an imaginative fiction, the vignette suggests that direct access to these reasons is not possible because reason has been racialized into yes or no. The novel proper will attempt to grant us unmediated access to these reasons, but at least in the preface *No-No Boy* insists that these Japanese American reasons cannot be known; they can only be *figured*. The vignette's narration of the Japanese American soldier's reasons does not lead, as we might expect, to his own reasons but to those of his no-no friend. Maintaining that the two share "another kind of uniform" (xi), the vignette proposes that the disloyal no-no boy is *formally* identical to the loyal Japanese American soldier. In the tiny space of this little fiction, the preface calls on the productive confusion between rhetorical and grammatical questions to suggest that yes and no cannot be formally differentiated, and in emphasizing their visual confusion the vignette suggests an aberrant itinerary for no: the no-no friend is not disloyal; his no means something else.

No-No Boy invites the reader into a literary space where the racial or linguistic sign can exceed its referential logic, where yes and no, despite the political pressures exerted on them, can be rhetorical. As de Man concludes, "Rhetoric radically suspends logic and opens up vertiginous possibilities of referential aberration. . . . I would not hesitate to equate the rhetorical, figural potential of language with literature itself."[43] Within the carefully constructed space of this fiction within a fiction, no and yes can mean other than their proper and referential meanings. Outside of this literary space the conditions for rhetoric are far bleaker. The vignette's persistent identification of the Japanese American soldier as Japanese American is telling, as is its need to differentiate him as "a *good* Japanese-American who had *volunteered* for the army" (x, my emphasis) or as "the Japanese-American soldier of the *American* army" (xi, my emphasis). The vignette recognizes that this differentiation is necessary—it distinguishes the nisei soldier from his family, who are "still Japanese-Japanese, or else they would not be in a camp with barbed wire" (x)—even as it acknowledges that the distinction is entirely rhetorical; these differences are eliminated by the fact of internment itself. Indeed we could argue that the vignette is quite aware of the profound distance between the Japanese American subject and the deracinated, self-determining subject because agency, for the racialized subject, must consist of withholding his reasons, of refusing to say what he means. Clearly *No-No Boy*'s concerns extend beyond the immediate circumstances proscribing Japanese American speech in this historical period. Its stakes are exponentially higher.

Masculine Self-Authoring

If the preface protests the racialization of reason by refusing to represent Japanese American reasons, the main body of the novel seeks the opposite: it portrays the no-no boy's struggle, from his own perspective, to represent his reasons. In one of the novel's infamously long interior monologues, Ichiro's miscarried speech act is attributed to his "weakness," his loyalty to his mother, but it quickly becomes clear that much more is involved. In Ichiro's words, "I do not understand what it was . . . that made me destroy the half of me which was American and the half which might have become the whole of me if I had said yes I will go and fight in your army *because that is what I believe and want and cherish and love*" (16–17, my emphasis). Unlike the nisei soldier from the preface who can refuse to say what he means, the no-no boy *cannot* say what he means and is unable even to know, in Derrida's little play on words, what he intends or wants to mean. Such is the epistemic violence of race and gender under Japanese internment that the no-no boy cannot occupy the space "proper" to the subject, his wanting-to-say. For the WRA and the War Department, "no-no" had to be equivalent to a self-declaration, so what does it mean for the novel to portray Ichiro's "no-no" as the loss of meaning, as a result of "forgetting" his reasons/reason? In a key passage that the novel will reprise in its final scene, Ichiro walks alone on a darkened street, which turns into a small synecdoche for all of America. As he puzzles over why he said no in the first place, he finally recalls his reason: "My reason was all the reasons put together. . . . I remember a lot of people and a lot of things now as I walk confidently through the night over a small span of concrete which is part of the sidewalks which are part of . . . the nation that is America. *It was for this that I meant to fight*, only the meaning got lost when I needed it most badly" (34, my emphasis). Ichiro "meant" to fight; he intended, in other words, to say yes, but with this loss of meaning the relentless drift of the sign is revealed, and in the wake of its exposure the subject's intentions and his meaning break apart. We would not be wrong to surmise that Ichiro is the fully imagined version of the no-no boy from the preface, the friend who shares the Japanese American soldier's form, but what I find more compelling here is why the novel presents the no-no boy's speech act as a linguistic and semantic crisis, as a scenario in which the speaking subject loses his conscious control over meaning.

As de Man understands it, Archie Bunker's anger conceals his despair when confronted by a linguistic structure he cannot control; here the no-no boy's rage, hopelessness, and desolation are racialized versions of this rhetoricity. The rhetorical question, in de Man's reckoning, is not a pretty ornament, as rhetoric was typically depicted in the Renaissance, to be plucked from a "garden of eloquence."[44] Instead the rhetorical question marks an unrelenting site of profound unease, an irresolvable impasse between grammar and rhetoric where meaning, in *No-No Boy*'s phrase, will inevitably get lost. This is why *No-No Boy* casts its protagonist's epiphany in the passive voice: "the meaning got lost," the novel insists, to underscore the impersonality of this semantic crisis, the "semiological enigma" that de Man identifies as "rhetorical."[45] For *No-No Boy*, as for de Man, the rhetoricity of the sign opens up a frightening abyss between meaning and intention, in which language can no longer be trusted as a vehicle for communication. If the Japanese American soldier from the novel's preface can afford to be a bit more coy about revealing his reasons, for the various no-no boys populating the novel proper the consequences of saying or not being able to say what they mean is far more unforgiving. The image of the no-no boy as an infant (from Latin *in-fans*, "unable to speak") is a powerful reminder of representation under race, but when this infantilized imagery is extended to the nisei veteran—Bull, Ichiro's erstwhile tormentor, is depicted as "an infant crying in the darkness" (250)—then it is obvious that the novel is considering a structural problem involving representation under conditions of coercion, even if those conditions have been reappropriated via the category of Asian American literature as an affirmative identity politics.

Patricia P. Chu takes us directly to the novel's quarrel with the self-determining subject and the representational scenario supported by such a subject when she argues that *No-No Boy* belongs to a "demi-canon" of texts defined by masculine tropes of self-authoring. For these texts, Asian American subjectivity is presumed to be male. According to Chu they delineate "a racialized anxiety of authorship in America" because they are simultaneously involved in struggles to define masculinity, to establish authorship, and to construct a literary tradition, all of which prominently feature a desire for white women and the abjection of the immigrant mother.[46] Rhetorically speaking this demi-canon shares a common set of "tropes of authoring as fathering and self-authoring as self-fathering." While Ichiro may not be an author figure, there is nonetheless a productive resonance between the no-no boy's inability to represent or author himself and the self-authoring trope as a function of Asian American subjectivity. Like its deracinated philosophical counterpart, the intending subject of reason, the self-authoring subject is also a figure invested in masculine agency in relation to representation. *No-No Boy* explores this masculine self-representation by dramatizing the struggle of nisei males, in the preface as well as the novel proper, to represent themselves—to be, in Chu's phrase, "self-authoring." While the novel recognizes the rhetoricity of language, what de Man calls the "referential aberration" of the sign, its concern is with the specific historical circumstances under which these linguistic tensions become insupportable, unsustainable. If *No-No Boy*'s response to the self-authorizing subject of metaphysics is to expose his abstraction as the privilege of deracination, it nevertheless refrains—as might be construed by its title—from questioning the masculine and heteronormative investments of this subject.

The novel proper returns to the more typical structure of the rhetorical question as it presents a generalized scenario in which the nisei male, whether no-no boy or veteran, is unable to answer or say what he means in response to questions about his identity. For example, *No-No Boy* begins by informing us "Two weeks after his twenty-fifth birthday, Ichiro got off a bus at Second and Main in Seattle" (1), trading on the birthday and the homecoming to suggest a sort of symbolic rebirth. But such hopes are immediately dashed because what our protagonist encounters as soon as he steps off the bus is the interrogative scenario of the loyalty questionnaire. At the bus stop Ichiro meets Eto, a nisei veteran, who demands that Ichiro declare himself by saying yes or no. For the loyalty scenario to appear right as the novel begins suggests, in one sense, that a remorseful no-no boy can make a different choice; this time he can say yes instead of no. Why, then, does the novel *repeat* his miscarried speech act rather than rescript it? The rhetorical question hints at why this might be. Eto is initially friendly until he realizes that Ichiro is a no-no boy:

> The eyes confronted Ichiro with indecision which changed slowly to enlightenment and then to suspicion. He remembered. He knew.
> The friendliness was gone as he said: "No-no boy, huh?"
> Ichiro wanted to say yes. He wanted to return the look of despising hatred and say simply yes, but it was too much to say. (3)

Like the interrogative structure of the loyalty scenario, this exchange involves a rhetorical question: Eto doesn't require an answer; Ichiro cannot offer one. The novel makes a point of telling us that "Ichiro wanted to say yes," but since he cannot articulate his "intention to say something meaningful," as Derrida glosses it, the novel makes it evident that Ichiro is by no means a self-authoring subject. If Derrida's deconstruction of the sign depends on the role of writing to disrupt the apparent presence of speech, in the scenario that *No-No Boy* imagines the emasculated nisei male's desire to say something meaningful cannot even enter language. *No-No Boy* informs us that the simple yes its protagonist wants to say is "too much to say," and we might think of this "too much" as also a kind of excess, a surplus of rhetoricity when what is needed, what is required is the impossible simplicity of referential language.

As the Eto scene continues, the novel comments on the inability of the interrogative scenario to make visible the interiority it seeks to represent and offers up a striking image of blindness to describe this failure. Ichiro "shook his head once, not wanting to evade the eyes but finding it impossible to meet them. Out of his big weakness the little ones were branching, and the eyes he didn't have the courage to face were ever present. If it would have helped to gouge out his own eyes, he would have done so long ago" (3–4). In the handful of lines that separate Eto's hailing of Ichiro as a no-no boy and the sentences just quoted, Eto's eyes become the disembodied proxy for the disciplinary gaze of the state and for Ichiro's own conscience. The "ever present" eyes that Ichiro cannot evade recall Foucault's reading of the panopticon as a metaphor for the disciplinary nature of modern society. Wiegman helps us connect this "visual modernity" to the new concept of race that arises in the nineteenth century. Elaborating on the epistemic shift that redefines race as simultaneously visual and hidden, Wiegman observes that "the conformation of the body to a racial script that precedes and instantiates the subject in a relation of subjection does not depend, in any uncomplicated way, on what the eye sees. . . . In the deeply wrenching knowledge of an eye that constitutionally misperceives, in the loss of an epistemological assurance in the referent . . . the logic of race attached to a corporeal essence is challenged at its most fundamental level of bodily belief."[47] If race, as Wiegman argues, stands for the misperception and misalignment of seeing and knowing, then the violent image of self-blinding that *No-No Boy* gives us here—Ichiro gouging out his own eyes—argues powerfully against the referential logic of the visual as a vastly inadequate framework when confronting race. Remembering that *No-No Boy*'s preface insists on yes and no as sharing "another kind of uniform," the novel disturbs a certain type of referential logic that fails to get at the intrinsic rhetorical potential of the linguistic sign. Despite a disciplinary gaze that is, as Wiegman suggests, "inscribing visibility everywhere,"[48] the loyalty scenario as staged by *No-No Boy* is a technology that fails not only to ascertain but to differentiate Japanese American reasons: Eto does not see, Ichiro is blind, the difference between yes and no is rhetorical. When Irma Szikszai-Nagy remarks that "interrogatives that are not real questions . . . are all Janus-faced," she illuminates what the novel is getting at here when it stages the limits of an all-powerful and invasive gaze that fails to "see" because it relies on a referential logic equating the visual with what *can be seen*.[49]

The novel's juxtaposition of the loyalty scenario with Ichiro's "rebirth" suggests that the problem of representing "no-no" reasons does not obtain at the level of the individual. The repetition of Ichiro's original no suggests that his inability to speak is not the result of a bad choice, an error that can be revised by an act of self-authoring, but rather the consequences of a structural problem. The novel formally registers this awareness in the Eto scene by depicting its effect on Ichiro as a linguistic version of internment: "The walls had closed in and were crushing all the unspoken words back down into his stomach" (3). Epistemic violence means that the no-no boy may be released from one type of incarceration, but he remains within another kind of coercive structure, one in which he has been infantilized as a subject unable to say what he means. We might consider the novel's repetition of the loyalty scenario and its original outcome as its formal commentary on the material and political conditions of Japanese American representation. It uses this repetition to signal its status as a novel, a literary text engaged in an act of re-presentation. Repetition, we might say, serves as *No-No Boy*'s means of "thinking" about the structural tensions involved in coercive representation, and it gives a slightly different emphasis to Ling's exhortation by indicating how the novel thinks about the "work" of fiction. As a point of entry into a deeply repetitive novel—similar scenes and characters, even the same phrases reappear—repetition offers us a way to theorize this formal behavior.

As previously mentioned, the novel's awareness of its own operations does not extend beyond certain gendered and sexualized limits. *No-No Boy*'s staging of Ma or Emi's interiority, for example, fails to operate at the same consistent level of complexity that has characterized its reflections on nisei male interiority. Several critics have noted the especially problematic portrayal of Ma because it seems to rehearse the same anti-Japanese rhetoric that the novel has condemned elsewhere. Chu, for instance, remarks of Ma that "she is just the sort of nationalist, anti-American, Japanese nut who was conjured up by the American press and military to justify placing Japanese Americans into camps."[50] Within *No-No Boy*'s representational economy the Japanese (m)other must be narratively foreclosed for the nisei male to attain representation. This (m)other both emasculates and infantilizes her son: her desire turns him into a no-no boy. In a key passage at the beginning of the novel, directly following Ichiro's confrontation with Eto, Ichiro returns home for the first time to be greeted without emotional fanfare by his mother. Disappointed and angry, he retreats to his room: "It was to please her, he said to himself with teeth clamped together to imprison the wild, meaningless, despairing cry which was forever straining inside of him. . . . It was she who opened my mouth and made my lips move to sound the words which got me two years in prison and an emptiness that is more empty and frightening than the caverns of hell" (12). Here the issei mother has transformed her son into a sterile womb: Ichiro thinks of himself as "an emptiness that is more empty and frightening than the caverns of hell." More troubling, though, is the depiction of the issei mother's desire as a violent act of ventriloquism: "It was she who opened my mouth." Aping the fifth-column rhetoric of racists like DeWitt, the no-no boy imagines the alien (m)other invading his consciousness and dispossessing him of his reason such that he cannot even speak, much less intend, for himself.

Later in the same passage the protagonist thinks, "Pa's okay, but he's a nobody. He's a goddamned, fat, grinning, spineless nobody. Ma is the rock that's always hammering, pounding, pounding, pounding in her unobtrusive, determined, fanatical way until there's nothing left to call one's self" (12). Because the novel uses a narrative direction to introduce the thoughts that follow—"he said to himself with teeth clamped" (12)—we are to understand that these are Ichiro's thoughts, not the novel's, and thus we can disagree with the character's perception of Ma as "pounding" and "hammering" in a way that belongs, in this phallocentric logic, to the heteronormative Japanese American male. Again it is Ichiro's belief, and not necessarily the narrator's, that Ma's gender perversion has turned the Japanese males in her radius into subjects defined by lack, that is, into "women": her son becomes a sterile womb, her husband a "nobody." But if we move from the perspective of the protagonist to the representational economy of the novel as a whole, we find that there may be a deeper alignment between the protagonist's consciousness and the values of the novel. As Chu comments, with regard to this demi-canon, "the use of the issei *mother* to represent the abjected Japanese traits seems fundamental to such texts rather than accidental."[51]

Refusing the Self-Authoring Model: "Feminism"?

In the paragraph directly preceding the passage discussed above, *No-No Boy* presents a troubling narrative ploy with regard to its representation of Japanese female "reasons." This paragraph is one of the few places in the novel where we are given access to Ma's thoughts, but as we shall see, the narrative direction confuses rather than distinguishes the origin of these thoughts.

> "I am proud that you are back," she said. "I am proud to call you my son."
> *It was her way of saying that* she had made him what he was and that the thing in him which made him say no to the judge and go to prison for two years was the growth of a seed planted by the mother tree and that she was the mother who had put this thing in her son and that everything that had been done and said was exactly as it should have been and that that was what made him her son. (11, my emphasis)

What, exactly, is the status of the passage proceeding from Ma's declaration of pride? The narrative direction "It was her way of saying" suggests that what follows is an interpretation of Ma's statement, but who interprets, and what exactly is being interpreted? Does the direction indicate the voice of the omniscient narrator in the act of presenting Ma's reasons from her perspective? Or, more likely, is this the same narrator we have encountered throughout, omniscient narration as focalized through

Ichiro, such that what is being presented as Ma's reasoning is in fact the narrator's report of how *Ichiro* is interpreting her thoughts? Compare, for example, a similar scene portraying the disclosure of Ichiro's reasons. Here Ichiro belatedly understands his reasons for refusing to enlist: *"And then Ichiro thought to himself:* My reason was all the reasons put together. I did not go because I was weak and could not do what I should have done. It was not my mother, whom I have never really known. It was me, myself"* (34, my emphasis). Setting aside this apparent gesture of self-authoring—"It was me, myself"—my interest lies in the narrative direction introducing these reasons. The colon inserted after the narrative direction, in addition to the shift to the first person, clearly indicates that these are Ichiro's thoughts. We are, in this sense, being given symbolic access to his reasons. Why the no-no boy's reasons are made clearly evident, as opposed to those of the Japanese American soldier from the preface, has to do, I believe, with the novel's defense of the no-no boy as someone who is forced by his own government to misspeak himself. The novel's reliance on its long interior monologues should be regarded as part of this defense.

Indeed *No-No Boy*'s efforts are ultimately homosocial; they are directed toward repositioning Ichiro from the infantilized position of no-no boy, of being without speech, toward a heteronormative masculinity, in which he can replace, if not speak for, the nisei veteran. And yet its conclusion problematizes the model of masculine self-authoring that it has idealized. It is significant that the novel is far less interested in the representation of female issei reasons, at least in comparison to the elaborate measures it has taken in withholding or disclosing male nisei reasons, especially because this is a novel preoccupied with the complications of speaking and being spoken for. Chu, however, issues a quick caution when she wonders "whether the novel's antifeminism can be so simple."[52] If not an inchoate feminism, might *No-No Boy*'s refusal to turn its protagonist into a self-authoring subject be, at the very least, a far from simple "antifeminism"?[53] The final lines of the novel reprise the language of a previous scene, the one in which Ichiro belatedly discovers his reasons. Here again we find the attempt to turn the tiny synecdoche of a single city street into the whole of a nation that can include even no-no boys: "He walked along, thinking, searching, thinking and probing, and, in the darkness of the alley of the community that was a tiny bit of America, he chased that faint and elusive insinuation of promise as it continued to take shape in mind and in heart" (251). The emphasis on "thinking" hints at the undisclosed reasons we encountered at the beginning of the novel, but these haunting final lines send the no-no boy back on his quest for meaning, into the solitary darkness. While it is true that Ichiro has traveled quite a distance from the bleak despair that characterized his homecoming, the novel ends by putting him in a gentler version of the predicament with which he began: "He couldn't see it to put it into words, but the feeling was pretty strong" (250–51). At the end of the novel Ichiro remains unable to say what he intends, to put his reasons into words, and it is his failure to inhabit the model of masculine self-authoring that grants us, in the novel's words, some "glimmer of hope" (250).

No-No Boy and Rhetoric

No-No Boy's literariness is difficult to defend. The novel's language is deceptively simple, and its characteristic style—most memorable, perhaps, in the long interior monologues—consists primarily of run-on sentences tumbling so swiftly into each other that they risk losing sense. The sparse commentary on No-No Boy's aesthetics tends to avoid the category's traditional preoccupations with beauty, pleasure, or truth. Instead these discussions take the position that the novel's style is intentional or oppositional.[54] Lowe, for instance, considers its "unconventional style" as "refus[ing] the development, synthesis, and reconciliation required by traditional canonical criteria." For her the novel articulates a distinctively Asian American aesthetics defined "by contradiction, not sublimation, such that discontent, nonequivalence, and irresolution call into question the project of abstracting the aesthetic as a separate domain of unification and reconciliation."[55] Lowe's comments on *No-No Boy* are regrettably brief as they occur in the context of a chapter principally concerned with delineating the potential critique that the institutionalization of Asian American literature offers the university at large. Ling takes a different approach. His task is to situate the novel's aesthetic choices within the limited discourses of its day and to explain how these racial, social, and commercial limitations worked in concert to restrict recognition of *No-No Boy*'s "literariness" and "rich human potential." For him *No-No Boy*'s style is best explained by "authorial design," which he indicates with a set of related terms, such as "authorial ploy," "rhetorical strategy," and, most often, just "strategy," which occurs again and again. Accordingly he argues that the novel's style should be regarded as "linguistic and syntactical innovations," implying that if readers find *No-No Boy* jarring or dissatisfying, they are experiencing the novel as its author intended. He insists, for example, that "the syntactic stasis that entraps Ichiro is, in this sense, [not] a passive reflection of Okada's transparent intentionality. . . . Rather, it is simply a rhetorical strategy that Okada uses to enhance the effects of his depiction of Ichiro's moral plight."[56]

To defend *No-No Boy*'s literariness, Ling has to resort to the author as an originator and a source of meaning for the text, a notion that has been attacked from different quadrants since the New Critics dismissed it as the intentional fallacy. But in making this move, Ling has redoubtable aesthetic company. It is this kind of language that Terry Eagleton identifies with the ideology of the aesthetic, arguing that "The emergence of the aesthetic as a theoretical category is closely bound up with the material process by which cultural production, at an early stage of bourgeois society, becomes 'autonomous.' . . . The idea of autonomy—of a mode of being which is entirely self-regulating and self-determining—provides the middle class with just the ideological model of subjectivity it requires for its material operations."[57] Glancing back to *No-No Boy*'s preface, we could say that the novel argues quite strongly against precisely this kind of autonomous subject. The rest of the novel too refuses this self-authoring model for its characters, whether "loyal" soldier or "disloyal" no-no boy. In the postwar world depicted in *No-No Boy*, signs are perpetually subject to coercion or drift, and no assurances can be made about intentions, authorial or otherwise. Indeed we might take note of Lawson Inada and Frank Chin's epiphany, memorialized in the critical essays bookending the reissued version of *No-No Boy*, that the author is dead, and no amount of effort, supernatural or otherwise, can raise his shade. As the complicated rhetorical activity moving through the pages of *No-No Boy* shows, the person of the author is not only missing but insufficient for predicting what the novel can mean, for explaining its figurative activities, and for directing the interpretive permutations that it has undergone and will continue to undergo.

I do not argue, as Lowe or Ling have, that *No-No Boy* offers a different route to the aesthetic. While this approach is both laudable and important, it sidesteps what I see as the most compelling part of the novel. What makes *No-No Boy* so powerful and enduring is not its aesthetics but the tension between its crude style and its rhetorical activity, which is immensely complex. *No-No Boy* is not "beautiful" in traditional aesthetic terms.[58] It is crude, didactic, and repetitive. Compared to a contemporary like Ellison's *Invisible Man*, for example, or assessed according to traditional aesthetic criteria, *No-No Boy* would surely fall short. Indeed it is because the novel is profoundly moving and persuasive, a scenario it presents in the preface, that it calls out for rhetoric, that traditional terrain where questions of figurative complexity and affective suasion are brought together. It is less that the novel taps into a different type of aesthetics and more that the category of the aesthetic is inadequate for handling the figurative densities of a text like *No-No Boy*. Ward Farnsworth's quip, "Rhetorical figures also show up often, of course, in a lot of bad speech and writing," while humorous, nevertheless gives us a point of entry into the rhetoricity of texts like *No-No Boy*.[59]

By way of concluding, I want to briefly return to the novel's preface. I have already discussed how the vignette disturbs the referential reading of yes and no, but in the section preceding the repetition of "I got reasons," the preface suggests a way of thinking about race in relation to rhetoric. When the Japanese American soldier begins to tell the blond lieutenant about the internment, the lieutenant finds it hard to believe: "The lieutenant listened and he didn't believe it. He said: 'That's funny. Now, tell me again.' The Japanese-American soldier of the American army told it again and didn't change a word. The lieutenant believed him this time" (xi). The first time the account is told, the lieutenant—the reader within the scene—finds it incredible. He dismisses it as joke. The second time the story is told, the lieutenant is persuaded, but the preface stresses the fact that the Japanese American soldier "didn't change a word." The exact same story elicits two divergent responses from the lieutenant, but the *text* in question remains the same. In other words, the preface insists on the precarious possibility that the same sign, the same form can mean something else, and in the difference between the first iteration of the story and the second lies the potential for the sympathetic imagination to brush against the other. The referential aberration that is opened up in the same form, a conundrum that *No-No Boy* presents again and again, is not accessed through aesthetics. It is available to us only through rhetoric.

No-No Boy's preface uses the figure of the rhetorical question to offer a complex reading of Japanese American intentions as a "story." As a fiction, the no and the yes, sharing a uniform, also share a place of referential aberration and thus the potential for resignification. Just as linguistic texts do not bear singular meanings for the signs they inscribe, so too racialized bodies can be shown as sites of possibility and alternative meanings. By foregrounding the rhetorical nature of language as a relationship between signs that produce meaning and potentially go awry, we reinvigorate the reading of Asian American literature at the same time that we resist the illusion of the sign's transparency—even when it is under pressure to be its most referential, to be its most truth-bearing, when it is at its most seductive and most dangerous.

Maxine Hong Kingston's *China Men* follows her critically acclaimed *The Woman Warrior* by telling the men's stories of working in and immigrating to the United States. Recounting the experiences of great-grandfathers, grandfathers, fathers, uncles, and brothers, *China Men* takes us from the sugarcane plantations of Hawaii to the laundries of New York City, from the canneries of Alaska to the railroads of California and behind the front lines of the Vietnam War. Like its predecessor, it is a hybrid of fact and fiction, but it is also a far more fragmented narrative, drawing on a wide array of textual sources from different historical periods, literary traditions, and genres. As in *The Woman Warrior*, the storyteller is a Chinese American daughter-narrator, but her duty here is both more ambitious and complex: she must imagine herself in the place of her often openly misogynist male ancestors while wrestling with their exclusion from and exploitation by the United States. One of *China Men*'s primary aims, as Kingston explains it, involves telling "American history poetically" by picking up where William Carlos Williams's *In the American Grain* leaves off.[1] To take up this task, however, *China Men* must first confront the institutionalized erasure of its subjects from the historical record, as well as from family memory. Given the high political stakes of reconstructing this missing history—a necessity that *China Men* is acutely cognizant of—why does it insist on making its subjects appear by disappearing them?

While *China Men* may not be as wildly popular as *Woman Warrior*, it is nevertheless a touchstone Asian American text and Kingston herself easily the most recognizable if not most widely taught Asian American author. This indisputable canonical status is what makes the following revelation, disclosed in a 1991 interview, all the more remarkable: there Kingston is reported as saying about "The Laws," "I didn't even write that part" and that "my editor . . . wrote it to make it sound really legal, journalistic, and not my language."[2] What are we to make of this extraordinary statement? And what does it mean for an author as identified with Asian American literature as Kingston to say that "The Laws" is not her language? Let us take this declaration as our point of entry into what Christopher Lee has called the "post-identity turn" of Asian American literary criticism, which involves the persistence of identity "as affective investments, means of knowledge production, and modes of ethico-political engagement and imagination" despite the multiple and sustained critiques of Asian American identity since the 1990s.[3] Lee cautions that "post-identity" should by no means be understood as a periodizing term because criticisms of Asian American identity have been in existence since the moment Asian America itself sprang into being. The recent surge of interest in questions of Asian American form and aesthetics, however, magnifies what Colleen Lye has called Asian American identity's "limitless tendency toward fragmentation" by turning away from the identity altogether as the critical energy for the literature.[4]

Early debates over the definition of Asian American literature tended to disagree about which ethnicities to include or exclude, but they almost never questioned whether Asian American identity should be the basis for the literary tradition. As a result, as Lye has observed, "the past 20 years have witnessed a publishing boom in literature by U.S. authors of Asian descent, but a scarcity of paradigms for its reading." What she calls the old paradigms—"synecdochic" or "ethnically aggregative" approaches to the literature—have never been very reliable for describing the formal features of Asian American literature, and until the past decade sociopolitical approaches to the literature have prevailed to such an extent that scholarship on form or aesthetics has been conspicuously absent. Lye's essay considers three new paradigms for studying Asian American literature, but it is the final model that is most relevant here. As she sees it, two possibilities unspool from defining Asian American literature as "literature that makes claims (or can be read as making claims) to Asian American political representation": the first would involve expanding Asian American literature to include nonliterary texts; the second would "delink" as she puts it, "the criteria for textual inclusion from authorial descent."[5]

Such moves, as Lye's roster of scholars demonstrates, are already occurring in the field, but I want to explore how Kingston's recusal of authorship offers a refinement on Lye's second possibility. The rhetorical name for the type of language Kingston invokes when she says "The Laws" is "not my language" is apophasis, which means "denial" in Greek. As a rhetorical figure apophasis involves affirming by denying, and it is this kind of figurative activity, I will argue, that we find in *China Men*. Figurative activity is not, as Kingston inadvertently puts it, the language of the author. It does not belong to the individual, nor can it be reckoned the property of living persons because it is part of a vast linguistic tradition reaching as far back as Greek antiquity and persisting today in the rhetorical patterns we can identify in Asian American writing, a tradition about as far removed from that of classical rhetoric as can be imagined. To insist on the rhetorical tradition—on highly codified patterns of language rather than the author—as the source of figurative activity is not, as we may initially think, to altogether dismiss the role of the ethnic author. What it does demand, however, is the redefinition of the role of the author in relation to the linguistic behavior of the literary text, which functions and operates beyond, as it were, the death of its author.

While the person of the author is extremely useful in explaining the aesthetic qualities of the text, what Sue-Im Lee designates as "deliberate choices in form, genres, traditions, and conventions," the author and her intentions are less useful in describing the kind of figurative activity at work in Asian American writing precisely because of the provenance of these ancient patterns.[6] By redirecting our attention to the language of Asian American literature, "not my language" offers us a paradigm wherein the author identified as Asian American writes in a language not her own. In this sense Kingston's claim that "The Laws" is "not my language" enables us to disarticulate the author from the figurative activity of the text without compelling us to give up altogether the sociopolitical importance of the ethnic author. As a rhetorical figure handed down from classical antiquity, apophasis lies beyond the biological author's sphere of influence. At the same time, that it is apophasis and not some other trope at work here is of utmost importance as it yokes together the linguistic behavior of this particular text (*China Men*) to a highly specific historical problematic (and, conveniently, to the rhetorical strategy of its author).

This chapter explores *China Men* as an example of the literary response to the condition of necessity, which is manifested in the text as the compulsion to correct the historical record, either by supplementing its omissions or by exploring different strategies of responding to this absence. As we may suspect, *China Men* responds in a rather unexpected way to the condition of necessity. On the one hand, it insists on the necessity of referential representation. The daughter-narrator wants the "real stories" of her male ancestors, but confronted by her father's silence and the absent historical record, she has to concede, "I'll tell you what I suppose from your silences and few words, and you can tell me that I'm mistaken. You'll just have to speak up with the real stories if I've got you wrong."[7] *China Men* calls on apophasis, the figure of negation or denial, to navigate its political obligation to referential representation and the negating activity of its representational strategies. In this way it makes use of the formal tension implicit in apophasis itself as a figure caught between saying and unsaying. Through apophasis *China Men* shows itself to be indebted to a particular Asian American history, even as its turn to apophasis—a trope and a discourse that is found elsewhere—demonstrates how *China Men* as a literary text exceeds its immediate historical context. By transforming Chinese exclusion into a rhetorical figure, *China Men* remains in touch with its specific problematic while at the same time multiplying the historical usages of its linguistic patterns.

Necessity

China Men is deeply shaped by its historical problematic of Chinese exclusion, so much so that its self-appointed task is to reconstruct and sometimes reimagine the missing histories of these Chinese Americans. At the same time, however, it is intensely aware—more so than any other Asian American text of the period—of the difficulties of responding, as a literary text, to the necessity of counteracting the historical absence of Chinese Americans by getting the stories "right." In one well-known quote, Kingston acknowledges the potential friction between what she calls "pure history" and the literary text. Speaking about "The Laws," she explains, "The mainstream culture doesn't know the history of Chinese Americans, which has been written and written well. That ignorance makes a tension for me, and in the new book I just couldn't take it anymore. So all of a sudden, right in the middle of the stories, plunk—there is an eight-page section of pure history. . . . There are no characters in it. But on the other hand, maybe it will affect the shape of the novel in the future. Now maybe another Chinese American writer won't have to write that history."[8] We could say that "The Laws" represents *China Men*'s most obvious and explicit intervention in the epistemology of Chinese exclusion, as nowhere else does it take up and rework the official record itself in such a sustained way. But Kingston's own characterization of this segment as "plunk" in relation to the rest of *China Men* shows she is aware of navigating the tension between the imperatives of "pure history" and the literary. Apophasis as it occurs in *China Men* is the figuration—the conversion into figurative language—of the historical experience of Chinese exclusion. It is therefore not the content of Chinese exclusion or the absence of Chinese Americans in *China Men* that we are tracking but the formal and figurative expression of this history.

If apophasis is the literary response to necessity, the precipitating historical problematic at work is Chinese exclusion and its far-reaching consequences. As a book about "the men's stories," as Kingston puts it, *China Men* focuses on the conditions specific to Chinese men, their sexuality, their imaginative lives, and the forms that their resistance took to what Elaine Kim has characterized as "genocidal American laws and policies."[9] In the context of Asian immigration to the United States, the Chinese were the first to enter in large numbers, and doing so, they encountered the American variant of Orientalism, which portrayed them as alien, foreign, and inassimilable. Officially designated "aliens ineligible for citizenship," they were prohibited by the 1790 Nationality Act from naturalizing. From 1882 to 1943 exclusion laws prevented the entry of Chinese workers, while other laws targeted them for special taxation or denied their right to landownership. Historian Madeline Y. Hsu describes the tremendous impact of immigration exclusion on the early Chinese population: in 1882 approximately forty thousand Chinese entered the United States; by the following year, after these laws went into effect, the numbers declined to eight thousand, and by 1885 fell to just twenty-two. At the same time Chinese sexuality, already perceived as deviant, was regulated by a series of laws excluding the entry of Chinese women in 1875 and then preventing interracial unions with whites. As Kim notes, the severely skewed sex ratios of men to women—in 1860, 19:1, in 1880, 27:1—turned Chinatowns into "bachelor societies."[10]

Although *China Men* is mainly concerned with Chinese exclusion, the problem of Asian exclusion has been a central

issue for the field of Asian American studies. Historian Gary
Y. Okihiro notes, for example, that when Asian subjects appear
in American historiography, they do so "most prominently as
objects of exclusion."[11] Asian American historiography thus
begins by contesting Asian exclusion, as Ronald Takaki demonstrates in the opening pages of *Strangers from a Different Shore*:
"We need to 're-vision' history to include Asians in the history
of America."[12] In literary history we might look to the cluster
of Asian American literary anthologies appearing in the 1970s
for a similar stance on exclusion. David Leiwei Li observes that
"The anthologies seem to constitute a two-step ethnic nationalist's project that begins with a critique of exclusion and is followed by the reconstruction of a lost tradition."[13] If the typical
response to exclusion in Asian American studies has involved
recovering or reconstructing these missing subjects, *China
Men*'s response—as early as 1977—is all the more striking. Even
as it acknowledges the importance of getting these stories right,
it nevertheless turns to a range of apophatic strategies to negate
the positivist representation of these fathers in the very act of
representing them.

China Men is a collection of stories told from the point of
view of different generations of Chinese male immigrants,
loosely drawn from Kingston's family lore. While *China Men*
did not achieve the overnight success that *Woman Warrior* did,
it too was a recipient of the National Book Award.[14] Its six main
stories, each of which follows a male ancestor or family member,
are divided by twelve short segments. These segments comprise
Chinese versions of Ovid and Defoe, retellings of Chinese classics
and folktales, and include Polynesian myths, diary fragments,
newspaper accounts, and a catalogue of anti-Chinese legislation.
Criticism on *China Men* has been extensive. It tends, however,
to concentrate on questions of intertextuality, genre, history,
or sexuality and has yet to consider the nature of its figurative
activity.[15] This is not to say, though, that critics have not been
attentive to Kingston's imaginative wordplay. Li, for example,
demonstrates his awareness of just how central this linguistic

play is to the title when he argues that *China Men* resignifies the racist term *chinamen* by transforming it into the literal translation of *zhong guo ren*, Mandarin for "Chinese people."[16] I want to contribute to this extant scholarship by accounting for *China Men*'s figurative activity, which I believe constitutes its most ambitious and significant intervention.

Apophasis is not an esoteric figure, even though the term itself may not be immediately familiar. It encompasses a vast range of material concerned with the limits of expression, and its traditional topics involve meditations on Being, God, and the limits of language. Negative theology, perhaps the least abstruse of these, attempts to describe the characteristics of a transcendent God by giving an account of what He is not. In a magisterial survey of apophasis in Western culture and thought, William Franke considers as apophatic any type of "self-negating discourse" and defines it further as "concentrat[ing] on the unsayable and generat[ing] discourse deliberately out of this experience." The etymology of the term (*apo*, "from" or "away from," and *phemi*, "assert" or "say") gives rise to yet another strain of apophatic thought that involves unsaying, including, as Franke puts it, "languages that cancel, interrupt, or undo discourse."[17] Apophatic discourse has no recognizable generic or disciplinary boundaries; it is found in a wide range of traditions both Eastern and Western, from literature to religion, philosophy, the social sciences, and the fine arts. Despite its ubiquity, however, it has remained marginal to the Western intellectual tradition, which tends to privilege what Derrida has called a "metaphysics of presence." For Michael Sells, who focuses on a particular strain of negative theology, apophatic discourse entails an infinite "linguistic regress," in which the attempt to state the ineffable must in turn be unsaid: "Any saying (even a negative saying) demands a correcting proposition, an unsaying. But that correcting proposition which unsays the previous proposition is in itself a 'saying' that must be 'unsaid' in turn." This persistent movement, which Sells describes metaphorically as a "circular turning back," offers a different perspective on the referential.

Apophatic discourse does not do away with the referential, but the motion of constantly turning back on itself leads Sells to call it "transreferential," a sense of the referential "beyond" the linear motion typically associated with referentiality.[18] We might be tempted to regard silence, the absence of language, as the purest form of apophasis, but as Franke reminds us, apophatic discourse necessarily involves language, however deficient and inadequate. Even this so-called absence is a highly created one, involving "methods and modes of silence" that persistently point toward the limits of what can be expressed. Apophasis, Franke concludes, "can actually be apprehended only in discourse."[19] Hence apophatic discourse demands a more complex view of language, especially when it appears, as it will in *China Men*, as that which must not, will not, or cannot be said.

As a rhetorical figure apophasis has two senses: *negatio* (denial) and proof by elimination, but it is the first sense that is most common. Richard Lanham explains the former as "pretending to deny what is really affirmed" and classifies it as a form of irony called *occultatio* (concealment), which involves "emphasizing something by pointedly seeming to pass over it."[20] For Reginald Gibbons, commenting on apophatic poetry, "the apophatic is a negative that is not straightforward, and can imply something that is in fact present despite the absence or inadequacy of a name for it—such as the nature of God—or present as an absence, like meaningful negative space in a sculpture. But in poetry the negative space is linguistic." As a rhetorical figure, apophasis proceeds, as Gibbons goes on to suggest, "by indirection."[21] For *China Men* it is this sense of apophasis as a negation that is "not straightforward," that moves "by indirection" that will be most important. Despite the significant role that apophasis has played in exploring the limits of representation, studies of apophasis have yet to connect this figure or discourse directly to questions of race, gender, or sexuality. *China Men* contributes to this body of scholarship by plunging it into the realm of history, of race and gender in relation to structures of power, and it disturbs the typically exalted frame of apophatic reference by making it confront the politics of denial and unsaying.[22] Again and again *China Men* will give us apophatic scenarios that emerge directly out of the predicament of representing a subject without a historical referent: a subject made absent, expelled, under interdiction.

In exploring the role of apophasis as an unquiet trope in *China Men*, I argue that apophasis occurs as a figure here in multiple senses of the term: the rhetorical trope, the historical person, and the rhetorical means by which literature takes up a particular historical problematic. With regard to apophasis, I am trying to describe a kind of figurative activity that is not restricted to Asian America but that nonetheless draws on a specifically Asian American history. The activity I explore is entirely rhetorical; that is, it involves a particular linguistic situation, one that can and does occur elsewhere, in a multitude of contexts, and yet is always concrete and particular. The rhetorical bridge of apophatic language is what concretizes *China Men*'s figurative activity and opens it up, at the same time, to much larger conversations, enabling Asian American literature to enter into these other discourses in such a way that the new questions it poses in this old language disturbs its traditional preoccupations.

Not Your Father

David L. Eng begins his elegant reading of *China Men* by acknowledging its historical problematic: "These Chinese American male laborers lack official documentation—a history of visible images—a lack that threatens to consign their existence to oblivion." Since his point of departure is the image, and more specifically the photograph, Eng directs our attention to the myriad ways *China Men* "reworks" dominant history by disrupting our ways of looking. In so doing, he argues, it teaches us "radical new methods of looking" that involve looking "askew" and "awry."[23] I want to recast his insights into literary terms because *China Men* is, first and foremost, a written text. What if the lesson to be learned here does not concern the image at all but a far more rudimentary problem? I argue that *China Men*, especially in its opening vignettes, poses fundamental questions concerning the relationship of race to the literary text. Modern definitions of race tend to emphasize its visual qualities; race is envisioned, in this sense, as an image. In the literary text, however, no images appear, and the sole medium is language and language alone. What, then, does it mean to "read" race if race no longer consists of a set of images?

One of the most typical and accessible methods of getting at race in the literary text has been to read for content. While this reading practice has proven itself as a powerful strategy for analyzing racial and gendered hierarchies, something more is required for *China Men*, not only because it is a text whose subject matter, by definition, cannot be "said" because absent but because its two opening vignettes refuse to provide any such content whatsoever. These vignettes, "On Discovery" and On Fathers," thus suggest a way to connect race to the literary text without resorting to a content-driven approach. Their staging offers us an alternative way to conceptualize what constitutes the racial—or, more properly, racialized—text. The vignettes both involve rather startling scenes of misrecognition. "On Discovery" concerns a violent metamorphosis: a male explorer searching for Gold Mountain is brutally transformed into a female servant. "On Fathers" presents a case of mistaken identity: as children, the narrator and her siblings confuse a stranger for their father. On the most basic level what these misrecognition scenarios mean for a text like *China Men* is that however urgent and significant its role in countermanding Chinese exclusion, such a text cannot be treated simply as a referential narrative. On yet another level these vignettes are self-conscious reflections about figurative activity, about figuring—translating into distinctly literary terms—a particular historical problematic. Read together they offer another model for thinking race in the literary text as a kind of textual trace, as a type of rhetorical movement, one that demands an entirely different set of interpretive practices.

As numerous critics have noted, "On Discovery" borrows its scenario from a nineteenth-century Chinese novel, Li Ruzhen's *Flowers in the Mirror*, in which the scholar Tang Ao, accompanied by his comical brother-in-law, embarks on a quest for immortality.[24] In one of their adventures they come across a land ruled by women, where Confucian gender norms have been inverted. In Kingston's version, Tang Ao has been converted into an explorer in search of Gold Mountain (a Chinese term for California), and it is he, not the brother-in-law (as in the original), who undergoes the agonizing transformation into a woman. Many critics treat the vignette as a historical allegory for the experience of Chinese male immigrants in the mid- to late nineteenth century. It is peculiar, therefore, that "On Discovery" makes no reference to the race or ethnicity of its characters; none of the physical features—skin color, hair, eye shape—that have come to stand in for racial difference is mentioned. In fact "On Discovery" makes a point of identifying Tang Ao solely as "a man, named Tang Ao" (3). There are of course situating references that hint at his ethnic background: an allusion to the reign of Empress Wu, during which this mythical Land of Women is discovered, and a parenthetical aside referring to an idiomatic expression identified as Chinese (the needle's "nose"). There are also references to Chinese cultural practices like foot binding. Given Tang Ao's name and his placement in a book called *China Men*, the reader is meant to assume that both he, and the world of the fable, are Chinese, but the fact that the vignette chooses *not* to mention his race at all—refusing, in this sense, to racialize him—is a highly created gesture. It is even more significant in the context of Chinese labor migration to North America, which, as Lisa Lowe and Caroline Yang have argued, was profoundly racialized.[25]

Sparse as it is, "On Discovery" provides at least a slim referential framework for situating its ethnic context. "On Fathers," however, refuses even this much. No hint of race or ethnicity appears in the second vignette. The single allusion, scanty at that, is the term *BaBa*, with which the children greet the stranger: "Father! BaBa!" (6). Since "BaBa" immediately follows "Father," the reader assumes that one explains the other, but the vignette leaves "BaBa" untranslated, and no other information is offered to identify the term. No mention is made of which language is being spoken here or why. Like "On Discovery," these omissions too are charged gestures. As before, the stranger is identified simply as "a man," and no physical descriptions are given of him, the children, their mother, or their father. In refusing to assign a racial identity to these characters, or even to hint at their ethnicity by identifying the sole non-English term, we might say that "On Fathers" is positioning itself against a conceptual framework that would normalize race as the proper way to understand this scenario. The absence of racial or ethnic references disturbs the otherwise Orientalist discourse that might obtain, marking these bodies as different (foreign, alien, other) from some unnamed norm (whiteness) and compelling such subjects, by various legal and social means, to understand themselves as "eccentric" (15). In refusing to stage racial awareness in visual terms, both vignettes suggest that so-called racial texts are more properly understood as having been racialized.

More important, though, the vignettes imply that neither race nor gender, at least within the bounds of the literary text, should be conceived as visual or even visible in any simple way. As Eleanor Ty has observed, we continue to rely on the visual nature of race: "Though thinking about race has shifted and changed over history, to a large extent, visibility is still the basis for discourses about difference."[26] To the extent that race has been recast in terms of the Saussurean sign, critics have sought to disrupt the logic equating physical appearance with racial meanings. If race is a sign, what it has yoked together—skin color and a racial "interiority"—is not only arbitrary but potentially discontinuous. Therefore Samira Kawash argues that "the modern conception of racial identity maintains an uneasy relation to the visual; the visible marks of the racialized body are only the signs of a deeper, interior difference, and yet those visible marks are the only difference that can be observed." Race, she concludes, "is therefore predicated on an epistemology of visibility, but the visible becomes an insufficient guarantee of knowledge. As a result, the possibility of a gap opens up between what the body says and what the body means."[27] A hasty reading of "On Discovery" might presume that Tang Ao's violent gender reassignment takes us to this gap in the visual logic of difference, but the vignette takes great pains to assure us that this is a true metamorphosis and not merely a cosmetic change. Tang Ao *literally* becomes a woman: "The tea was thick with white chrysanthemums and stirred the cool female winds inside his body. . . . Vinegar soup improved his womb" (4). As the transformed Tang Ao serves dinner in the great hall, the guests greet him as a female: "'She's pretty, don't you agree?' the diners said, smacking their lips at his dainty feet as he bent to put dishes before them" (5).

What the dinner guests see—the image of a pretty face and a pair of tiny feet—identifies Tang Ao as female. And yet what they "see," the vignette warns us, cannot be taken at face value. The diners are not prepared to encounter a sign that might go awry, and because they do not expect this wayward trajectory, they apply the most rudimentary of interpretive practices. In equating what they see—the image—to the real, they expect the sign to correspond, mimetically and reliably, to the "truth" of gender. For them no potential gap, as Kawash describes it, can exist between what this body looks like and what it might mean. But if the image offers no access to the discontinuity of gendering, the vignette indicates that it is in language, the medium of the vignette, and language alone that this semiotic gap can be grasped. In contrast to the diners in the vignette, the reader of the vignette is given a distinct advantage. In shifting from the perspective of the diners to that of the reader, "On Discovery" suggests not only a gap but a divergence between the seen and the real. The disconnect, though, is indicated in the *text* of *China Men*. The masculine pronouns in the passage above—"his dainty feet," "he bent"—hint at an altogether different history for the body now recognized as female, a history that is not visible to the diners and that cannot be rendered visible to them. The incongruity between what the diners see and what the reader understands is one that the image, at least as it is presented by "On Discovery," cannot make available. How, then, is the reader of *China Men* to learn to "read" a history that is missing? The second vignette directs us once again to language, but this time as a particular type of rhetorical movement.

From the Back

"On Fathers" begins with an intimate mistake: the children confuse their father with a stranger. To present this particular father as unknowable at the very start of *China Men* suggests that the daughter-narrator's task, to know and represent her fathers, will have to be an apophatic one. When the children first greet the stranger, the language of the vignette quite purposefully blurs the distinction between father and stranger:

> "Waiting at the gate for our father to come home, my brothers and sisters and I saw a man come hastening around the corner. Father! 'BaBa!' 'BaBa!' We flew off the gate; we jumped off the fence. 'BaBa!' We surrounded him, took his hands, pressed our noses against his coat to sniff his tobacco smell, reached into his pockets for the Rainbo notepads and the gold coins that were really chocolates" (6).

Nowhere does the vignette actually distinguish between the children's own father and this stranger; the impersonality of the pronouns *him* and *his* carry out the task of making the father and the stranger grammatically indistinguishable. Eventually the stranger speaks up: "'But I'm not your father. You've made a mistake'" (6). The children, however, are not entirely convinced, and the next lines again imply that stranger and father are interchangeable, if not identical:

> "We went back inside the yard, and this man continued his walk down our street, from the back certainly looking like our father, one hand in *his* pocket. Tall and thin, he was wearing our father's two-hundred-dollar suit that fit *him*

just right. *He* was walking fast in *his* good leather shoes with the wingtips" (6, my emphasis).

As other critics have observed, *his, he,* and *him* can refer to either the stranger or the father, further increasing the misrecognition effect.[28] Moments later the right father arrives, and the vignette concludes: "We ran *again* to meet him" (7, my emphasis). The force of the *again* returns us to the joyous scene of mistaken reunion, just as the pronoun *him* erodes our certainty in which father, exactly, is being greeted.

Although the proper subject does eventually appear—"our own father" (7) the narrator tells us—the end of the vignette propels the reader back to the original misrecognition with which the episode began. The vignette does not identify these father figures as Chinese, but the repeated denials ("I'm not your father," the stranger protests; "No, that wasn't your father," the mother concurs) can be said to *figure* a history entirely specific to Chinese America. Legal prohibitions in place from the end of the nineteenth century to the mid-twentieth made it difficult, if not in some cases impossible, for Chinese men to establish families in the United States. That the father's own children do not recognize him, that they make such a personal error, suggests yet another complication in Chinese American history: the phenomenon of paper sons. During the exclusion era Chinese continued to immigrate illegally by purchasing fake papers identifying them as children of U.S. citizens.[29] So widespread was this practice that a federal judge in 1901 declared that "if the story told in the courts were true, every Chinese woman who was in the United States twenty-five years ago must have had at least 500 children."[30]

In transforming the stranger into a father and the father into a stranger, "On Fathers" insists that the china man as a subject cannot be "known," even for a narrator who is also a daughter, and hints that the narratives to come—all stories about fathers—may be even more problematic than they initially appear. As the vignette's title proclaims, the misrecognition scenario poses as a problem the general place of the father and the symbolic economies that he anchors. Susan Koshy elaborates the broader ramifications here when she uses the example of the Asian bachelor to suggest that "normative models of family, gender, and nation are unable to capture the historical variations in, and dynamic quality of, these arrangements and ties." She goes on to explain, "'Bachelor' Asian males were often married and had wives and children in their homelands. Some subsequently married and had children in the United States and maintained two households over a lifetime; some slowly gave up one family and acquired another; some had one family, developed another, and then reunited with the first."[31] In other words, the particular instance of the Asian bachelor illuminates the normative (naturalized) subject of paternity and gender in the nineteenth- and twentieth-century United States.[32] The legacy of paper or fictive kin demands a similar rethinking of kinship, family, and identity under race. Estelle T. Lau argues, for example, that these complex transnational networks "disturbed basic family structures but created new ones." Sustaining these paper families involved elaborate deceptions that had to be maintained for generations, and, as Lau points out, "even bona fide United States citizens had to study these newly created 'family trees,' for if their answers failed to convince the immigration officers or if they failed to jibe with those given by their paper relatives, they, too, were vulnerable to deportation."[33] Because the fictions extended by these "papers" had to be lived out, there is something about the nature of Chinese America that is not only fundamentally textual but figurative because the distinction between what is real and fictive, referential and literary can no longer be easily distinguished.

The history of Chinese exclusion may explain the misrecognition scenarios at the beginning of *China Men*, but none of this history makes its way directly into the vignettes. In fact, given their prominent scenarios of violent gendering, it is gender, not race, that concerns them. How, then, are we to understand these figurative scenarios as pertaining to race, to Chinese American men, and not just men in general? I would argue that it is precisely because "On Fathers" does not make reference to race (with the exception of "BaBa," if that linguistic trace can be counted as race at all) that the vignette renders a powerful lesson in the work of figurative activity. By giving us no content to fall back on—no explicit mention of race or ethnicity—"On Fathers" forces the reader to rely solely on figurative resources. In other words, it is because race does not manifest itself in these vignettes that it must be conjured through figurative activity. It would be no great leap to connect the recurrent denials presented by "On Fathers" to apophasis, the figure of negation, but the vignette has something more sophisticated in mind than simple negation. The repetition of the phrase *from the back* calls even more directly on the tradition of apophasis by borrowing an Old Testament language for theophany, the manifestation of God. As Franke observes, there is a long and venerable tradition of biblical interpretation "keyed to the apophasis, the silence and negativity, of the Word," and he cites the theophany at Sinai recorded in Exodus as "foundational" because it "dramatically highlights the sublime transcendence of the divine that makes seeing God fatal and representation of him illicit, if not impossible."[34] There are in fact two theophanies at Sinai in the book of Exodus. It is the second of these I am concerned with, as it is there that we find the biblical echo of the phrase *from the back*. When Moses asks to see the face of God, he is told that he will be granted instead a glimpse of His back because the unmediated experience of God's presence is fatal to humankind: "As My Presence passes by, I will put you in a cleft of the rock and shield you with My hand until I have passed by. Then I will take My hand away and you will see My back; but My face must not be seen."[35]

Biblical scholar Brevard S. Childs points out the exegetical problems in this passage: "Of course, a tremendous anthropomorphism is involved, but the extreme caution with which it is used is an eloquent testimony to the Hebrew understanding of God."[36] What Childs characterizes as a "tremendous anthropomorphism," a reference to God's face, hands, and back, suggests that the figurative activity in the passage is already occurring at two removes: it is prosopopoeia (personification) appearing within an apophatic passage concerning the unsayable nature of God. At the same time, this figurative activity, however unverifiable, is the sole means of accessing that which cannot be accessed. Nahum M. Sarna notes, for example, that "no human being can ever penetrate the ultimate mystery of God's Being. Only a glimpse of the divine reality is possible, even for Moses."[37] If God can be glimpsed at all, as these verses from Exodus suggest, it must be from behind, as He is departing the scene of representation, as it were. Put another way, *from the back* does not tell us what Moses is capable of "seeing"; it registers instead the apophatic experience of *not being able to see* God's face, only His back. No theophany as such exists in *China Men* of course. Its concern is not with failing to see the face of a transcendent God existing beyond or outside of representation but with a far more vulnerable kind of father, one whose "existence," as the narrator says in a subsequent chapter, "was outlawed by Chinese Exclusion Acts" (151). How might this kind of subject, one under interdiction, enter into representation? "On Fathers" suggests that he can do so only "from the back," by turning away and leaving the scene—that is, through denial and negation.

From the back occurs twice in "On Fathers." The first time it is uttered by the narrator, warning of the mistake she has made in confusing a stranger for her own father: "from the back certainly looking like our father" (6). The second time, uttered by the mother, the phrase indicates how a subject barred from being a father might become one: "He did look like BaBa, though, didn't he? From the back, almost exactly" (7). *From the back* is a reminder that these missing subjects have no empirical referents; representing them will therefore involve figuration, an activity without guarantees. Accordingly the narrator's encounter with the stranger/father occurs "from the back"; that is, it consists of a scenario in which the subject of narration is made to leave the frame, to depart the scene. What *from the back* describes is a certain figurative motion, and it is this tropological *motion* of turning (from Greek *tropos*, "a turn"; Latin *tropus*, "figure of speech") that enacts rhetorically the gesture of negation. *From the back* thus directs the reader of *China Men* not to "look" at race in the context of the literary text, as if it could be grasped as a set of images, but to *read* it as a set of textual and rhetorical traces. *From the back* constitutes a rhetorical version of the historical circumstance known as Chinese exclusion. Together these negations and their peculiar rhetorical movement remember, in figurative form, a historical problematic (Chinese exclusion) that is no longer recognizable *as* Chinese exclusion. To put it differently, the negations and rhetorical motions that occur here are conspicuously crafted gestures that *figure* a highly created historical absence. "On Fathers" presents its Chinese American male subjects "from the back" because they are missing (prohibited), made up (fictive or fraudulent), or simply wrong (misrecognized). So why does *China Men* choose to repeat their historical effacement here? In presenting these Chinese males "from the back," *China Men* restores to the bachelor figure—those "unfamilied men" (117)—a kind of reproductive capacity denied to him by exclusion laws: "from the back," a stranger can be recognized *as* a father. *China Men* puts negation to figurative use such that *from the back* restores kinship to the stranger, making it possible for him to not only be mistaken for a father but, to be, in the narrator's words, "our own father." From the back, turned away from the viewer, any china man, despite the historical interdictions on his sexuality, has the potential to be a father.[38]

The vignette's title proclaims its authority to speak for all fathers, a rhetorical way of bringing together these unlikely father figures: one so exalted He must not be seen, another so abjected he cannot be seen. What would it mean, therefore, to take seriously the vignette's audacious claim to speak universally about fathers by means of the historically specific Chinese father? Another way to frame the question would be to ask what it means for *China Men* to put a trope like apophasis to use, and how this troubles the extant critical discourse on apophasis. Apophasis involves negation and unsaying, but its traditional subject matter is divine or metaphysical. *China Men*, on the other hand, is a profoundly profane text whose subject is entirely historical: the racialized, sexualized, gendered subject of nineteenth- and twentieth-century legislation. These vastly asymmetrical situations—the unsayability of God, a deity beyond human language; the unsayability of a subject made absent by and in history—are brought together rhetorically. The limitations of the unsayable in *China Men* are, in the historical sense, constructed; by unsaying its subject matter, these apophatic strategies thus return us to history, something that the apophatic tradition, by the nature of its objects of study (God, Being, language), tends to eclipse or transcend. In fact it is because *China Men*'s figurative activities are bound so strongly to its historical problematic that it can shed light on what is not being asked or said within the apophatic tradition itself.

Ah Goong: Nobody's History

More than any other chapter of *China Men*, "Grandfather of the Sierra Nevada Mountains," third in the sequence of father stories, is explicitly concerned with how to tell a history when empirical evidence of that history is either inaccessible or unrecorded. The chapter begins with a reference to the infamous Golden Spike Ceremony, the joining of the transcontinental railroad at Promontory Summit, Utah, on May 10, 1869. In the official photographs of the ceremony no Chinese appear, even though a small contingent was present and responsible for setting the final spike.[39] The preceding chapters are also shaped around historical silences, but unlike "Grandfather," palpable traces of the past remain in those earlier narratives: the narrator's father in "Father from China" may refuse to speak of China, but it lingers in his "wordless male screams" (13); the great-grandfathers may have been prohibited from speaking in "Great Grandfather of the Sandalwood Mountains," but they "planted" words in the earth like the cane they cultivated, words that eventually prompt the narrator to marvel at "what stories the wind would tell" (118). "Grandfather" is sandwiched between an interchapter about a Polynesian trickster god who dies in the earth ("On Mortality Again") and the formidable catalogue of a century and a half of Chinese exclusion acts. Its protagonist is Ah Goong ("grandfather"), one of thousands of Chinese who helped build the railroads, none of whom is officially remembered in the narrative of the nation: "There is no record of how many died building the railroad" (138), the narrator reminds us. In recounting Ah Goong's story, *China Men* pays tribute to these unrecognized china men, "the binding and building ancestors of this place" (146), but in doing so it turns to a particular aspect of apophasis, one that unsays the very thing being said.

As it turns out, Ah Goong is not simply missing, but excluded—"Driven Out" (146), the narrator insists—from the scene of representation. "Grandfather" makes this point by commencing with a familial act of exclusion, exposing how the reality recorded by the photograph is in fact a representation. The chapter begins with the narrator contemplating Ah Goong's absence from the family photo album: "In the family album are group pictures with Grandmother in the middle, the family arranged on either side of her and behind her, second wives at the ends, no Grandfather" (127). Playing out the imagined scene in her mind, she speculates that "the family hurried from clothes chests to mirrors without explaining to Grandfather, hiding Grandfather" (127), and imagines her mother intervening: "My mother, indignant that nobody had readied Grandfather . . . would have slipped him into the group . . . *but Grandmother chased him away.* 'What a waste of film,' she said" (127, my emphasis). Reconstructing the original scene allows the narrator to show us the work of exclusion, work that is elided by the reality effect of the photograph, which is taken as historical truth. Ah Goong's exclusion from the family photograph is an intimate version of the more violent exclusions he experiences as a Chinese worker, barred from citizenship and banned from the social, cultural, and reproductive life of the nation. As the narrator observes, "While the demons posed for photographs, the

China Men dispersed. It was dangerous to stay. Ah Goong does not appear in railroad photographs" (145). These multiple exclusions suggest a structural condition that determines the mode in which his story (history) can be told.

The statement "Ah Goong does not appear in railroad photographs" is a constative; it states or reports on a fact and as such is part of that everyday class of language called ordinary or referential. As the passage that follows makes clear, however, this statement is also oddly figurative because it will act out, "perform," in Austin's sense, Ah Goong's absence from the very sentences that denote him. "Ah Goong does not appear" is the first of many negative constructions initiating an apophatic cascade, one that confers on these constatives a performative aspect, a figurative dimension. By the end of the passage these figurative maneuvers will ensure that Ah Goong will most definitely not appear. Although the passage begins by seeming to attribute Ah Goong's disappearances to his own ingenuity, it soon becomes clear that more than cunning is involved:

> Good at hiding, disappearing—decades unaccounted for—*he was not working* in a mine when forty thousand chinamen were Driven Out of mining. He *was not killed or kidnapped* in the Los Angeles Massacre. . . . He *was lucky not to be* in Colorado when the Denver demons burned all chinamen homes and businesses, nor in Rock Springs, Wyoming, when the miner demons killed twenty-eight or fifty chinamen. . . . Ah Goong *was running elsewhere* during the Drivings Out of Tacoma, Seattle, Oregon City, Albania, and Marysville. . . . And when the Boston police imprisoned and beat 234 chinamen, it was 1902, and Ah Goong had already reached San Francisco or China, and perhaps San Francisco again. (148–49, my emphasis)

Ah Goong may not appear in railroad photographs, but he does not appear in this account of history either: "He was not working in a mine . . . not killed or kidnapped." These negations do not offer much in the way of information, and yet they are entirely referential since what they describe is Ah Goong's factual absence from places and events. In offering us reference through negation, this apophatic passage seems to demand a different understanding of the referential. By presenting a list of places where Ah Goong does not appear, "Grandfather" reaches for what Sells has termed the "transreferential" aspect of apophasis. If *China Men* is transreferential, however, it is so in a different sense than Sells would have us understand it, as a "linguistic regress" involving a perpetual saying and unsaying. According to him, apophasis "cannot dispense with reference, but through the constant turning back upon its own referential delimitations, it seeks a momentary liberation from such delimitations."[40] For *China Men*, however, there is no rhetorical motion that approaches, in Sells's words, "a circular turning back" because there is no antecedent or previous saying that can be narratively undone. Instead *China Men* grapples with what Franke considers the "ultimate apophatic expression": silence or absence.[41] If "Ah Goong does not appear in railroad photographs," as the narrator insists, then for *China Men* the transreferential must consist of a different kind movement, one that involves the confusion of reference and rhetoric.

The incidents alluded to in the passage quoted above are actual historical events, but they are certainly not familiar episodes of American history, if they register at all in our national consciousness. As historian Sucheng Chan has pointed out, there were regular outbreaks of violence against the Chinese during the nineteenth century, but they were often poorly documented. In her discussion of violence against Chinese miners in California, for example, she concludes that "there is no accurate record of all the Chinese miners who were injured and killed."[42] *China Men*'s inventory of these events presents an occluded and ugly version of American history, rooted in economic exploitation rather than equal opportunity, racial exclusion rather than inclusion, and white hegemony instead of democracy. In referencing this history *China Men* renders it visible, but if this is meant to be a history, it is one that is curious indeed because it recounts these events in the negative: we are given only a list of places where Ah Goong does not appear. This account is also missing its historical referent, the actual Chinese men and women who were killed or kidnapped, beaten or imprisoned. *China Men* cannot tell their story—no record exists—so in the place of the actual referent, we are given Ah Goong, the wrong subject or father. If the original historical subjects have disappeared, the men and women to whom these events occurred, whose history is being presented here? At the same time because the passage is quite firm about the fact that Ah Goong does not appear, we cannot conclude that this account is about him either. Indeed it is because Ah Goong does *not* appear that he is able to figure, to stand in for, these nameless others. In this regard we should consider as instructive *China Men*'s repeated reference to Ah Goong by a generic rather than a personal name (*gong* means "grandfather").

Kingston's neology for the variations on Chinese exclusion is "Driving Out" (145), a phrase that the narrator repeats again and again. Why, then, does *China Men* "drive out" the very subjects whose narratives it seeks to represent? All these disappearances might suggest that *China Men* has merely led us into a transreferential abyss, but this is not the case. If "Grandfather" struggles with recounting a history defined by absence, *China Men*'s solution to this challenge is to put apophasis to work with highly productive, albeit problematic consequences. The apophatic sequence we encountered above is not merely negative; it is also referential; yet, in being referential, it is also figurative in a complicated sense. These referential sentences *do* something; they are performatives in the sense that Austin taught us: they make the subject Ah Goong disappear, and in doing so they cast these referential statements into a figurative mode. To negate Ah Goong is to disappear him, to make him absent from his own story, but in repeating the originary gesture of exclusion in the context of the literary text, *China Men* makes the original negation capable of much more than mere negation. Within the parameters of "Grandfather," these negations *figure* a history that would otherwise simply not surface, or do so with great difficulty. This history, because it does not appear in the "visible" archive, the dominant historical narrative, can emerge only in this way, by means of figurative activity, to be sure, but more specifically by forcing the referential statement of absence into a figurative register. It is only by negating Ah Goong in this way that these others, these numerous and unremembered china men, can appear. And yet because this history can exist only in figurative activity—in and as these series of negations—it remains, like all literary figuration, ultimately unverifiable.

"Grandfather" ends with rumors of Ah Goong's death, but his disappearance from the archive, personal and official, is so complete that even the narrator is unsure of how to end his story. Falling back into the mythic voice of "On Discovery," the narrator relates several versions of his demise: "Some say he died falling into the cracking earth. . . . Some say the family went into debt to send for Ah Goong, who was not making money. . . . It cost two thousand dollars to bring him back to China" (150). A little later she reconsiders: "Maybe he hadn't died in San Francisco, it was just his papers that burned; it was just that his existence was outlawed by Chinese Exclusion Acts" (151). The great earthquake of 1906 proved an extraordinary stroke of luck for the Chinese since the resulting fires destroyed the Hall of Records. Lau indicates that for paper sons, "the subterfuge grew even more popular, as many Chinese claimed to have been born in the United States and the government found itself without the means to disprove these claims."[43] In terms of the resident Chinese community Takaki notes, "The fires destroyed almost all of the municipal records and opened the way for a new Chinese immigration. Chinese men could now claim they had been born in San Francisco, and as citizens they could bring their wives to the United States."[44] The narrator strikes a similarly optimistic note: "Every China Man was reborn out of that fire a citizen" (150).

If every china man is a citizen because nobody has papers, "Grandfather" ends, formally speaking, with the same structural condition that it has struggled to overcome: the absence of Chinese on paper and in the historical record. *China Men* drives Ah Goong out of his own narrative to remind us that he, like the nameless other china men he represents, is not merely absent but made so. There is no body (nobody) in the archive, and it is precisely because "Grandfather" is nobody's story that Ah Goong and these nameless others can survive in this text insofar as they survive *as* disappearance, *as* negation. Again and again Ah Goong is made to appear by disappearing. In this way he figures the kind of negative work we have come to associate with apophasis itself. Figuring history for us in this way, Ah Goong mediates the place where a constellation of questions about representation, history, and literature cluster.

Writing the Laws

The chapter called simply "The Laws" presents over a century's worth of legislation against the Chinese in the United States. Some of these entries, however, also involve litigation attempts by various Chinese Americans to appeal discriminatory treatment. The entries begin in the late nineteenth century and proceed chronologically to 1978. Most critics, even those otherwise attentive to the literary qualities of *China Men*, tend to understand "The Laws," as Te-Hsing Shan does, as a *"strictly historical account,"* or, as Linda Sledge does, as a "purely factual testimony of Chinese-American legal history."[45] Such an approach follows Kingston's own lead (she regards this chapter as "pure history"). It also responds to the cues of the highly impersonal language that distinguish "The Laws" from other parts of *China Men*. In a 1991 interview Kingston draws attention to her deliberate shift in language here, explaining, "I wanted to say, 'There's poetic language and there's legal language.' I was contrasting the language of feeling, where you could make friends with the characters and feel for them, with this formal, distanced language."[46] We might say that this recourse to referential language has a rhetorical function: it seeks to persuade the reader that "The Laws" is an authoritative and legitimate counternarrative to mainstream history. But as we have observed elsewhere in *China Men*, when such language occurs within the boundaries of the literary text, its referential aspect does not preclude it from exercising a figurative function.

The few critics who have commented on the literariness of "The Laws" have done so all too briefly. Donald C. Goellnicht, for example, comments on its "ironic" tone and placement: "By imitating the monological voice of authorizing History—the history imposed by the dominant culture that made the laws—this section uncovers both the dullness of this voice and its deafness to other, competing voices, those of the minorities suffering legalized discrimination."[47] Jinqi Ling directs our attention to the rhetorical nature of "The Laws," arguing that its strategic placement at the center of *China Men* illuminates a "submerged" narrative linking the interchapters of the book. This intercalated structure produces a strong formal tension between the heroic mode of the father stories and the subtle feminist critique of this mode as manifested by the interpolated fragments, which tell a different story, one of violation, humiliation, and trauma: "Such a deliberate structural subversion of unmediated history problematizes Kingston's invocation of 'Gold Mountain Warriors' inscribed in the traditional Chinese seal as innocently celebratory, and provides the ground for the female narrator to tell untold stories about China men in her own terms." While Ling asserts its "several important rhetorical purposes," he does not specify precisely about "The Laws," and the structural direction of his reading maintains a certain distance from the figurative activity of the text itself.[48]

Before I begin my own reading, I want to point out several places where we might discern the highly stylized nature of "The Laws." For example, while it is indisputable that these laws are presented sequentially, their framing is a different matter. Kingston's account begins in 1868, presumably to highlight the disparity between the actual treatment of the Chinese and the rights guaranteed them by the Burlingame Treaty. As if to remind us of this gap, the relevant passage from the treaty floats above the first entry. But there is certainly earlier legislation in the books against the Chinese. Chan points out, for instance, that California passed a Foreign Miners' Tax in 1850 that "was enforced primarily against the Chinese."[49] In 1854, to cite another well-known example, the Supreme Court of California determined in *People v. Hall* that Chinese could not testify against whites in court. My point is not to quarrel with "The Laws" but simply to indicate that its framing—where it begins, where it ends, which entries are included or excluded—is one place where the text bears the marks of its own imagining. When we begin to look for it, we can see evidence of the narrator's activity everywhere in "The Laws." More often than not the narrator's opinions or positionings are openly flagged. The entries for 1896 and 1898, for example, eschew objectivity to characterize the outcomes of two Supreme Court cases as victories: *Yick Wo v. Hopkins* is described as "a victory" and *United States v. Wong Kim Ark* as "another victory" (155). Elsewhere the narrator "corrects" the law. In the 1878 entry, an extensive inventory of discriminatory laws passed against the Chinese, the narrator reports that occasionally these laws would be overturned as unconstitutional, but lest we mistake these repeals as the rule rather than the exception, we are told, "The repealed laws were often reenacted in another form" (154). In other places the narrator interrupts the chronological account of the laws to demonstrate Chinese agency or resistance. Following several entries from the late 1880s—the prime years of Chinese exclusion—an entry dated 1889 is added, which informs us that "Chinese pooled money to fight the various Exclusion Acts in the courts" (155) and proceeds to delineate one of these cases. Parenthetical asides are also employed, acting as supplements to the law by indicating what they have left out. The entry for 1880, for example, reports that the Burlingame Treaty was modified to restrict Chinese entry into the United States. The narrator, however, reminds us that the real motivation for the American concession to the Chinese government was economic self-interest: "In return (so as not to bring about

limits on American entry into China), the American government promised to protect Chinese from lynchings" (154).

"The Laws" is also plotted. Even though these events are
chronological, they are nonetheless shaped, and this shaping
offers us a story, a narrative about the Chinese in America. For
instance, the first entry does not begin with a date like the rest
of the entries; instead it presents a narrative point of origin: "*The
First Years*: 1868, the year of the Burlingame Treaty, was the
year 40,000 miners of Chinese ancestry were Driven Out" (152,
original emphasis). Since Chinese immigration to the United
States begins in earnest in the 1840s, the designation of "The
First Years" should alert us not only to the selection of this particular moment but to its significance as the point of departure.
If this version of Chinese American history has ignominious
beginnings—the Chinese are "Driven Out" despite the terms of
the Burlingame Treaty—its end is heroic, or rather it is precisely
because its beginnings are ignoble that its conclusion is all the
more triumphant. Despite 110 years of legislation aimed at "out-
lawing" their existence, the Chinese have managed to survive
and even, after the Immigration Act of 1965, thrive: "In the last
decade, the ethnic Chinese population of the United States has
doubled. The 1980 census may show a million or more" (159).
While the historical experiences portrayed in "The Laws" are
demeaning, the plotting of this chapter produces what is ultimately a narrative of heroic survival.

What lends this narrative more weight and authority is the
"journalistic" and "legal" language of "The Laws." This is language, in other words, at its most referential, its purpose solely to
convey information rather than draw attention to itself. And yet
despite its claim to referentiality, to merely state preexisting facts,
"The Laws" is not, strictly speaking, a referential text. Nowhere
in "The Laws" does its referent—the laws themselves—actually
appear. In fact, with the exception of the epigraph, which cites
a portion of the Burlingame Treaty, "The Laws," despite its title,
is conspicuously missing the laws. The ones we encounter here
are paraphrased, with the occasional fragment incorporated as

a direct quote. In making its referent absent, "The Laws" enacts an apophatic gesture that suggests a formal similarity to the Chinese absence from the historical archive. The assembly of verbs in "The Laws" collectively perform a shared rhetorical motion, that of negation: beginning with "Driven Out" (152), we move to "barred," "prohibited" (153), followed by "banned" and "forbade" (154), "turned back," "deported," "expel" (155), then "segregated" and "excluded" (156), et cetera. Rhetorically speaking, the Chinese "exist" in the law as exclusion; their rhetorical imprint appears in the official record as negation. By disappearing the referent, what "The Laws" stages is not just a representation of the law but the *rewriting of law* at the hands of a Chinese American daughter-narrator. In other words, because "The Laws" has made the laws absent, what it presents to the reader is a literal and audacious writing of Chinese exclusion. In fact because "The Laws" rewrites the source of Chinese exclusion itself, we could say that it, more than any other part of *China Men*, represents the kind of political intervention imagined by the founders of the Asian American literary tradition.

In conclusion, let us return to the self-negating gesture with which this chapter began, Kingston's statement that "The Laws" is "not my language." In a subsequent clarification she specifies that her editor "*edited* 'The Laws'" and explains that while she wrote the section, "his work is within the purview of editing, not writing."[50] I want to take Kingston's clarification here very seriously because it helps us think through the complications of being the "author" of *China Men* while, at the same time, acknowledging the impersonal rhetorical lineage of this kind of language. At the very moment in which the identity politics of Asian America might carry the greatest force, in a segment staging the counternarrative to Chinese exclusion, Kingston's claim that "The Laws" is "not my language" suggests that her recusal is no mere absence but *an apophatic strategy*. Gorazd Kocijančič indicates what is at stake here: "The word 'apophatic' denotes in Greek a 'technique' of thought, a technique of denial. . . . The word is related to the Greek word 'apo-phasko,' 'apophemi,' which means 'I say no,' 'I deny,' and the noun 'apophasis,' which means 'denial,' 'negation.'"[51] In other words, Kocijančič suggests that as a *technique* these apophatic gestures can be found anywhere, irrespective of disciplinary or national boundaries. In this way, we can think of Kingston's negative gesture as reworking the usual circuitry between the rhetorical tradition and Asian American literature. On the rhetorical plane, insofar as the recusal of ethnic authorship constitutes a technique of apophasis, what matters more is that this apophatic strategy, this rhetorical technique occurs. What it means for "The Laws" to be a text is that it continues to perform the writing (or rewriting) of Chinese exclusion regardless of who is writing or not writing "The Laws." That the figurative activity of "The Laws" *continues to function* is what disarticulates it, as writing, from the rhetorical absence of its author. On a political level, of course, the question of authorship is of paramount importance; it is, after all, the organizing impetus for Asian American literature as self-determined and culturally distinct, which is why Kingston's recusal, given her status as a canonical Asian American author, is all the more remarkable. As a limit case for the Asian American author, *China Men* offers an outstanding example of how we might understand the enduring power and complexity of Asian American writing without requiring the author as the origin of this textual activity.

One might think that Kingston's absence in "The Laws" denudes it of its force as a Chinese American intervention in historiography, but this is where apophasis, the figure of negation or denial, offers a different way forward. If an apophatic gesture brings "The Laws" into being, this same rhetorical strategy, a rhetorical technique "alien" to Asian America, is also what drives the linguistic behavior here and elsewhere in *China Men*. Gibbons makes a strikingly similar insight about apophasis itself when he observes that apophatic thought is not "native" to English-language speakers: "It's not that the scarcity of apophatic poetic thinking in English is a defect; it is simply a difference.... The interesting thing for any poet, it seems to me, is to *open up in one's own language resources of poetic thinking from elsewhere.*"[52] Gibbons's phrasing echoes uncannily Kingston's own. Whether as a technique or as a resource "from elsewhere," these apophatic gestures, both inside and outside of *China Men*, mean, first of all, that *China Men* cannot be treated as a simple or simply referential example of Asian American writing. It is quite obviously in conversation with, and intent on troubling, a far broader range of literary, rhetorical, and historical traditions. At the same time we cannot disregard Kingston as the author of *China Men* because her self-negating language links her to the linguistic activity and the historical problematic precipitated in *China Men*. That this text draws on apophasis, a trope "from elsewhere," to articulate its subject matter means that we must not only rethink what we mean by "Asian American" in relation to the race-identified author, but more important, that figurative activity itself can no longer be understood or studied as merely formal or purely linguistic.

Like the texts discussed in previous chapters, *China Men* poses different questions—historical, racial, gendered, and sexualized—of a rhetorical tradition unused to accommodating these questions. By means of these multiplying apophatic gestures, *China Men* demands that we enlarge its frame of reference beyond Chinese or Asian America. Restricting its subject matter to Asian America ignores what this text is doing with apophasis and misses what these apophatic strategies, as employed by *China Men* and its author, are asking of the tradition of apophasis. What might it mean, for instance, for "china men" to *figure* the ancient and theological trope of apophasis? In constructing these rhetorical bridges, my purpose has been to imagine alternative trajectories for the racial sign with the hope that in doing so we might be able, in Kandice Chuh's words, to imagine that sign otherwise.

3 / Catachresis: *Blu's Hanging* and Error

The 1998 award controversy over Lois-Ann Yamanaka's novel *Blu's Hanging* was a tumultuous event for many reasons, but the turmoil it caused and the painful schisms it exposed pushed literature to the forefront of Asian American politics with an urgency we have not seen since the days of *Aiiieeeee!* Of the several issues raised by the controversy, one of the most contentious involved the alleged bias of the Association for Asian American Studies for endorsing a novel with such obvious Filipino stereotypes. The heated debates that ensued took up entrenched positions for aesthetics or for politics, but the very familiarity of this divide served as a potent reminder of a relationship that the field has grappled with from the beginning and has yet to satisfactorily resolve. What made the controversy even more charged was the additional complication of Hawaii's local culture, which serves as the setting for Yamanaka's novels and which has been largely "invisible," as Viet Nguyen has observed, to the continental imaginary of Asian America.[1] As the controversy gathered momentum, the award's supporters found themselves defending the autonomy of aesthetic production and denouncing Yamanaka's critics for failing to grasp the complexity of literature. The award's protestors, on the other hand, took a differently problematic position by emphasizing Yamanaka's Japanese heritage, which rendered the recurring figures of Filipino sexual predators in her body of work all the more fraught. In contemporary Hawaii the plantation era's racial hierarchy has resulted in a social structure dominated by whites and local Japanese and defined by systematic racism against Filipinos.[2] The options, as they must have appeared to participants at the time, seemed polarizing and bleak: either one had to treat the novel as racist for reinforcing the racial asymmetry of Hawaii's local culture, or one had to privilege the "ambiguity and complexity" of literature over the politics of the community, as the petition defending the award put it.[3] Neither side, it seemed, could break the stalemate between an aesthetics devoid of politics and a politics purged of aesthetic activity.

In the decade and a half since the controversy, the critical landscape of Asian American studies has changed dramatically, making available different methodologies and theoretical paradigms. While some of these new critical urgencies have appeared in the scholarship on *Blu's Hanging*—queer critique and racial melancholia come to mind—for the most part treatments of the novel have not progressed much beyond the initial positions staked out by the controversy.[4] The recent approaches to *Blu's Hanging*, for example, have yet to take the novel's aesthetic qualities into consideration as part and parcel of its other concerns. What this means for scholars of the novel is that there is no coherent account of its formal specificity, generic interventions, and figurative behavior.[5] At the same time, however, it is easy to understand why the aesthetic, a category traditionally concerned with disinterested judgment, has had such a dismal track record with this novel in particular. Candace Fujikane, a vocal critic of the uses to which the aesthetic was put before and during the award controversy, argues that a highly restrictive version of the literary shut down the possibility of discussing the novel's relationship to racism. Referring to similar debates surrounding Yamanaka's *Saturday Night at the Pahala Theatre* in 1994 (also nominated for an AAAS award), Fujikane recounts that local Filipino readers had been told "that if they read Yamanaka's representations as racist, they do not know how to grasp the complexity of literature." While she does not explicitly mention aesthetics as the culprit here, the reference is clear in her conclusion: "We can see that literary criticism was being used to uphold systems of racism by rendering local Filipinos as 'deficient' readers of literary texts and 'deficient' readers of race."[6] Aesthetics fares no better in Mark Chiang's account of the award controversy. For him, the association of the category with disinterested and autonomous representation is so ingrained that aesthetics necessarily functions, as it did in relation to *Blu's Hanging*, as a claim to autonomy that denies its relation to capital and power. Chiang's approach to the estrangement of aesthetics from politics is to argue that *Blu's Hanging* should be understood as Yamanaka's "response to her critics," such that the Filipino characters "serve as figures for those in the local community who object to Yamanaka's representation of them." As Chiang understands it, the novel's primary aim is to legitimate Ivah's (and by extension, Yamanaka's) authority to represent the community: "*Blu's Hanging* strives to legitimate Ivah's representation of the local community as superior because of its disinterest and innocence, but her representation means erasing the mechanisms of representation and their implication for relations of power."[7] From this admittedly brief outline, neither the literary nor the aesthetic as they have been conceived in relation to *Blu's Hanging* seems to offer much traction for a criticism simultaneously invested in the political *and* the figurative since the choices presented so far have been either to forgo the question of the literary altogether or to collapse the issue of aesthetics into politics by making the two identical.

Error

If aesthetics and literariness are compromised points of entry for the novel, why return to them at all? Why should the novel's behavior as a literary text matter, given Fujikane and Chiang's sharp criticisms of these approaches? It matters because what I am calling the novel's figurative behavior—its literariness—can teach us something about representation, especially when it engages the issue of race and racism. Here I want to redirect Chiang's argument concerning the field's lack of theorizing about representation and shift it away from the category of the aesthetic and toward the place of figurative activity. Chiang casts the controversy and the novel as a conflict between those doing the representing and those being represented. While he differentiates between political and aesthetic representation (in the sense that the first requires consent and the second functions without it), his account of representation remains relatively simple, as he lines up the former with identity and realism and the latter with difference and antirealism.[8] These binaries are heuristic for Chiang, but instructive nonetheless. His concern, as he explains later in the essay, is that if the novel makes Uncle Paulo represent the "violence of the literal," then "to equate the literal with violence or power implies that the figurative is somehow free of the stigma of power."[9] What happens, though, when representation refuses to align with the neat polarities Chiang assigns to it here? If we find, for example, the figurative deeply embedded in both violence and power, or the literal understood as a necessary and figurative mistake?

What we want, I think, is a theory of representation that can accommodate a more complex notion of referentiality, one that can account for its potential errancy, for its aberration or rhetoricity. This is where an investigation into the novel's figurative activity, its highly patterned use of language, can take us beyond the current stalemate between aesthetics or politics. To borrow from an insightful though problematic observer of figurative activity, I quote Cleanth Brooks, who notes, "Whatever statement we may seize upon as incorporating the 'meaning' of the poem, immediately the imagery and the rhythm seem to set up tensions with it, warping and twisting it, qualifying and revising it."[10] These warping and twisting effects are not, of course, reserved for poetry alone, especially when we remember that literary language has been habitually understood as a turn away from proper usage (from Greek *tropos*, "turn," and Latin *tropus*, "figure of speech").[11] Indeed the twisting effects Brooks describes are produced by rhetorical activity, a fundamental part of language itself and an activity that requires us to scrutinize the relationship—no longer symmetrical, and often unpredictable—between words and their meaning. But to insist on this figurative activity is not, as critics of the novel have feared, to claim that *Blu's Hanging* is removed from violence or power, from its historical context. What it does mean is that we need more than "sociological readings," as Wendy Motooka terms them, to describe the novel's activities.[12]

While it is true that attention to figurative activity has customarily been the purview of literary training, it would be a mistake to assume that literary critics have a monopoly on theorizing the sign as divergent or discontinuous. Theories of race, gender, and sexuality have long offered powerful examples of such theorizing. To borrow an example from ethnic studies, Gary Y. Okihiro reminds us that "comparative ethnic studies is the study of power, and its locations and articulations around the axes of race and ethnicity, gender, sexuality, class, and nation."[13] In rebuking the field's detour into identity politics, Okihiro urges us to remember that race, ethnicity, gender, sexuality, class, and nation are *figurations* of power relations. To cast his point into literary terms, it is only when we grasp race, ethnicity, gender, et cetera as the means by which power relations are re-presented as something else that we can begin to critically intervene in the politics of identity. Figurative activity rearticulates the precipitating historical problematic of the literary text, but because this historical problematic is *figured*, translated into figurative language, it is no longer simply straightforward or referential.

Blu's Hanging calls on the trope of catachresis, the figure of abuse, to present race, gender, and sexuality as improper yet indispensable names for power relations. In previous chapters we explored how literary texts responded to conditions of defiance, coercion, and necessity. Here we turn to *Blu's Hanging* for the literary response to error, specifically to indispensable error, when the word in question is simply wrong but no other term exists to describe the phenomenon at hand. Chiang's reading of the controversy describes precisely this catachrestic predicament: "In the *Blu's Hanging* case, the primary categorical error was to apply the rules and assumptions of political representation to literary representation."[14] If the award's protestors were forced into this necessary error by the lack of symbolic capital, the resources that the novel musters to deal with error take us into a more complicated realm of rhetorical behavior. The figures we encountered in previous chapters were relatively straightforward; neither the rhetorical question nor apophasis, for example, tried to hide or disguise its figurative nature. With catachresis we confront a far more unquiet figure, as it insists on its activity being wrong, a misuse of language, but also necessary, whether because it is the only term available or because what it seeks to name does not exist.

Blu's Hanging's historical problematic is the plantation economy of Hawaii's colonial history, which the novel has figured as the catachreses of race, gender, and sexuality. Cynthia Wu beautifully captures these historical complications in her depiction of the novel's backdrop: "The polycultural demographics in Hawai'i originated from its plantation history in which a racially, ethnically, and linguistically diverse work force emerged from a complex set of forces involving not only agricultural capital, but also carefully orchestrated negotiations between the United States and Japan, legislated subduing of the Hawai'ian kingdom, and a multiplicity of colonialisms in Korea and the Philippines."[15] If aesthetic representation is as straightforward as critics of the award have claimed, why does *Blu's Hanging* stage race, gender, and sexuality in scene after scene as catachrestic sites of visual misrecognition and profound error? These catachreses are the literary means by which the novel connects the abuses of figurative language to the material conditions of empire.

Catachresis 1: Asian America

Catachresis is not an Asian American trope, but because it names an indispensable error it has been widely adopted as a byword for Asian American identity. In Greek it means the "misapplication" or "misuse" of a word.[16] In Latin it is translated as *abusio*, "abuse." We find an early definition of catachresis in Quintilian's *Institutio Oratoria*, a famous rhetorical manual of the classical world: "the practice of adapting the nearest available term to describe something for which no actual term exists."[17] Whereas Quintilian differentiates catachresis from metaphor (in which another term is available), other rhetoricians understand it as merely an extreme or forced metaphor. Richard Lanham, for example, describes catachresis as an "implied metaphor, using words wrenched from common usage."[18] These finer points of classification aside, what is important here is that catachresis announces itself, whether "wrenched" or misused, as a kind of language whose figurative errors are *necessary*. Gayatri Chakravorty Spivak parses catachresis to stress the indispensability of its error: "In other words, no other word will do, and yet it does not really give you the literal meaning in the history of the language, upon which a *correct* rather than catachrestic metaphoric use would be based."[19] In catachresis words lose their literal sense, and yet this is an error that we cannot do without, a referential crisis that explains why the trope has been so congenial for describing the limits of the term *Asian American*. In Susan Koshy's well-known formulation, "'Asian American' offers us a rubric that we cannot not use. But our usage of the term should rehearse the catachrestic status of the formation. I use the term 'catachresis' to indicate that there is no literal referent for the rubric 'Asian American,' and, as such, the name is marked by the limits of its signifying power."[20] But if an understanding of catachresis in relation to Asian America has featured prominently in the field's cultural criticism, this does not yet explain what the trope, with its ancient resonance, is doing in *Blu's Hanging*, a novel whose context is radically foreign to the rhetorical tradition that once flourished in antiquity and in the European Middle Ages and Renaissance.

Nguyen's approach to *Blu's Hanging* as representing "the limits of Asian America" may help us make the rhetorical connections here. While Nguyen does not refer to catachresis, his argument suggests an affinity for the trope. For him Yamanaka's novels are not Asian American at all; instead they represent Hawaii's local culture, an entirely separate cultural formation. Consequently he proposes to "read Yamanaka's work not so much as examples of Asian American literature but as examples of something that Asian American literary criticism has claimed as its own." *Asian American*, in other words, is the wrong term for the novel. The misuse of *Asian American* as a catachresis for Hawaii's local culture allows us to glimpse a deeper history of colonial encounters. As Nguyen explains, "Asian American studies feels safe to claim Yamanaka's novels and the culture they represent as Asian American, despite the fact that it may in doing so 'operate unexpectedly in the service of American imperialism.'"[21] The claim to local culture, however, has its own difficulties because it masks the "settler colonialism" of Asian-descent immigrants. Claiming the novel either as "local" or "Asian American" is thus equally problematic.

Blu's Hanging is set on the island of Molokai. It follows the Ogata children—Ivah, Blu, and Maisie—as they try to come to terms with their mother's death from an overdose of drugs taken to prevent a recurrence of leprosy. The novel's working-class Hawaii, defined by poverty, racism, and sexual violence, features repeated scenes of human and animal exploitation. It is a far cry from the multicultural paradise so familiar to the tourist imagination. Unlike their middle-class Japanese peers, the Ogatas are stigmatized by their poverty, but their ethnicity positions them socially above the Reyes, their slightly wealthier Filipino neighbors. Narrated in the first person by Ivah, *Blu's Hanging* is a female bildungsroman involving a social mobility plot. At the end of the novel, she leaves home for an elite prep school that will pave the way to college. In the novel's most controversial and violent scene, middle child Blu is raped by Uncle Paulo, a Reyes neighbor. The leading scholarship on the novel is an important resource for situating the novel's reception and its politics with regard to the controversy and to Hawaii's local culture, but it is less helpful in explaining the novel beyond these immediate contexts. This is where an account of the novel's figurative activity may be useful. Catachresis breaks us out of the local context of the controversy and of Asian America because this linguistic pattern comes from elsewhere. At the same time, because the trope is localized—it translates the novel's historical problematic—while exceeding the parameters of *Blu's Hanging*, it redraws these national, cultural, and linguistic boundaries in important ways. We find evidence of this ancient rhetorical activity in *Blu's Hanging* because to the extent that it is a highly patterned use of language, the novel participates in the vast linguistic heritage of these widely circulating tropes and devices. Insofar as we find catachresis in this particular novel, with its highly specific historical problematic, its appearance here poses new and different questions of the classical rhetorical tradition. Tracking the unquiet presence of a trope like catachresis in a text like *Blu's Hanging* thus pushes in two directions: against the deracinated study of figurative language and against the identity politics reading of the novel.

Catachresis 2: Gender

One of the archetypal scenarios of the female coming-of-age story involves the onset of menstruation, the initiation into "womanhood." Why, then, does *Blu's Hanging* portray the protagonist's first menstruation or menarche as a mistake? When Ivah first begins to menstruate, she misidentifies the blood as diarrhea: "There are brown stains on my panties. . . . I wonder why my anus leaks diarrhea when it never leaked before."[22] The discontinuity between the body and its meaning is reinforced by the placement of this scenario within a greater discontinuity, a White Christmas dance in the tropics. The narrator explains,

"The day before the intermediate school's Christmas dance, 'Walkin' in a Winter Wonderland,' I start feeling sick. . . . I feel like I might have diarrhea, so I . . . sit for a long time on the toilet, pushing and pushing, cold sweat and sore stomach" (92). The alert reader will of course recognize the stains as menstrual blood, and this misrecognition scenario is by no means unusual for such narratives, but my point is that the novel takes particular pains to draw out the error here. The protagonist is understandably confused about the nature of these stains, but the narrator, who narrates in the present tense from the perspective of the adult Ivah, should not be, and yet she manages to report the physical symptoms—cold sweat, sore stomach, brown stains—without identifying them, thus preserving the effect of the misrecognition. The scene implies not only that gender is something learned but, more important, that identity—gendered or otherwise—may simply be "wrong." There is an existing term for the brown stains that Ivah discovers, but because the novel presents her as mistaking these stains for diarrhea, we need to appeal to the figurative resources of catachresis. Lisa Freinkel comments, for example, that whether "understood as mixed metaphor or as the misapplication of terminology, catachresis is simply *wrong*."[23] Diarrhea implies not only the character's mistake in misidentifying the brown stains but, more generally, the potentially improper names that, in Koshy's formulation, we cannot not use for signifying this body, the most salient for this scene being the complex of gender, sexuality, and class. Janet Lee observes that within the matrices of heteronormativity and patriarchy, menarche is conflated with sexual availability and reproduction.[24] But menstruation, as Joan Jacobs Brumberg and others have elucidated, is also firmly bound up with class and nation. The protagonist's shame, as well as her understanding of herself as "dirty" (94), are perhaps more inculcated than allayed by the education she has received from "Time of Your Life," her fourth-grade health education class, which disseminates, as Brumberg has argued, a "middle-class sanitary ideal" involving "learning to menstruate the 'American way.'"[25]

Indeed, as the scene continues it becomes disturbingly clear that the protagonist's education into normative femininity involves both American assimilation and commodity culture: she refers to the sanitary products she requires by brand name alone, Tampax and Modess.[26]

If menarche itself constitutes a kind of threshold, the novel's staging of this key scene begs for a rhetorical understanding of how the body enters into language and culture. In rhetorical terms menarche itself suggests a kind of catachrestic motion. Patricia Parker explains that catachresis (Latin *abusio*, "abuse") and metaphor (Latin *translatio*, "transfer") were often confused in antiquity because both tropes involve rhetorical transfer.[27] As the passage from girl to woman, menarche also designates a type of "transfer." As Lee puts it, "What is crucial here is that this *juncture*, menarche, is a site where girls become women and gender relations are reproduced."[28] In calling menarche a juncture, she elucidates the rhetorical resonance that *Blu's Hanging* has built around its version of menarche as a transfer of meaning, where the name for this transfer (this *translatio* between one physiological stage and another) is the "wrong" one. By staging the name for this juncture as "wrong" (diarrhea rather than menstrual blood), the novel implies that gender and sexuality designate potential discontinuities for the body, and gestures as well to the other forces also at work here that generate similar errors: heteronormativity, patriarchy, class, Americanization. That Ivah so easily mistakes her menstrual blood for excrement suggests the patriarchal associations that have long identified menstrual blood as dirty or polluted; more fundamentally though it registers the cultural mediation of the body that feminist thinkers have called "gender." In displacing the gendered mind/body divide that has defined Western philosophy, Elizabeth Grosz urges us to imagine a model "where the join, the interaction of the two surfaces, is always a question of power."[29] The "join," in other words, between mind/body and sex/gender is a catachrestic one; the boundary between nature and culture is "joined" by rhetoric. If gender and sexuality are nothing more than improper names for power relations, they mark the site where power relations re-present themselves by taking on the catachreses of gender and sexuality. Because the novel assigns to Ivah an identity arc that is principally concerned with gender and sexuality, it must consistently ignore how these issues intersect with race or racism. With the exception of her occasional run-ins with racist haoles, the protagonist is rarely troubled by questions of race or racism.[30] As we shall see, the arc connecting race and racism to sexuality is one that the novel has assigned to Uncle Paulo and the Reyes, and it is a trajectory that it carefully prevents from overlapping with the Ivah arc. In staging menarche as an error, the novel makes available a range of different questions having to do with class, gender, and sexuality, but *not* race. This occlusion in the Ivah narrative becomes significant later with regard to the novel's inability to imagine a more ambitious critique of power relations that would articulate the Ivah arc with Uncle Paulo's.

It is the novel's figurative activity, however, that grants us access to these insights, and this point is nowhere more evident than in the paratactic conclusion of the menarche scene. As the scene progresses, a short paratactic set of sentences relays the character's thoughts to the reader. The character's moment of recognition—it is blood, not diarrhea—is given to us as parataxis, the juxtaposition of clauses or phrases without conjunctions:

And then I know.
   "Go sleep early. You feel betta in the morning," Poppy tells me.
   Right before I sleep.
   How alone I feel.
   No Mama for me.
   Nobody to help me with this blood.
   Blood. (93)

The grammatical disconnect produced by parataxis emphasizes the disjointedness between the character and her understanding of her own body's processes. To understand the significance of these brown stains as blood and this moment as the threshold to "womanhood" evokes an entire discursive complex that is missing here, an absence that the character identifies with the lost maternal figure: "No Mama for me." The rearrangement of Ivah-character's thoughts into the paratactic form the reader sees above represents the re-telling of the past from a future time, but this retelling, this *re*presentation is presented as immediate and real, that is, as a "telling" rather than a *re*-arrangement. The temporal gap between the time of the narration and the events being narrated is not accessible, but it is made "visible" as the disconnected, paratactic phrases we see above. The temporal gap, in other words, is only glimpsed as *form*, as the paratactic rearrangement or representation of the character's thoughts.

If we can think of Ivah as being *staged* as narrating, we are better able to access the colonial history of the novel's language. The device of the first-person narrator reflecting on the experiences of her younger self is not an exceptional one. What makes this device remarkable in the context of *Blu's Hanging* is that the novel visually distinguishes the events being narrated from the narration of these events by using pidgin for the former and standard English for the latter. In a telling scene on the perceived inferior status of pidgin, the narrator relates her conversation with Miss Owens, a racist haole teacher from the mainland, who has just implied that Maisie's silence stems from a physical handicap. To this, the novel has Ivah respond, "'She not deaf.' Miss Owens gives me a sneering smile for my pidgin, I don't even care" (60). The shift from pidgin into standard English is quite seamless; there are no obvious intrusions that call attention to this shift, and yet what the shift indicates is a temporal lag measuring the distance between the time of the narration (adult Ivah narrating in standard English) and the events being narrated (child Ivah speaking pidgin). Shifts like these are frequent and common in *Blu's Hanging*; they are formal indices that suggest, in distinctly literary form, the novel's historical problematic. Since the use of pidgin is associated with the narrator's past and the use of standard English with her future, we might consider this a formal recognition of the problematic hierarchy intrinsic to the developmental structure of the bildungsroman: the mastery of standard English by adult Ivah firmly situates pidgin in a past she will inevitably and naturally outgrow.

The literary use of pidgin is itself fraught. Once considered a debased or broken version of standard English, it has survived persistent attempts at eradication by the English standard school system. Today, however, pidgin is the defining feature of Hawaii's local literature and, as Stephen Sumida notes, is considered "a language of agency, of self-determination."[31] But if Sumida identifies the use of pidgin with the postcolonial nature of Hawaiian literature, Yamanaka herself understands its literary usage differently. For her, writing in pidgin constitutes a reclaiming of one's "own" heritage, and involves affirming a linguistic practice once denigrated as inferior and ignorant. "It's nice now," she concludes, "that we have ownership of our own stories."[32] The claim to ownership, however, is a vexed one, as Susan Y. Najita explains, because pidgin itself is a colonial language: it is "a language that evolves out of the U.S. overthrow of the sovereign Kingdom of Hawai'i." She goes on to quote an early observer who describes it as a "language of command" facilitating the vast racial machinery of the plantation and its racial hierarchy of white planters, native Hawaiians, and immigrant workers. Pidgin is also inextricably bound up with attempts to suppress the Native Hawaiian language, as well as with efforts to Americanize the descendants of nonwhite immigrants. Hence Najita urges us to consider it as "simultaneously the language of the plantation, the site for preserving the Hawaiian language, and the site of critical anticolonial consciousness."[33]

While one could certainly make an argument that pidgin constitutes a form of linguistic catachresis, more compelling is how Yamanaka's understanding of pidgin as "ownership" takes us back to the rhetorical figure, since it is precisely the issue of ownership—of proper usage, proper names, and property—with which catachresis is concerned. As Freinkel observes, "At the heart of catachresis—*abusio* as the Latins call it—lies the *problem of proper use*."[34] Parker's reading of catachresis explains what is at stake in the issue of proper usage. Returning to the classical confusion between metaphor and catachresis, she suggests that this conflation arises not from "the presence or absence of an original proper term but [from] *the question of conscious control*." That is, catachresis (arising from the lack of an existing term) implies necessity, while metaphor (arising from the "transfer" of an already existing term) implies a "controlling subject who applies the figure at will." Ultimately this involves, in Parker's words, "no less than the mastery of language itself, the question of whether its movements control or are controlled by the subject in question."[35] Proper names, property, and the attendant questions of agency and ownership are also at the heart of identity politics, and this is where Parker helps us yoke the novel's figurative activity to the politics of the award controversy. Catachresis disabuses us of any simple notion that the author is a controlling subject exerting her will over language because first and foremost the premise of the trope is that the usage in question is incorrect, wrong. Second, catachresis is a rhetorical pattern inherited from elsewhere, from a remote and foreign rhetorical tradition, and its appearance in *Blu's Hanging* troubles the assumption that the author figure possesses language or its proper use. Hence we cannot say in any simple way that catachresis is a pattern that Yamanaka owns or controls. Recalling Najita on pidgin's colonial complications, we must be cautious about the identity politics narrative implicit in Yamanaka's claim to ownership, especially since the novel has been insisting on a notion of identity as a problem, as a necessary error, not a solution.[36] My point here is not to dismiss the important claims to agency that must and should be made in the name of identity politics but to guard against the occlusion of a critical consciousness, as Najita puts it, one that is muted by a narrative of agency and ownership. First-person narration, point of view, and present tense are some of the literary devices employed by the novel to generate a fiction of identity for Ivah, to naturalize her voice as that of the novel's and the novel itself as her ostensible self-representation. Because *Blu's Hanging* starts off by staging its pivotal scene of female identity as a misuse of language, it immediately complicates any easy notion we might have of identity in relation to linguistic ownership.

Catachresis 3: Uncle Paulo

If the novel initially stages Ivah's menstrual blood as excrement, it quickly corrects this error. In adjusting this mistake it pulls back from a potential critique of gender as error by offering the correct interpretation; that is, it normalizes the heteronormative and patriarchal matrix within which menstruation is associated with shame and reproductive sexuality. The next misrecognition scenario the novel presents occurs at the site of race; in the same sentence it will suggest that Uncle Paulo, though "being" Filipino, does not "look" Filipino at all. While each of these scenarios can be understood separately as catachrestic—power relations are mistaken as race and gender—the novel is unable to recognize their mutual imbrication in the same originating historical problematic, and thus is unable to fully realize the far more powerful critique that would follow from articulating them as consequences of a plantation economy under empire. That there is no existing term in the representational economy of the novel for the connection between these two scenarios except by the name of Filipino racism is the most formidable catachresis here. I turn now to a reading of Uncle Paulo to try to elicit some of the hidden linkages between the seemingly disparate histories of gender, sexuality, capitalism, and colonialism.

The Uncle Paulo character is a pedophile, a proud defiler of high school virgins, a rapist and drug dealer. There is little in his characterization that redeems him from being anything more than a set of animated stereotypes involving Filipino sexual rapacity, violence, and depravity. The novel's perspective and its narration, channeled as they are through Ivah, work to restrict the reader's imaginative access to the character. Given these obvious roadblocks, *Blu's Hanging*'s staging of Uncle Paulo is arguably even more complicated than its staging of Ivah. His appearances in the novel involve disavowals of the visual cues marking him as Filipino, active obstructions of our view through multiple framings, and challenges to his self-identification as Filipino. Since the sharpest criticisms of the novel revolve around the stereotypical presentation of its Filipino characters, what ought we to make of the novel's peculiar approach? Indeed, it is surely significant that for the first two-thirds of the novel, *Blu's Hanging* refuses to identify the Reyeses as Filipino. Quite early on, it informs us that the Reyes nieces are half-Japanese, and that one of these nieces is proud of her "Spanish" heritage, but no further information regarding their racial status is forthcoming. Uncle Paulo himself is not explicitly identified as Filipino until the tenth chapter of a seventeen-chapter novel, and when he is named as such, this identification is immediately problematized. Up to this point, then, it is the reader, alert to the racial cues of a multiracial local Hawaii, who must identify the Reyeses as Filipino.

What can the novel mean by arranging things this way? In the key scene where Uncle Paulo is first identified as Filipino, we are given some clues. There Blu asks Maisie whether Uncle Paulo "no look like Davy Jones to you? I mean, he Filipino, but he no look like one kinda haole-ish Monkee to you?" (138). By identifying Uncle Paulo as a Filipino who looks like an actor from a reality television show, the novel opens up a distance between the Filipino subject and "looking," if not "being," Filipino. Furthermore because the novel presents this relationship as a disavowal, it suggests that "being" Filipino, at least for Uncle Paulo, involves not looking Filipino and looking like someone else.[37] If Uncle Paulo fails to look Filipino while remaining in some way "Filipino," the recognition of certain bodies as Filipino—their racialization—must necessarily consist of a *mis*recognition. The racial logic of identity, in which racialization involves matching up a set of physical features to a corresponding sensibility or consciousness, is disturbed here. By describing him visually as "one kinda haole-ish Monkee," the novel suggests that being identified as Filipino for Uncle Paulo may involve some form of passing. In the context of African American literature, Samira Kawash has argued that the passing body represents a profound epistemological crisis: "Between the 'perception' of whiteness and the 'knowledge' of blackness, an abyss opens up, an abyss that threatens not only confusion but the very orders of being." In other words, rather than shoring up a racial logic, passing brings about its disintegration. Kawash puts this in literary terms: "The possibility that the body, which is meant to reflect transparently its inner truth, may in fact be a misrepresentation and that its meaning may be illegible threatens the collapse of the system of racial ordering and separation on which the hierarchical distribution of social, political, and economic opportunity is based."[38] In the crisis of seeing and knowing that the novel names "Filipino," we have a visual structure that resembles the form of catachresis, the figure of abuse and improper usage. In addition to opening up a gap between seeing and knowing, the novel suggests that race—"Filipino"—is what sutures this gap, but it can only do so catachrestically. Such a gap between representation and its referent finds some affinity with the gap or absence that catachresis attempts to repair by borrowing, with some violence, an improper term for an object defined by lexical absence.

Like "diarrhea" in the previous scene, "Davy Jones" operates catachrestically for "Filipino." Not only does this scene insist that Uncle Paulo fails to properly designate or represent his race, but that neither "Filipino" nor "Davy Jones" are proper names for him. In fact, by identifying Uncle Paulo with Jones, the novel pushes the impropriety of proper names even further since the producers of *The Monkees* (NBC, 1966–68) hired Jones to play "himself." The show revolved around a struggling rock band modeled after the Beatles. Unlike the other band members who hailed from southern California, Jones was British, but he, like the rest of the cast played a "character" with his own name. As one of the producers explained, "We didn't even look at actors, and we didn't look for experienced rock 'n' roll groups because we wanted *guys who could play themselves.*"[39] In other words, the casting decisions of the producers strove to achieve what Matthew Stahl calls the "authenticity effect." If Jones is a musician hired to play himself, the blurring of "reality" and "television" through performance adds yet more density to the novel's staging of Uncle Paulo. In the scenes that follow, the novel will put the character again and again in roles that he is made to perform, asking us to entertain a much more complex view of race and ethnicity in relation to the visual and the known.

The novel uses two devices, reported speech and multiple framings, to show us why Uncle Paulo can appear in the novel only as a stereotype. The first few references that the novel makes to Uncle Paulo all occur as reported speech. He is first mentioned in an anecdote that the narrator relates; she has heard this story from her brother, who was told the story by Blendaline, a Reyes niece: for New Year's Eve, Uncle Paulo and other boy cousins entertained themselves by tormenting cats. The next reference is also reported speech: the narrator reports what her friend Mitchell was told by Evangeline, another Reyes niece: Uncle Paulo marks his conquest of high school virgins by tying black lace to his car's antenna. The device of reported speech alerts us to the framing of this character. The character does not speak for himself; instead his actions are relayed by other speakers. In the next instance of reported speech, the novel uses an additional device: framing. In this scene the Reyes family and Blu play a game of cowboys and Indians. When Blu is abandoned midgame, Ivah and Maisie must come to the rescue. This time it is Mitchell who informs Ivah, "We were playing a game of cowboys and Indians with Uncle Paulo, who suggested that we take a hostage, so he looked around and said, 'Grab the fat ass, he make good stew,' and proceeded to tie up your brother. Uncle Paulo told him not to worry—Blu was actually Clint Eastwood and the hero of the movie, so they'd get F Troop to set him loose in no time. But they didn't" (153). Several framings are at work in this passage: the story is told to the narrator by Mitchell; Uncle

Paulo plays the role of an Indian in the children's game; and we find yet another allusion to an American television show from the 1960s. *F Troop* (ABC, 1965–67) takes place shortly after the Civil War and spoofs the conventions of the western. Set in a fictionalized Wild West, it relates the comic misadventures of a group of army misfits and their partnership with a local Native American tribe, the Hekawi. "F Troop" may now be a term for bungling ineptitude, but the novel's allusion to the series evinces the imaginative and symbolic power of American popular culture. That Uncle Paulo, already a "Filipino" who looks "white," is cast in the role of the Indian adds to the complex representational moves the novel is making here. Playing on the fine line between performance and reality, the reference to *F Troop* further troubles the visual logic of race since the actors hired as Hekawi tribe members were, of course, non-natives playing the role of natives.[40]

The novel stages Uncle Paulo through multiple framings to designate a preexisting framework of representation in which his figure has been inserted, and outside of which he cannot be visible. By staging I mean the novel's awareness of *how* it is presenting him and also, to extend this theatrical language, the roles he is made to play and the stage (the preexisting framework of representation) on which he is made to enact these roles. When the novel stages Uncle Paulo as playing a series of roles, it is saying, effectively, that it is not presenting "Filipinoness" but its problematic and troubled re-presentation. To the extent that these roles—Davy Jones, Indian—are fictional, they are errors, but insofar as these roles are the means by which the figure of Uncle Paulo can appear before the reader, they are also indispensable as they determine how he can be seen or recognized. Since the novel portrays these roles as visually unreliable, as mistakes and misrecognitions fundamental to colonial performance, it warns us to be wary of the easy promises of the visual, in which "looking" Filipino is equated with "being" Filipino. However, because Uncle Paulo is not just a racialized figure but also a figure identified with a potentially queer sexuality (he has intercourse with both sexes), we might consider these multiple stagings as formal indices of yet another trajectory for his representation that cannot find expression in the preexisting frameworks that determine the novel's imaginative repertoire.[41]

If Uncle Paulo consists of a series of roles, these roles are scripted by colonial histories that do not appear on the main stage of the novel, as it were, and yet they hover in the wings and direct from afar the cultural scripts through which they exert material and imaginative force. Sociologist Moon-Kie Jung demonstrates how the widespread stereotypes of Filipinos as violent or depraved were the result of the particularly violent "mode . . . of colonial incorporation" inflicted by the United States on the Philippines. In fact the importation of Filipino labor into Hawaii was understood as part of American colonialism: white planters, Jung states, "saw Filipino labor migration as an extension of the U.S. colonial project in the Philippines."[42] The multiple framings of Uncle Paulo in Blu's Hanging are the means by which the novel calls our attention to the preexisting colonial frameworks—F Troop and the conquest of the West, Filipino stereotypes as signifiers of U.S. imperialism—that set the stage for how the subject racialized as Filipino can appear. So when Blu's Hanging stages the children's game of cowboys and Indians, it makes the American frontier reappear in Hawaii to reveal a colonial history that the novel never alludes to otherwise. Hawaii itself, as well as the Philippines, is part of the new American frontier being constructed at the turn of the century, even though no direct acknowledgment of this occurs in the novel. There are cultural traces, however, of this forgetting. Before the scene involving F Troop, the novel has made repeated references to actors like John Wayne and Clint Eastwood, to iconic westerns like The Good, the Bad and the Ugly, and made allusions to a Wild West, replete with gun-slinging cowboys and hangman's nooses. The "myth of the frontier," as Richard Slotkin observes, has framed American history as a story of the "discovery, conquest, and settlement of the West" ever since Frederick Jackson Turner identified the frontier as the essence of the American character. Slotkin goes on to argue that the frontier myth is deeply racialized: "In its original form, developed between 1780 and 1850, the myth depicts America as a racial entity: a white Anglo-Saxon Protestant nation, which defines itself by destroying or subjugating a 'nonwhite' enemy—Native Americans and Mexicans."[43] This backdrop renders the novel's staging of the frontier especially fraught, as the children's game of cowboys and Indians superimposes multiple arcs of colonialism, past and present. The game suggests the colonization of Hawaii as part of an American "empire of bases," in Najita's phrase, but it also indexes a less visible colonialism, one that calls itself "local" to claim its place in Hawaii on the basis of shared oppression during the plantation era.[44] Native Hawaiian leader Haunani-Kay Trask argues, "Modern Hawai'i, like its colonial parent the United States, is a settler society; that is, Hawai'i is a society in which the indigenous culture and people have been murdered, suppressed or marginalized for the benefit of settlers who now dominate our islands."[45] In Blu's Hanging the game of cowboys and Indians is all that remains of these entwined histories of colonial violence and erasure.

I want to linger on the staging of this game because a complex argument concerning the perils of identity politics is hinted at here by making Uncle Paulo play the role of the Indian. Recall that in the scene above Uncle Paulo says of Blu, "Grab the fat ass, he make good stew." If we follow the novel's lead in recognizing Uncle Paulo as a figure that does not look Filipino, that is, if we understand his function in the novel as playing the "role" of Filipino, then a far-ranging critique of multiple colonialisms—plantation, U.S., Asian settler, and Asian American—is made possible. This is so because in the context of this game the Uncle Paulo figure stands in for, erroneously and yet indispensably, the native other *who cannot be figured*, who can appear only through the scrim of colonial discourse. Playing the role of the Indian, Uncle Paulo can be said to *figure* as catachresis the native other who does not otherwise appear. Up to this point, the novel has refused a simple stance on its representation of

Filipinoness, but if we gloss over this meticulous and careful staging of the roles Uncle Paulo is made to play, our access to the epistemic violence of colonialism is blocked. In other words, if we understand Uncle Paulo merely as Filipino, as the subject of racism, he assumes this identity at the expense of erasing the indigenous native—Native Hawaiian or American Indian—in whose role he has been cast and whose figuration now cannot even be glimpsed.[46] This longer history of colonial erasure, however, is made available if we attend to what the novel means by staging him in this complicated way.

This staging mechanism suggests the figurative work accomplished by the deployment of these Filipino stereotypes, at least with regard to Uncle Paulo. In the specific context of Hawaii, Chiang argues that stereotypes about Filipino sexuality do not in fact index sexuality at all, but the relationship of Filipino labor to the plantation economy: "Stereotypes of sexual deviance reflected the perceived economic threat of Filipino labor."[47] While appearing to refer to Filipino subjects, these stereotypes point elsewhere, indicating something else entirely. Let us imagine, in the context of the novel, that these racial stereotypes are useful catachreses that can aid the politically engaged reader by disclosing a suppressed history of economic, sexualized, and colonial violence. They can do so, however, only by borrowing, in error, someone else's name. If "Filipino" is viewed as a catachresis, an improper name for the self, it gives us figurative access to multiple forms of colonialism: the dispossession of native peoples in Hawaii, the mainland, and the Philippines, as well as the "settler colonialism" that goes by the name of "local."

Catachresis 4: Racism

So far the novel has employed the term *Filipino* to index the discontinuity of the racialized body, the erasure of the indigenous, and the reterritorialization of Hawaii as American frontier. In the final scene I will discuss, "Filipino" has a different task; its place is to mark a critique that cannot be named within the novel and can be referenced only by its catachresis: racism against Filipinos. In this key scene Ivah and the children have just returned from Mrs. Nishimoto's, a mainland haole immigrant who exploits them for child care and domestic work. They encounter Uncle Paulo, who is departing after delivering some marijuana to Poppy. Blu greets Uncle Paulo, telling him that Ivah has forbidden him to associate with Blendaline, his erstwhile girlfriend. Uncle Paulo then launches into a two-part speech condemning Japanese racism and white racism against Filipinos. As other critics have noted, the scene is significant for being the one place in the novel where its protagonist's Japanese privilege in relation to Filipinos is openly acknowledged; also relevant is the fact that Uncle Paulo is used as the mouthpiece for this criticism. But what seems more important is that the novel cannot articulate the real historical problematic at work, not even when it is able to acknowledge, however indirectly, the structural similarity between the Ogata children and Filipinos: both parties are economically exploited by whites, and this exploitation is a consequence of Hawaii's colonial history.

The scene begins with Uncle Paulo complaining to Ivah, "Whass wrong with my niece playing wit' yo' bradda? What, he mo' betta than her 'cause he Japanee? Fuck, Japs for think they mo' betta than everybody else, fuckas. Especially the Filipinos. Fuck, everybody for spit on Filipinos, shit" (207). If Uncle Paulo's complaint makes a glancing reference to Japanese racism as part of a greater racial hierarchy, one rooted in the plantation era, it all too quickly returns to racism as the source of the animus. In his next outburst another hint at the plantation economy appears, but is quickly redirected. When he learns that the children are working for Mrs. Nishimoto, "'Thass another one,' Uncle Paulo mutters. 'Fuckin' haoles. They mo' worse than the Japs the way they act like we just a truckload of fuckin' brownies picking pineapples for minimum wage. Fuckas all hate us Filipinos'" (207). Despite the reference to the pineapple industry, what is being condemned here is not the racialized economic disparities of the plantation system but white condescension:

"they act like we just a truckload of fuckin' brownies." The hint that some cause other than racism is responsible for these structural inequities is left unrealized. The end of Uncle Paulo's speech returns, as above, to an indictment of racism: "Fuckas all hate us Filipinos."

The issue here is not that the novel is unable to recognize racism against Filipinos but that its representational economy cannot articulate the larger historical relationships within which racism against Filipinos forms just one moving part. Within the parameters of the novel Uncle Paulo's awareness of this distant history can be articulated only as racism against Filipinos. If the novel so far has cast serious doubt on the referentiality of "Filipino" as the name for the self, in this scene it complicates the trajectory of this term even further by having Uncle Paulo, in a rare act of self-representation, identify himself as Filipino: "us Filipinos," he declares above in reference to haole disdain. But in the very same passage, the novel also demonstrates that "Filipino" is not really a proper name because what it designates is not an "authentic" self but a colonial interpellation into a racialized structure of economic exploitation: "a truckload of fuckin' brownies picking pineapples for minimum wage." In fact the term *Filipino* is itself a colonial catachresis. It is not the "name" for the subject but a historical term for what Amy Kaplan calls the "violent belongings" of American imperialism.[48] The term's etymology derives from the Spanish "(las Islas) Filipinas," literally "the islands of Philip," and indicates an even earlier colonialism by remembering Philip II of Spain, in whose name the islands were claimed in 1565.[49] If the character Uncle Paulo can comprehend this history only as "Filipino," the reader alert to figurative activity is able to recognize what the character cannot: that "Filipino" here marks a racialized, classed, and sexualized position in an exploitative structure of power under colonialism that is *historicized* as the catachresis "Filipino."

By presenting this "name" and its chain of colonial histories as a way of understanding how these subjects are hailed by a historical expression of unequal relations of power, the novel suggests that the proper referent for "Filipino" is not histori-cal Filipino subjects but *the history of multiple colonialisms*. Hence this scene is crucial insofar as it registers, in a disjointed and irregular fashion, the novel's incomplete attempts to con-nect anti-Filipino racism to the other moving parts generated by the plantation economy: colonialisms new, old, and settler; the interlocking of gender and sexuality within the matrices of heteronormative privilege; ethnic and class stratification; American commodity culture. Ironically enough, the novel is able to acknowledge, however obliquely, the structural similar-ity between the Ogata children and Filipinos vis-à-vis white economic privilege. Uncle Paulo's reference to "picking pineap-ples for minimum wage" is echoed by Poppy's comment in the same passage that the children have been "fuckin' doing slave work for that highfalutin haole" (207). Uncle Paulo's reaction to Mrs. Nishimoto—"Thass another one"—registers this common ground. But despite this structural recognition of economic exploitation, the novel cannot bring their separate arcs together. Indeed, it formally separates the two parts of Uncle Paulo's speech (his criticism of Japanese racism against Filipinos and his indictment of white racism against Filipinos) by inserting an interjection by Poppy. On the heels of Uncle Paulo's denuncia-tion of Ivah, the novel interpolates Poppy's question:

> "Where you was?" Poppy asks again, but not mad, just a
> little louder.
> "We was helping Mrs. Nishimoto."
> "Thass another one," Uncle Paulo mutters. (207)

As the second part of Uncle Paulo's speech concludes, the novel moves us directly from his indictment of white racism against Filipinos into the domestic space of the Ogata home, and the rest of the scene shifts focus entirely by concentrating on the children's bedtime rituals and Poppy's absence from them. No further attempt is made to articulate what are once again com-pletely separate narrative arcs. Diegetically speaking, the cri-tique of a racialized plantation labor hierarchy, and the violent colonial histories it names, is unavailable to both Uncle Paulo, as a character, and Ivah, as the narrator. But there *is* a name for what the novel cannot articulate, and that name is catachresis. For J. Hillis Miller, it is a trope that "makes present in a borrowed name what otherwise has no name and could not be named as an immediate and literal presence." It is the name for "something which has no literal name," and what has "no literal name," in the context of *Blu's Hanging*, is a profound critique that could rework the familiar circuitry of identity politics.[50] It is only when we understand "anti-Filipino racism" as a catachresis for that which has no existing term—the critique of a deep history of multiple colonialisms—that we can grasp the catachrestic nature of all identities, which are produced by political and rhetorical activity, and generate a reading of the novel that breaks through the original impasse of the award controversy by rearticulating the relationship of aesthetics to politics.

Having shown how the novel's turn to catachresis demonstrates the liabilities of an identity politics stance that understands "Filipino" as simply referential, I want to conclude by responding to Chiang's call to theorize representation. As he points out, one factor behind the intractability of the arguments over *Blu's Hanging* and its award controversy was the lack of any sustained theorizing of representation itself. An attendant problem was the assumption during the controversy and persisting in its critical afterlife that literary and political representation were to be carefully kept apart. What drops out in the clear-cut distinction between politics and aesthetics is the critical effort of guarding against such easy binaries. To remind us of this task, Spivak asks us to consider the productive tension that we find in Marx between these two senses of representation, *Vertretung* (replacement) and *Darstellung* (portrayal). The former involves representation in the political sense (your elected official "wearing your shoes," as she puts it); the latter involves representation as portrait, representation in the theatrical or literary sense. "The thing to remember," she reminds us, "is that in the act of representing politically, you actually represent yourself and your constituency in the portrait sense, as well. . . . So that you do not ever 'simply' *vertreten* anyone, in fact."[51] In other words, the tension between these two senses of representation requires us to approach politics, whether of the identity variety or of the elected kind, as quite inextricably entangled with a presenting-again that depends on aesthetic and rhetorical activity. It is this productive tension that has been forgotten in the controversy's narrative of identity politics coded as simple resistance or as simple antiracism. The tension between both senses of representation must be carefully scrutinized. The difficult lesson of *Blu's Hanging*, if such a lesson can be drawn here, is not to dispense with the error, the catachresis of identity—however painful, however asymmetrical—but to attend, meticulously and persistently, to the figurative conditions of their emergence. This task, which a critic sensitive to figurative activity can perform, may be where the supplement of literature finally meets politics.

4 / Allegory: *Native Speaker* and Deceit

Chang-rae Lee's *Native Speaker* tells the story of Henry Park, a second generation Korean American employed by a private intelligence agency for his ability to play the role of an Asian American. In the course of the novel he brings about the downfall of a Horatio Alger figure, an Asian American politician from Queens, one of New York City's most diverse boroughs. In a series of escalating events, amidst accusations of illegal donations and money laundering, the politician's mayoral campaign ends in a firestorm of xenophobia, terminating in a raid by the Immigration and Naturalization Service (INS) of his supporters, many of whom are undocumented immigrants. Soon after *Native Speaker* was published, its extraordinary prescience was revealed as these imagined scenarios came to pass. In 1996, a year after the novel came out, the discovery of illegal fundraising activities among members of the Democratic National Committee erupted into the scandal problematically dubbed "Asian Donorgate." John Huang, a high-level Clinton appointee and the most visible of these figures, was accused of accepting foreign donations from Asia. Spurred by the media and select political figures, allegations of campaign finance violations quickly transformed into fears of a national security breach at the hands of a Chinese spy ring. The accounting firm hired to investigate the Democratic donor list, not immune to the frenzy, proceeded to target donors with Asian names, interrogating them about their citizenship status. In 1999, four years after *Native Speaker* was published, the second half of "Asian Donorgate" unfolded, culminating in the arrest of Taiwanese American scientist Wen Ho Lee on suspicion of nuclear espionage conducted on behalf of the People's Republic of China.[1] In the fall of 2000, the hysteria of "Donorgate" finally began to subside: Lee was acquitted of all but one count of mishandling classified information, the campaign finance scandal was exposed as wrongdoing on the part of certain individuals, and threats of meddling by the Chinese government or acts of Asian American espionage were firmly debunked. However rough this sketch of events, it should be clear that *Native Speaker*'s central conceit draws on a deep well of American Orientalism and taps into a readily available discourse of Asian deceit, treachery, and inscrutability revolving around the Asian figure as a perpetual foreigner and inassimilable alien. But if *Native Speaker* objects as strongly as it does to this Orientalist discourse, why does it challenge this discourse by presenting us with an Asian American protagonist who is both a spy and a traitor?

Native Speaker represents the most cynical Asian American treatment of race we have encountered so far. In the world of the novel, race and ethnicity consist of little else than a meticulous and lifelong series of performances. The protagonist, alienated from mainstream whiteness and the culture of his immigrant parents, believes that his "truest place" in America is as an outsider and a traitor. Accordingly he and his fellow operatives specialize in "ethnic coverage," gathering information on their own kind at the behest of shadowy transnational corporations and foreign governments. In spite of its cynicism, though, *Native Speaker* is also an unabashedly assimilist text, as it features a protagonist yearning to be unmarked, to be a native speaker of the land. Through its ethnic operatives, the novel explores the desire to be free of ethnicity, to be liberated from what

Rey Chow has called "coercive mimeticism," a form of subjection such that the ethnic subject must perform ethnicity in order to be visible. At the thematic level *Native Speaker* gives every indication of rejecting this mimeticism: its assortment of spies are racial impersonators, its protagonist is symbolically married to *the* native speaker, a white American speech therapist, whom he desires for her lack of what he calls "mystery." At the thematic level, we might say, the novel depicts the longing for referential transparency. At the figurative level, however, it offers a rather different scenario: there, it interrupts the desire for referential transparency by staging race, whether Asian or white, as a type of rhetorical activity with inexplicably allegorical effects.

Native Speaker calls on allegory, the figure of double meaning and other-speaking, to figure its historical problematic, the discourse of Asian deceit. Previously we considered the response of literary representation to political conditions of defiance, coercion, necessity, and error. In this final chapter, we will consider literary representation under the condition of deceit. In earlier chapters evidence of figurative activity was relatively easy to discern. Those tropes, while unquiet, were nevertheless quite obvious about announcing their rhetorical behavior. Antanaclasis, for example, repeated a word in a different sense; the rhetorical question took on the grammatical form of a question; apophasis used negation to affirm. In *Native Speaker*, however, figurative activity involves dissimulation and deceit. As a mode of concealment or hiding in plain sight, this allegorical behavior is expanded by the novel to include a range of different activities: ethnic spying, which dissimulates by pretending to be without disguise; native speaking, which imagines itself as speech without accent; whiteness, which camouflages itself as a race without race; and Henryspeak, the novel's narrative style, which disguises itself as referential language. Like Okada's *No-No Boy*, *Native Speaker* is yet another text that insists on the inscrutability of the racial sign; it, too, is excruciatingly aware of the dangerous political liability of asserting such obscurity. Unlike *No-No Boy*, however, this novel is intrigued by the notion of Asian deceit, an idea that flickers in and out of view depending on the specific historical moment but remains at all times a part of the reservoir of American Orientalism. We might consider, for example, the illegal immigration of Chinese during the exclusion era, a phenomenon that Tina Chen has termed the "paper son industry," to get at the incredible scope, complexity, and permanency of this discourse.[2] As historian Madeline Y. Hsu sees it, the legacy of Asian deceit is a direct product of American exclusion: "These laws cemented the outsider status of Chinese Americans: although they failed to prevent Chinese from migrating to the United States, they ensured that most who did come after could only do so illegally."[3] If such laws forced would-be Chinese immigrants to become "imposters," adopting false identities to enter the United States, those same laws made it imperative for them to continue practicing these deceits in their new lives. For Chen this history means that Asian American identity must be understood as a "politics of impersonation."[4]

This sense of necessary duplicity also informs allegory, both as a genre of allegorical composition and as a type of interpretation, allegoresis. This chapter will not differentiate between the two, preferring instead to move between the two traditions to take advantage of a broader range of critical resources. In a world transformed by the unending war on terror, it seems all the more urgent to theorize the desire on the part of the United States, at the vanguard of these efforts, for a new white language. Jasbir Puar indicates the very material embodiment of this desire when she observes of Guantánamo Bay, "The name of the detention site, Camp X-Ray, suggests in itself a profound yearning for the transparency of these bodies, the capacity to see through them and render them known."[5] *Native Speaker* turns to the figure of allegory to insist that there can be no such thing as a white language, no discourse of the sign, racial or linguistic, that is free of mystery.[6]

Deceit

The notion of Oriental inscrutability or Asian deceit is of relatively recent vintage. The longer tradition of Orientalism from which it springs, however, spans millennia, reaching back to classical antiquity. Historian Gary Y. Okihiro discerns an early version of Orientalism in the fifth century BCE writings of Greek physician Hippocrates even as he cautions us against treating this discourse as homogeneous or timeless. However distant or transformed, it is this Orientalist legacy that informs the first European and American encounters with Asia. As Okihiro writes, "Asians entered into the European American historical consciousness long before the mid-nineteenth-century Chinese migration to 'Gold Mountain' and, I believe, even before Yankee traders and American diplomats and missionaries traveled to China in the late eighteenth century."[7] From the early twentieth century onward, fears of Asian modernity and immigration materialized in the form of fictional characters like Sax Rohmer's Fu Manchu, the half-caste evil genius who threatens Western civilization with his diabolical cunning. In the middle of the twentieth century hysteria over a supposed Japanese fifth column led to the mass incarceration of Japanese Americans. During the cold war the suspicion of Chinese as communist sympathizers led to the formation of the Chinese Confession Program, which offered naturalization to Chinese willing to inform on others. At the beginning of the twenty-first century Special Registration, an initiative of the Department of Homeland Security, targeted Arabs and South Asians as the latest Orientals under suspicion.[8] Officially speaking, from their first entry into the United States in the late eighteenth century to 1952, immigrants of Asian descent were designated "aliens ineligible for citizenship." Cultural critic Lisa Lowe points out the ideological task accomplished by this symbolic "alien" status: "The project of imagining the nation as homogeneous requires the orientalist construction of cultures and geographies from which Asian immigrants come as fundamentally 'foreign' origins antipathetic to the modern American society."[9] Over and above the homogeneity of the abstract citizen, the Asian immigrant has been instrumental to securing the imagined community of the United States as a white republic. As Chen observes, "Pervasive ideas of Asian Americans as somehow never being able to be 'American' enough . . . coalesce into the figure of the Asian American as spy or alien, a figure whose foreign allegiances make it not only possible but probable that his/her claims to American-ness are suspect or, in other words, impostured."[10] In the late twentieth century this long discourse of deceit and treachery organized itself around narratives of Asians as spies or traitors.

These historical mutations suggest that there may be something deceitful, as Colleen Lye has observed, about "Asiatic racial form." For Lye "the visuality of Asiatic racial form has a distinctive character insofar as the sense of its deceitfulness or mystery always points to the presence of something not shown. To put it another way, we recognize the Asiatic as a figure for the unrepresentable."[11] Giving us a deeply historicized account of Asiatic form, Lye examines a vast assortment of documents, texts, and archives to inquire whether such a form always takes anthropomorphic shape with the consequence, as Joseph Jeon explains, that racialization becomes international and global: "Rather than understanding it simply as a mechanism through which white supremacy reproduces itself, she argues that racialization develops because of its ability to suit the often contradictory political and economic necessities of a rapidly expanding nation with imperialist aspirations."[12] While recognizing the far vaster scope that Lye asks us to consider, what I am struck by, and what this chapter is concerned with, is how closely her description of Asiatic form resembles both the language of allegory and the language used by the novel for the Asian American spy's distinctive brand of espionage. While allegory does sometimes take anthropomorphic form, as in the medieval personification of the vices or virtues, it occurs in *Native Speaker* as a way to theorize deceit or mystery as particular kinds of rhetorical activity. Lye's work opens up various and multiple ways to think about the possibilities of Asiatic form. Taking just one of these compass points, we might ask whether there is a rhetorical version of Asiatic form and, if so, what it would "look" like. Given *Native Speaker*'s preoccupation with referential transparency in relation to race and espionage, the question of the visual seems particularly pertinent. What would it mean to approach the rhetorical figures in Asian American literature as a set of linguistic patterns that are visually apparent but semantically opaque? This chapter is an attempt to begin to answer some of these questions.

Allegory is commonly defined as saying one thing and meaning another, but such simplicity belies the vast and ancient tradition that comprises the allegorical tradition. From Greek antiquity to the medieval and early modern periods, allegory was understood as an "obvious double order of correlated references, one literal and the second allegorical."[13] Etymologically the term means "other-speaking" (*allos*, "other," and *agourein*, "speaking"). Modern readings of allegory, however, tend to emphasize its affinity for alienation, distance, and difference. Its poststructuralist version in particular stresses its innate capacity for destabilization and subversion. Paul de Man's well-known reading of allegory, for example, understands it as offering a deconstruction, at a secondary level of signification, of its own textual operations: "The resulting narratives can be folded back upon themselves and become self-referential."[14] Indeed, allegory is a figure that veers between the extremes of obscurity and referentiality. Jon Whitman explains, for instance, "The more allegory exploits the divergence between corresponding levels of meaning, the less tenable the correspondence becomes. Alternatively, the more it closes ranks and emphasizes the correspondence, the less oblique, and thus the less allegorical, the divergence becomes."[15] These formal tensions resemble a similar set of pressures with regard to the Asian American figure, which also vacillates between being too referential (too obviously racialized) and too opaque (inscrutable, alien). Theresa Kelley's characterization of allegory helps illuminate the legacy of alterity it shares with the Asian American figure. Kelley depicts allegory as the "abjected 'other' to be cast out in the name of modernity" and declares that "allegory *is* alien, its ancient rhetorical status as 'other speech' survives all other adjustments."[16] It turns out, in this figurative sense, that allegory constitutes a rather fitting, albeit ominous rhetorical figure for the Asian American subject.

The connections that *Native Speaker* makes between allegory, Asian Americans, and espionage are anticipated by several centuries in the work of the Renaissance rhetorician George Puttenham, who "Englishes" the original Latin term for allegory (*allegoria*) by renaming it the "Figure of False Semblant or Dissimulation." For Puttenham allegory is "the chief ringleader and captain of all other figures" because, as his editors note, he understands the rhetorical figures as deceptions, first and foremost. The canniest affinity that Puttenham presents for us between allegory and the Asian American spy lies in the former's nature as a "courtly figure," mastery of which is a necessary skill for the Renaissance courtier-poet. Insofar as the courtier is also an actor, engaged constantly in acts of social "counterfeiting," this Renaissance figure suggests an early prototype for the modern-day Asian American since both are roles that demand an aptitude for impersonation.[17] When Angus Fletcher introduces allegory as "a fundamental process of encoding our speech," he elucidates its intrinsic affinity for the activity of espionage.[18] The world of espionage, as John Cawelti and Bruce Rosenberg describe it, is a distinctly allegorical one: "Nothing is what it seems and everything is potentially dangerous. Only the agent knows something of the truth."[19] *Native Speaker* draws together these dormant affiliations by making them appear as Lelia's infamous list, the catalogue Henry's wife has secretly compiled of his attributes. Representing her attempts to understand her enigmatic spouse, Lelia's list makes use of recognizably allegorical traits—surreptitious, alien, and even antiromantic—as descriptors for Asian American stereotypes, thus articulating the resonance between them as figures at once alien and inscrutable.[20]

Native Speaker is set in a 1990s New York City and commences with Lelia's departure for a trial separation. In her absence the protagonist starts to reevaluate his profession, his upbringing by his Korean immigrant parents, and his lifelong effort to assimilate. The novel is narrated by Henry in the first person, and its action develops in two related plots: his tenuous efforts to reconcile with Lelia after the death of their mixed-race son and his growing inability to perform the role-playing necessary to his profession. A series of flashbacks to previous missions and to early scenes from his marriage and childhood culminate in a disastrous final assignment, during which Henry infiltrates the mayoral campaign of John Kwang, the self-made politician from Queens. Kwang's campaign implodes under charges of corruption, and by the end of the novel an INS raid aided by Henry's intelligence has ended Kwang's career. Afterward a disillusioned Henry quits the agency to assist Lelia in the ESL classroom. Criticism about *Native Speaker* is extensive and rich, but this scholarship either tends to promote deracinated approaches to the novel's form or to deploy referential reading practices in the pursuit of sociopolitical analysis.[21] Both critical trends, however, are complicated by the novel's opening pages, which immediately problematize the referential treatment of any text, whether identified as "literary" or "Asian American." In the past decade a new formalism has revitalized literary study, but it has yet to consider in a sustained way the relationship of figurative activity to race. What we want and need is a reading practice that can make the connections between the novel's concerns with race and its concerns with a particular form of figurative activity. On the other hand, our thinking on race, as sociologist Howard Winant has observed, has not advanced much beyond the well-trod concept of social construction: "If race is both objective and illusory, if it is *both* a way of ordering and explaining the social world *and* of making it opaque and mysterious, that is more than a peculiar phenomenon in social science. That is a compelling theoretical problem."[22] While Winant makes no reference to the literary as a way into the conundrum he has laid out for us, I do so here to suggest that as a literary text, *Native Speaker* supplements the social sciences by staging how something like race can be, as Winant puts it, simultaneously objective and illusory, both a way of explaining the world and rendering it more mysterious. In turning its historical problematic into figurative language, the novel gives us a literary point of entry into the theoretical problem of race and representation.

Henryspeak

In *Native Speaker* allegory appears primarily as a kind of figurative activity that disguises itself as referential language, as a type of language lacking opacity and artifice. The clearest example of this kind of behavior is Henryspeak, the novel's term for referential language used so precisely that it is forced into double meaning. As a way of dissembling, Henryspeak calls directly on the allegorical capacity for deceit, an aspect Puttenham captures well with his renaming of allegory as "False Semblant or Dissimulation," where "semblant," as Puttenham's editors gloss it, means semblance or appearance.[23] Henryspeak brings together a set of related ideas about referential transparency, espionage, and Asian inscrutability to explore the cunning of signs whose operations consist of hiding in plain sight. In one strained conversation Lelia inquires after Henry's current assignment, and he responds by describing it as "*sensitive* and *evolving* but going well."[24] When the novel has Lelia call this Henryspeak, it acknowledges that he is being intentionally misleading, that he is double-speaking, in the Orwellian sense, but also speaking "falsely," as a nonnative speaker. The final addendum to Lelia's list identifies Henry as a "false speaker of language" (6), a phrase that clarifies the potential for double meaning by presenting two different semantic meanings in the same grammatical structure: Henry is both a deceitful (false) speaker and an imposter, a nonnative speaker of English who has learned to speak like a native. But there is more at stake here than a difference of semantics. What the novel recognizes is the narrator's ability to exploit the expectations brought to bear on referential language—that words say what they mean and mean what they say—to say something else entirely. In this sense Henryspeak taps into the ancient allegorical sense of enigma, wherein hidden meaning paradoxically lies in plain sight, nowhere evident except in the words themselves.[25] The introduction of Henryspeak leads immediately into the narrator's confession, which concludes the first chapter by presenting a linguistic mode of hiding in plain sight in which the hidden is disguised by appearing as the all-too-evident.

The confession scene remembers an Asian American history troubled by compulsory acts of confession and self-declaration. From the interrogations of Chinese "paper sons" during the exclusion era to the Japanese American loyalty questionnaire of World War II, from the Chinese Confession Program of the cold war to the Special Registration of Muslims in the post-9/11 period, the Asian American subject has been "guilty" of being inscrutable and potentially treacherous.[26] We know from Foucault that the confession is a vexed form insofar as it produces an array of devices—the self, experience, referential language— that it relies on but cannot verify. Chow extends Foucault to argue that Asian American literature, or ethnic literature more generally, is predicated on self-referential gestures that are "tantamount to performing a confession in the criminal as well as noncriminal sense. . . . It is to admit and submit to the allegations (of otherness) that society at large has made against one."[27] The novel manipulates this confessional mandate by having its Asian American narrator "confess" in Henryspeak. The "secret" that he reveals through confession, however, is what is already apparent: "I lied to Lelia. For as long as I could I lied. I will speak the evidence now. My father, a Confucian of high order, would commend me for finally honoring that which is wholly evident" (6). Playing on two senses of *evidence* (what is readily apparent and proof), his evidence makes clear only what is already known; it involves no new revelation.[28] Seeming to volunteer a confession, he presents only what is "wholly evident," what is already obvious. Acknowledging this linguistic elusiveness with an ironic aside ("honoring that which is wholly evident"), he suggests that no hidden truth, no deeper meaning will be made known since "the truth, finally, is who can tell it" (7). Deploying the strictest sense of the referential (taking it literally, so to speak) and speaking only the evidence (what is already evident), the narrator manages to speak altogether otherwise. Here the novel plays with the "purest" form of the referential, which, taken too literally, becomes instead a form of other-speaking, that is, allegorical. Kelley's caution regarding allegory is felicitous here: it is a figure, she argues, that "needs to be read, not simply looked at."[29]

In the second part of his confession, the narrator appears to address the reader directly: "And yet you may know me. I am an amiable man. I can be most personable, if not charming and whatever I possess in this life is more or less the result of a talent I have for making you feel good about yourself when you are with me" (7). This disclosure too is carefully worded, connecting the literalness of language—the words on the page—to the curious effect of being unseen: "In this sense I am not a seducer. I am hardly seen. I won't speak untruths to you, I won't pass easy compliments or odious offerings of flattery. I make do with on-hand materials, what I can chip out of you, your natural ore" (7). Again employing its referential sleight of hand, the narrator does not lie ("I won't speak untruths"), but he manages nevertheless not to speak "truly" (honestly). Never speaking falsely ("I am not a seducer"), adding nothing that is extraneous ("easy compliments") or false ("odious flattery"), he speaks only what is already evident. Hiding in plain sight, this spy is "hardly seen"; hard to see because he offers only what is evident, he resists being seen (through). Declaring that he is not a seducer, that he "won't speak untruths," the narrator disclaims rhetorical excess—persuasion in the form of seduction or flattery. Instead he claims to present only what is already there, "on-hand materials" and "natural ore." By announcing his lack of rhetorical ornamentation he claims to speak evidence, yet by speaking only the "evident," he contrives to speak otherwise. Maureen Quilligan helps clarify what is happening here when she argues that in the context of allegory, the literal meaning of a text is in fact "metaphorical" as the term *literal* literally means "letteral" (from *literra*, letter). Quilligan explains, "The 'other' named by the term *allos* . . . is not some other hovering above the words of the text, but the possibility of an otherness, a polysemy, inherent in the very words on the page." She insists that "the key to the story's meaning lies in the text's language—its most *literal* aspect."[30] By returning us to the "most literal aspect" of the text as the place of the other, Quilligan offers us a different reading of the literal *as* the figurative, a scenario employed to great effect by the novel. In yet another echo of Kelley's insight that allegory must be read and not just looked at, Henryspeak suggests that the "most literal aspect" of the words on the page— their arrangement, their ordering, in short, their form—can be *too* plain to see. If a lesson can be extracted from Henryspeak, it is a reminder to read Asian American literature as figurative (and potentially allegorical), even when it appears to be entirely referential.

With Henryspeak as our guide, let us turn to Lelia's list, which represents the most explicitly referential text in the novel. The list represents Lelia's numerous and failed attempts to "read" Henry. It serves as a kind of reference work about the inscrutable Asian, standing in for the Other as such. Although the narrator disclaims its encyclopedic status, saying, "Eventually I would understand that she didn't mean the list as exhaustive, some-thing complete, in any way the sum of my character or nature" (1), he nevertheless acknowledges its authority to represent him by informing us, in the very first line of the novel, "The day my wife left she gave me a list of who I was" (1). We can think of the list as a referential text at its most rudimentary. Both its form and its use of purely denotative language trade on the fact that lists involve language at its most referential and least figurative. Indeed, we might think of them as nothing but reference. The novel's staging of Lelia's list reinforces this referential effect. It is reproduced *as* a list, centered in the middle of the page and set off from the rest of the text. This staging increases what is at stake here as what Lelia's list presents is a set of stereotypical Asian American attributes:

You are surreptitious
   B+ student of life
   First thing hummer of Wagner and Strauss
   illegal alien
   emotional alien
   genre bug
   Yellow peril: neo-American
   great in bed
   overrated
   poppa's boy
   sentimentalist
   anti-romantic
   _____analyst (you fill in)
   stranger
   follower
   traitor
   spy (5)

The most negatively charged traits recall the Orientalist discourse of Asian treachery, foreignness, and deceit that the novel has set out to contest, and yet what is remarkable is that *Native Speaker* turns the list, referential language at its starkest and most spare, into an exercise in imaginative reading.

When Lelia gives Henry the list, she warns him, "This doesn't mean what you'll think" (4). Her parting advice should be understood as both an intelligence truism and an exhortation to think allegorically about seemingly referential entities like race and Asian American literature. In lists language appears at its most self-effacing, its most self-evident, and yet the narrator is staged as approaching the list as if it had "literary" qualities. Initially he mistakes it for a "love poem" or "dulcet verse." Later, once he realizes what it is, he nevertheless "appreciated its count, the clean cadence" (5). A list is without story, without plot or rhetorical behavior, yet the protagonist is portrayed as imagining himself in the place of its author—"I imagined her scribbling something down in the middle of a recipe" (5)—and he eventually concludes, "I came to know the list intimately as my own, as if I alone had authored it" (14). *Native Speaker* asks us to treat referential texts, even ones as minimally textual as the list, as invitations to the imagination. But there is more: Henry destroys the original after making three copies: one is kept in his wallet, another is mailed to "historicize" it (4), and the last one ends up tacked to the wall of an East Village bar. The final iteration of the list is turned, quite literally, into something else: "The Yerrow Pelir," an alcoholic drink described as an "emetic concoction of Galliano and white wine" (14). The novel's staging of the list asks us to treat the referential text as something that might very well take on a different form—a poem, a verse, or a drink. More important, by showing us how the staging of the list invites the reader into acts of the imagination, a task tradition-ally appointed to literature, the novel suggests that referential texts are, if not strictly allegorical in the typical sense, at least minimally rhetorical.

In a later scene the novel takes this further by showing us that Asian American texts are collections of textile metaphors with a motion of their own, a kind of "turning" that, by repelling our ability to see through it, defies the illusion of referential trans-parency. In doing so *Native Speaker* follows an old terminology identifying figurative or literary language with the "turn" or deviation from proper meaning. "Turn," Judith Butler reminds us, "was an English term for 'trope' in the seventeenth and eigh-teenth centuries," and the term *trope* itself owes its etymology to the Greek word for "turn."[31] In drawing attention to this figura-tive activity, I seek to demonstrate the serious limitations of ref-erential reading with regard to Asian American literature. Given the heightened burden placed on such texts to represent ethnic experience, it behooves us to refrain from treating the language in these texts as simplistic or transparent. In the content-driven approaches typical of referential reading, what is bypassed is precisely the texture of literature, the way figurative activity works to refract and sometimes obfuscate the meaning of the text. Literature, as Gayatri Chakravorty Spivak has often said, cannot be a "blueprint" for society; it is the unverifiable space of the figure and one of the last great instruments for training the ethical imagination.[36] In paying such close attention to this figurative activity, it is my hope that this exercise can help us better theorize race and racialization as processes subject to similar vexation, errancy, and reimagining.

"Looping": Troping Asian America

I want to make a small detour to explore how the novel's use of tropological language presents a different approach to Asian American literature, not as narratives of identity but as narratives about figurative activity or textual activity more broadly. For obvious reasons the novel's psychoanalytic episodes have been treated as commentaries on Asian American identity. In these sessions Henry has been assigned to Dr. Emile Luzan, a Filipino psychoanalyst and Marcos supporter, whose practice he infiltrates by pretending to be a businessman with depression. The mission is initially successful. As the sessions continue, however, his cover is blown and the assignment is terminated. Later we learn that Luzan dies in a suspicious boating accident. In the scene I now turn to Henry is staged as suddenly losing control of his performance; what results is a mixture of half-truths and fictions that convinces Luzan his patient is "unraveling" (181). Here instead of an identity-based narrative, what Chen calls "a loss of self,"[33] the novel suggests that what drives the scene is textuality, which offers a more tangled and inconsistent model for representing race. While *Native Speaker* does not propose that Asian American subjectivity is allegorical, it does suggest that racialization may have a tropological trajectory; that is, far from being linear, equivalent, or corresponding, it may "loop" and "turn," obeying a rhetorical rather than referential relationship of signification.

In Henry's initial assessment of the Luzan mission, he describes himself as exerting total control of the performance, both of his "legend," the alibi he has prepared beforehand, and its execution: "I was elaborating upon my 'legend' consistently and Luzan accepted my pathologies" (22). Later he says, "I was developing into a model case. Of course I was *switching* between him and me, getting piecemeals of the doctor with projections in an almost classical mode" (22, my emphasis). "Switching," as he calls it, registers his finely tuned control over his actions, and it rests on the very notion that psychoanalysis has persistently tried to disturb: the self as a rational ego defined by consciousness. "Switching" also recalls, as Cawelti and Rosenberg describe of espionage, a "fantasy of invisibility" involving "voyeurism, self-concealment, and license."[34] Where things start to get interesting is the novel's disruption of this model, presenting it as falling apart, breaking down, and ensuring that it is no longer clear who or what is in control. Continuing from above, the narrator recalls, "For the first time I found myself at moments running short of my story, my chosen narrative. Normally I would have ceased matters. . . . But *inexplicably* I began stringing the legend back upon myself. I was no longer extrapolating" (22, my emphasis). For a first-person narrator the loss of narrative control—"inexplicably"—is surprising. His lack of narrative control over his story, his script, produces confusion and entanglement: "I was looping it through the core, freely talking about my life, suddenly breaching the confidences of my father and my wife. I even spoke to him about a lost dead son" (22). When the role-playing breaks down and the "real" intrudes, it does so messily, in such inconsistent and unpredictable ways that neither alibi nor self can be distinguished. Later when the narrator thinks back to this incident he tells us: "Inconsistencies began to arise in crucial details, all of which I inexplicably confused and alternated. . . . I told the kind brown-faced doctor that my son had suffocated while playing alone with a plastic garbage bag, or that my American *girlfriend* was conducting extended research in Europe, or that my father had recently taken *a second wife*" (181). "In another session," he concludes, "I might tell him another set of near-truths, forget my conflations and hidings" (181). Chen's "politics of impersonation" offers an insightful way into this scene. She argues for impersonation as a "critical trope" that elucidates both the constructed nature of Asian American identity and the agency of Asian American subjects. Impersonation entails a double action, enabling Asian Americans, in her words, "to establish their own claims to a U.S. American identity and to critique the American institutions that have designated them as 'aliens.'"[35] The novel's staging of Asian American identity in the psychoanalytic episodes elaborates on the tension that Chen's model seeks to explore, but *Native Speaker* troubles further the already fraught distinction between impersonation and imposture by implying that the spy is not an agent in control of his "performance."

While Chen's theory is immensely useful for clarifying the identity slippages between impersonation and imposture, it must rely on a stronger sense of agency, intrinsic to the idea of performance, than what is found in the novel. *Native Speaker*'s account of this episode proceeds somewhat differently; it suggests that what is being depicted in these psychoanalytic sessions is also a *text*. The narrative, as recounted by Henry, bears all the earmarks of a written text: it is composed of textual metaphors, it is scripted, and it has a generic form—the narrator thinks of it as an "autobiography," an "extensive 'story' of who we were" (22). In fact he explicitly says that he loses control of his *text*, what the novel calls his "chosen narrative" (22): "*inexplicably*," he says, "I began stringing the legend back upon myself" (22, my emphasis). No subject endowed with agency, in control of his performance, can be discerned here. The narrator's admission that what transpires in this scene occurs "inexplicably" is the first clue that something else might be driving the scene. Indeed, his narrative of the session consists of a series of textile metaphors: "looping through the core," "stringing back upon myself." These weaving metaphors (from Latin *texere*, "to weave") generate a confused narrative defined by "near-truths" and "hidings" (181). In other words, as metaphors, as tropological language, these movements defy Luzan—and the narrator himself—from deriving any clear sense of meaning or clarity of reference. More important, these textual metaphors move like tropological language; what are "looping" and "stringing back" but "turns" that recall the etymology of trope itself? In the novel's own language this rhetorical activity is unpredictable as it occurs "inexplicably," and also unverifiable as it is composed of "looping" and "stringing." "Looping" and "stringing" are the means by which the novel *figures* the unpredictable effect of racialization. The activity of looping is ultimately opaque; turning back on itself, it refuses the illusion of referential transparency. However, it does not give up referentiality altogether, as it figures the historical problematic of Asian deceit. To reframe these psychoanalytic sessions as narratives about textuality rather than identity offers us a point of entry into the formal specificity of Asian American literature. If we understand what transpires in these psychoanalytic sessions as textual effects, as generated by a certain kind of figurative activity, we can better grasp the novel's behavior as a literary text. This figurative activity does not lie within the control of the performer, author, or agent. If there is an agent here, it is the highly figured behavior I have been identifying as tropological language. Given the incontrovertible proof of this rhetorical behavior—the words on the page, as Quilligan would say—I find these ancient linguistic patterns more enduring and persuasive as a source for the language of Asian American literature.

"Looping" and "stringing back" suggest a turning motion that Butler associates with the inauguration of the subject. For Butler, who seeks to understand the rhetorical nature of subjection (how social relations produce the subject as their effect), subjectivity is inaugurated by a "figure of turning" resembling the motion of figurative language.[36] The subject of/to power is produced by a turning against or turning on herself, expressed in the form of guilt or conscience. Since the conversion into a subject consists of this very turning, and not some preexisting referent imitated by the trope, the "paradox of subjection," as

Butler puts it, also implies a "paradox of referentiality" as "we must refer to what does not yet exist."[37] Neither trope nor subject can be evaluated on strictly positivist or referential grounds, as they are themselves both figures and figures for figuration itself. When we consider that Butler's tropological structure is followed by a second rhetorical maneuver, a metaleptic reversal enabling the subject produced as the effect of power to imagine herself as the author of power, it becomes increasingly clear that these rhetorical effects work to problematize the notion of the author as an agent. By presenting as "Asian American" a subject whose guilt consists of being presumed alien, the novel reminds us that this figure is the subject of/to unequal relations of power constituting it as the figure of a "turning" it must persistently confess. Simultaneously the novel also argues against the abstract scenario of subjectivity that Butler helps us imagine by insisting on a specific history of subjection, one that is defined by a relentless referentiality and historicized as "Asian American."[38] If Butler shows us how subjectivity in general is produced by the motion of turning against, then the history of Asian American subjectivity articulates the political consequences of being identified as the figure of turning. As we have seen, the history of Asian American confession demonstrates just how vulnerable this particular subject is to being cast as spy, traitor, and foreigner, all of which are figures suspected of betrayal—a different kind of turning (on or against one's "own").

To argue, as I have, that Asian American referents are obscure and erratic at best or that a literary text enacts its own version of Butler's "paradox of referentiality" does not mean, however, that referentiality does not matter for *Native Speaker*. It is far from insignificant, as the novel's turn to allegory represents its attempt, as literature, to rework the referential relationship imposed on Asian bodies. In the long historical context "Asian American" may take on various meanings at different historical moments, but what remains constant is its "difference" from the norm, a difference that is understood in racial terms. Even as David Palumbo-Liu stresses the dynamic and mutually constitutive relationship of Asia to America, he reminds us that their "historical crossings" are "constantly compromised by the essential, racial separation of Asians from 'Americans,' a distinction buttressed by a belief system deeply ingrained in the American imaginary which insists on the essential difference of racialized peoples." Even Asian American achievements, he observes, "do not necessarily erase racial distinctions that leave Asian Americans susceptible to being redefined as 'foreign' at specific historical moments."[39] To return to "Asian Donorgate," the strength of this notion of Asian difference can be measured by the ease with which a simple matter of fundraising violations turned into a scandal of national security. As the *Asian American Policy Review* concluded in its assessment of the media coverage surrounding Huang, "The 'Asian connection' title itself reveals the racialization of the scandal."[40]

If referentiality works on the sociopolitical register to code certain bodies as Asian, the referential pressures given to Asian American literature encounter a different problem. There has always been a close relationship between Asian American identity and the literature called Asian American, but, as Lye observes, "in the context of what social scientists note to be continuingly weak racial formation, Asian American literature is arguably a primary force in the institutionalizing of Asian American social reality."[41] Presently a second wave of Asian American literary criticism, animated by the formal turn of the past decade, has bent its energies toward disarticulating the literature from the racial formation, but if Lye is correct, there will continue to be overlap and interference between the two. My effort here, and throughout the book, has been to bracket the usual connections made between the novel and its Asian American frame of reference and focus on its figurative activity. To my way of thinking, this figurative activity—"looping" and "stringing through" in the scene above—is a literary attempt to *think* the problem of racial referentiality. "Looping" and its correlates do not lead us directly to an Asian American referent, but this does not mean that Asian America does not make an appearance. It does so, obliquely, as the figuration of a historical problematic (the discourse of Asian deceit, betrayal, and espionage) unique to Asian America. *Native Speaker* calls on a set of tropes that move in similar ways—"looping," "stringing back"—to figure *the figuration* of Asian America as the subject of betrayal, the inscrutable Oriental. By their tropological motion alone these textile metaphors refuse us any simple referential glimpse of Asian American interiority. At the same time this figurative activity "remembers," in an unverifiable way, its originary historical problematic.

These tropes identified by the novel with Asian America, "looping" and so forth, perform a double duty: they serve as the figure for Asian America (they refer to it symbolically), and they index its figuration (its translation into figurative language) by a mainstream discourse that has projected its difference from the other onto that other as "Oriental inscrutability." The dominant position of this normative subject has enabled it to imagine its own position as transparent, a point that I shall return to later. "Looping" and its correlates perform one final task. They are not allegories in the traditional sense, but insofar as they serve as a secondary level of signification wherein the text comments on its own figurative operations, they are allegorical in the deconstructive sense. These textile metaphors are commentaries on the narrative being presented to us during the psychoanalytic sessions: they compare its effect to "turning." As allegories in the de Manian sense, then, these textile metaphors direct the reader to consider the tension between the narrated action and its figurative activity. In utilizing these particular tropes to call its referential authority into question, *Native Speaker* echoes nicely de Man's own textile trope for allegory as a self-referential text "folded back upon" itself.

On Paper

In my reading of Henryspeak I have been saying that *Native Speaker* utilizes a form of allegory as "false-seeming" in that it features figurative language disguised as referential language.

Insofar as the allegorist uses language to disguise a hidden meaning, Quilligan concedes, with Fletcher, that allegory sometimes does "disintegrate into a kind of double-talk, a process of verbal legerdemain designed to hide, rather than to reveal, meaning."[42] In my second example of allegory at work this kind of deceptive language is explicitly connected to Asiatic racial traits. As scholars like Okihiro, Robert Lee, and Lye have observed, the "model minority" and the "yellow peril" are not antimonies, as they seem to be; instead "yellow peril and model minority are best understood as two aspects of the same, long-running racial form, a form whose most salient feature, whether it has been made the basis for exclusion or assimilation, is the trope of economic efficiency."[43] This trope appears in diluted form in *Native Speaker* as a kind of efficiency or industry indissociable from deception. In the scene I wish to discuss, the narrator is reflecting on his failed marriage: "It's my brand of sloth, surely, that I could fail my wife so miserably but seem to provide all the necessary objects and affections" (160–61). His version of sloth, as we shall see, involves a tremendous amount of industry and, in this sense, recalls the language of Asiatic form. In tracking the shifts in the model minority from its cold war origin to its revamping during the "global restructuring of capital" in the 1980s, Lee argues that "the model minority has two faces. The myth presents Asian Americans as silent and disciplined; this is their secret to success. At the same time, this silence and discipline is used in constructing the Asian American as a new yellow peril."[44] The novel neatly captures this double resonance. The passage begins by hinting at the language of the model minority—the references to productivity, discipline, and persistence—then quickly veers into yellow peril territory: "On paper, by any known standard, I was an impeccable mate. I did everything well enough. I cooked well enough, cleaned enough, was romantic and sensitive and silly enough . . . was paternal, big brotherly, just a good friend enough . . . and then even bull-headed and dull and macho enough, to make it all seamless. For ten years she hadn't realized the breadth of what I had accomplished with my exacting competence, the daily *work* I did, which unto itself became an unassailable body of cover" (161). As Lye explains, the late nineteenth-century emanation of the yellow peril emerges within a discourse of American decline, "America's transformation into a 'business civilization' at the expense of its 'warrior' qualities," against which the military might of Japan, and the tremendous industry of the Chinese worker, combine to threaten the West: "The yellow peril fantasy is thus to be located within this constellation of discourses linking decline and industrialization, and a heroic age with the spirit of the frontier, which seized on Asia as both heir and rival to a decaying West."[45] We find a similar sense of Asia as combined threat and rival in *Native Speaker*'s version of the ethnic spy. The spy master Hoagland, for example, expounds on the "natural" aptitude for espionage found in Asian culture with its emphasis on discipline and self-effacement: "If I were running a big house like the CIA," he tells Henry, "I'd breed agents by raising white kids in your standard Asian household. Discipline farms" (173).

What's interesting and odd about Henry's industry, however, is that it produces *not* a mate who is extraordinary—brilliance or "virtuosity," as he says later—but rather a mate who is merely average: "I did everything well enough." And yet, even though the life he has created is undistinguished, nothing out of the ordinary, it nevertheless requires a tremendous amount of industry: "exacting competence" and "daily work," the narrator insists. It is the very ordinariness of these deceptions that grants them their "unassailable" quality. In other words, their deceptiveness, their ability to generate an "unassailable body of cover," lies precisely in the fact that they are so unexceptional. We have an echo here of Henryspeak but also of referential language as what philosopher J. L. Austin called "ordinary language," the language of the everyday. So successful is this strategy of deceit that it fools not just Lelia, as the narrator mentions in the passage above, but the practitioner himself: "And the surest testament to the magnificent and horrifying level of my virtuosity was that neither had I" (161). If Henryspeak presents a situation wherein the figurative disguised itself as referential language taken too literally, then here we have another variation wherein the capacity for deception lies in being ordinary. In this newest variation even the everyday—the "daily work"—is a place for double meaning ("body of cover"). "On paper" Henry was an "impeccable" spouse; in reality he was a failure, despite having done "everything well enough." By explicitly presenting the disconnect between figurative and literal meaning, *Native Speaker* asks us to reconsider what the "literal" meaning of allegory might be under Asiatic racial form. "On paper" is an idiom that has been in use since the late sixteenth century. In the context of the passage, it means "in theory" or "in principle," which is to be differentiated from what occurs "in reality" or "in practice."[46] That is, Henry is an "impeccable" spouse in theory; in practice he has deceived both himself and Lelia. In the context of espionage, the phrase takes on an additional meaning because even the "reality" comprises nothing but deceit; it turns out to have been an alibi or cover story. "On paper" is at once letteral (lexically speaking, that is, it refers to paper) and also figurative (it means that something is not what it seems despite what is in print). In the passage quoted above, "on paper" denotes a discontinuity (between appearance and reality), but in doing so it *functions* figuratively, as a figure of speech; there is no "paper," for example, involved. Crudely put, "on paper" has a double and contradictory meaning.

One of its meanings, its earlier meaning, is quite literal. The *OED*, for example, informs us that "on paper" means first "in writing, in print."[47] This first meaning possesses a literal or "letteral" character in that the word *paper* suggests a certain materiality, the fact of existing on the page. The second meaning that the *OED* gives to the phrase hints at a figurative sensibility: "in theory or in principle, rather than in practice or reality." This second meaning insists on a discontinuity, a gap between practice and theory. That the potential for these multiple meanings arises from the same phrase and that this phrase turns on the issue of the literal or letteral takes us, in a roundabout way, back to Quilligan. If we recall, she understands allegory as "a special potency in language—that it can create extra significations" and insists that "the 'allegory' is in the words written on the page, not in the words the reader says to translate the narrative action into allegorical meaning." What *Native Speaker* insists on, however, is not just extra meanings but contradictory ones that deconstruct the very letters that constitute them, what the *OED* defines as the "real" meaning of the phrase itself. For Quilligan the textual nature of allegory is essential: "allegories are always written," in that they consist of "texts, that is, words printed or hand-printed on a page."[48] This letteralness, the materiality of the words on the page, is what lends authority to her insistence that allegory's polysemy is literal, that is, intrinsic to the words themselves. *Native Speaker*, however, takes away our security in even the literal because it turns out to have been a figure of speech all along. The novel uses the phrase "on paper" as the vehicle of the literal—it is "in print, in writing"—to convey a meaning that is figurative through and through. The access to this double meaning, however, is possible only via text—the actual words we are reading on the pages of a novel called *Native Speaker*.

No White Language

Native Speaker's most ambitious and troubling move involves turning the linguistic norm, the native speaker into a figure of nonnative speaking or allegory. For the majority of the novel both Lelia and Henry have undergone a kind of education such that by the end, Henry has given up his work at the agency and learned that he must say what he means; Lelia, on the other hand, is transformed from someone seeking to represent the Asian other to someone who learns, from below, to speak in the place of the other. The novel's final scene takes place in a New York City public classroom, a utopian site for a robustly pluralist and thoroughly immigrant version of a multicultural America. Yet the move that the novel makes is unexpected; its goal is not, as we might expect of an Asian American novel, to replace the normative native speaker with an Asian American figure—a move, as Daniel Kim argues, that the novel makes elsewhere—but to convert the native speaker into an other among others. The novel bends its transformative energies, in other words, toward its white character.[49] For this metamorphosis to occur, however, certain differences, queer and Asiatic, must be reinstated for the transformation to take effect. The scene calls on both a stereotypical Asiatic racial form and a previous iteration of the term *queer* to aid in Lelia's conversion. In this final scene of education no corrective speech exercises occur, nonnative speaking is valorized, and all the foreign-language-speaking students are welcomed as citizens. This scenario marks the progress from a previous scene of American education, remembered by the narrator as an episode of cultural imperialism, in which an "ancient chalk-white woman" by the name of Mrs. Albrecht disciplines his "unruly" tongue by beating him with a ruler as he recites a verse from Shelley (233). In the new scenario the novel presents, Lelia's version of American education is a vast improvement. Instead of a disciplinary scenario, she provides, as the narrator describes it, "a form of day care, ESL-style" (348). Her pedagogy is entertaining, "a kind of multimedia show" that "uses bucktoothed puppets with big mouths, scary masks, [and] makes the talk unserious and fun" (348). As the scene continues it is clear that the novel wants to differentiate this scene from the previous one: here it is Lelia who undergoes the American education and it is Lelia who learns the lessons of reading, speaking, and writing the "difficult names" of these "foreign language speakers" (349). With Henry narrating, the haunting last lines of the novel leave us with a vision of another white woman, but this time she is "speaking a dozen lovely and native languages, calling all the difficult names of who we are" (349).

What we have by the end of the novel is a transformed native speaker; no longer the self-proclaimed "standard-bearer" (12) of the novel's beginning, she has become a figure of nonnative speaking. To call on an allegorical language here, Lelia has been converted into the figure of other-speaking. This is, following

Quilligan's cue, a most "literal" reading of allegory insofar as Lelia is not an allegorical figure—that is, she does not stand in for anything else—but is literally engaged in what the figure of allegory is said to do: other-speech or other-speaking. By staging her this way the novel slyly suggests that whiteness, despite its pretense of being self-evident or transparent, is also allegorical. To understand how important this transformation is we have to return to an earlier part of the novel, which extolled Lelia as the referential ideal, the figure of whiteness and referential transparency. The narrator, for example, understands his attraction to Lelia in terms of her referentiality and portrays her in idealized referential terms as "the worst actor on earth" (158). He ruminates, "Perhaps most I loved this about her, her helpless way, love it still, how she can't hide a single thing, that she looks hurt when she is hurt, seems happy when happy. That I know at every moment the precise place where she stands. What else can move a man like me, who would find nothing as siren or comforting?" (159). The rhetorical question at the end reminds us that her apparent transparency emerges in relation to his supposed obscurity and that we must not be taken in by such figurative persuasions. As a speech therapist, Lelia is the literal embodiment of the native speaker, which is, as Julian Edge argues, "a type of linguistic unicorn, well known in the myths and legends but impossible to relate systematically to a group of living beings. This native speaker is one of a set of idealised abstractions."[50] In the proliferating global spread of English-language teaching, the native speaker also serves an ideological function: "the supremacy of the native speaker keeps the UK and the U.S. at the centre of ELT [English language teaching]."[51] In the context of American multiculturalism, Liam Corley reads the scene as a deconstruction of the white native speaker. For him *Native Speaker* "points out instead in a dual movement that *native speakers*, like Lelia, cannot equate their whiteness with ownership of the language unless they repress the material histories of *other native speakers*, like John Kwang."[52] Min Song is troubled by a different aspect of this scene: "By the end of the novel, it is

Henry the narrator who is speechless." He suggests that Henry's silence and his persistent racialization associate him with the Korean comfort woman, figured in the novel as Ahjuhma and Kwang's sixteen-year-old hostess: "Henry returns to the private 'sphere' only to become, in fact, one of the very 'shadowy figures of Korean American women' who are placed at the margins of the novel."[53] If Lelia's conversion into the nonnative speaker pivots on the feminizing of the Asian male or the necessary erasure of other American natives, her new role also seems to require a Speech Monster. The latter is a "job" we are told that Henry happily occupies: "I like my job. I wear a rubber green hood and act in my role as the Speech Monster. I play it well" (348). By turning the sympathetic white female into a figure of native speaking, Native Speaker certainly rewrites the dominant racial, linguistic, and cultural norms, but her conversion (from vertere, "to turn") into the figure of other-speaking is achieved precisely through the erasure of these others: she is now the mouthpiece for the "dozen and lovely native languages."

Although Native Speaker demonstrates the political urgency for Lelia's conversion, it also worries over the irreducible differences that are obscured in the process of figuration. Insofar as she figures other-speaking, she also obscures it—a necessary effect, as David Lloyd would argue, of the process of representation itself, which he connects not only to whiteness but to the entwined developments of a Kantian aesthetics based on abstraction and a colonial chronology positing Europe as the telos of civilization.[54] Early scenes from the novel explicitly identify Lelia's referential transparency with her whiteness. When Lelia and Henry first meet, each tries to guess the other's ethnic background. Lelia is less certain about Henry's, but he immediately deduces her origins: "I guessed somewhere in the Commonwealth" (10). Lelia protests: "'I'm too easy,' she cried, 'You even got the Massachusetts part without trying. It's so depressing. You don't know what it's like. An ordinary white girl has no mystery anymore, if she ever did. Literally nothing to her name'" (10). To Lelia's plaint, the novel has Henry respond

"There is always a mystery. . . . You just have to know where to look" (10). This "lack of mystery" the novel suggests is a matter of perception. John Fiske refers to this as "ex-nomination," the technique by which whiteness refuses to be named and arrogates to itself the power of the norm and the universal.[55] The "mystery" of the white subject, unlike that of the racialized subject, looks like nothing—"literally nothing to her name"—and if it presents any mystery, it is one that can be easily seen through.[56] The status of whiteness from the vantage point of the twenty-first century, however, is in crisis. As Winant, Eduardo Bonilla-Silva, and Robyn Wiegman point out, today's whiteness looks nothing like it did in the past. The monolithic version of white supremacy may have been demolished, but white privilege still exists, now splintered into new and contradictory iterations: white antiracism, neoconservative calls for "color blindness," and white victimization. *Native Speaker*'s own concerns about whiteness are echoed by Winant's point about color blindness: "neoconservative racial ideology," Winant writes, gives a racially dualistic shape to whiteness because of "its commitment to formal racial equality and its professions of 'color blindness.'"[57]

The intractable material differences belied by this apparent formal equality is what the novel hints at when it has Henry assure Lelia, "There is always a mystery. . . . You just have to know where to look" (10). Although the novel refuses to allow her a deracinated status—the scene names her "a pale white woman" (349)—its recognition of her racial status is troubled by its concomitant "queering" of her voice: the narrator tells us, she "reads a tall tale in her gentlest, queerest voice" (349). In queering the accent of the native speaker, the novel hints at a different genealogy: how the norming of a specific accent has been forgotten and naturalized as the lack of accent. Of course it also calls on the previous, demeaning sense of *queer* as aberrant, strange, deviant. By making the term *queer* available to us, the novel enables a certain kind of bridgework. In the 1990s *queer* was resignified to name a broader range of positions invested in criticizing the normative or normalizing. As Michael Warner explains, "'Queer' gets a critical edge by defining itself against the normal rather than the heterosexual," but this is not the sense in which the novel uses it.[58] David L. Eng's inaugural remarks on the critical affinity between queer and Asian America are more apropos. Eng proposes that "queerness comes to describe, affect, and encompass a much larger Asian American constituency—whatever their sexual identities or practices—whose historically disavowed status as U.S. citizen-subjects under punitive immigration and exclusion laws renders them 'queer' as such."[59] The novel's queering of Lelia does not make these connections explicit; I draw these connections here to suggest the specific racial mode in which the novel casts her accent. What does *queer* mean in the pedagogical context of native speaking? Certainly it seems to involve a kind of accented English, that is, a nonstandard, nonnormative use of English. If so, does this not once again reinstate the accented English of these foreign-language speakers as nonnormative? Kim reminds us that in comparison to a recognizably "black" vernacular, accents are racially asymmetrical: "The 'instant American inventions' of the immigrant tongue generally are not perceived as constituting a vernacular; indeed, they are difficult to register as anything other than an accent or a 'broken' English."[60]

If Kim worries that immigrant Englishes will be perceived as "broken," the novel realizes his concerns by covertly associating Lelia's "queerest" voice with Asiatic form. In these public classroom sessions, we are told that Lelia uses "buck-toothed puppets with big mouths" (348). For a novel as sensitive to race and racial stereotyping as is *Native Speaker*, a description as loaded as "buck-toothed" cannot be insignificant. As Lee points out, "buck-toothed" is unavoidably racialized; it is part of "a tradition of racial grotesques that had illustrated broadsides, editorials, and diatribes against Asians in America since the mid-nineteenth century."[61] If the puppets used by Lelia in *Native Speaker* are not exactly in yellowface, "buck-toothed" registers the persistence and necessity of Asian racialization. These props, as the narrator tells us, are necessary to the kind of speech therapy envisioned by a figure like Lelia, someone who "makes the talk unserious and fun" (348). The queering of native speaking, then, depends on forgetting a certain history of Orientalism, the very same discourse that has targeted Asians as spies and traitors and represented them as forever mysterious. Yet the novel seems aware that such forgetting is necessary for the reboot of the "old" native speaker to be transformed into a nonnative speaker. The act of queering the sympathetic white mother is a progressive one, but it also demands a certain forgetting of race. Insofar as Lelia and Henry represent a mixed-race, nonreproductive, adoptive family, they figure what Eng has elsewhere called "queer liberalism," the desire on the part of gays and lesbians to occupy the same normative structures of kinship and family they once critiqued and from which they were once excluded. For Eng the practice of transnational adoption is crucial to this new formation, and yet he is disturbed that "queer liberalism relies upon the logic of colorblindness in its assertion that racial difference has given way to an abstract U.S. community of individualism and merit."[62] We find a hint of just such a family in the novel's concluding scene, which positions Lelia and Henry as symbolic parents to these foreign-language-speaking students. As the two hug and kiss each student good-bye, Henry openly compares them to Mitt, his dead child: "When I embrace them, half pick them up, they are just that size I will forever know, that very weight so wondrous to me, and awful" (349). By making the sympathetic white mother the normalizing figure through which a "dozen lovely and native" (349) differences must pass to be articulated, *Native Speaker* hints at the troubling prospects of formalization, the promises of the formal equality that we so eagerly, and necessarily, embrace in this queer liberal and postracial moment.

My reading of *Native Speaker* has tried to clear a space for the tension between its representation of the desire to be unmarked, to be "readable," and the rhetorical strategies that have persistently staged racial inscrutability. In the simplest sense, that the racial sign is opaque preserves the possibility that the Asian subject can exceed its racialization, be more than a spy or a traitor. As a corollary, if all racial signs are potentially allegorical, *Native Speaker* extends the burden of this opacity to whiteness, refusing its self-described transparency. Returning to the "Donorgate" scandal with which this chapter began, we might consider the discourse of Asian deceit as an impetus, as Michael Chang has urged, for imagining models of citizenship beyond the paradigm of assimilation, ones that can accommodate the ambiguities, multiplicities, and heterogeneities defining our American allegiances. Focusing on allegory, one difficult trope among many for figuring a historical problematic called Asian American, may help us work toward transforming the "text" of rhetoric and America. In a post-9/11 landscape the yearning for transparency, as Puar puts it, like its previous incarnations throughout American history, is increasingly more deadly and more costly. Here and throughout the book, I have argued that it is only when we are able to fix our attention on the formal activities of the literary text that we can discern the particularities of this desire to be seen (through) as a kind of white language. Cultivating the difficulties of the literary referential at the present moment may seem frivolous, if not elitist or simply out of touch, but it is precisely at such fraught moments that the task of worrying at the illusion of transparency, patiently and persistently, becomes all the more urgent.

Conclusion

This book has sought to persuade you of the fitness and the necessity of treating Asian American literature as a particular constellation of figurative activities, as a set of textual patterns and behaviors translating specific historical problematics distinct to Asian America rather than a group of identity narratives reifying the assignment of racial meaning. As an ancillary task, by emphasizing the ancient lineage of these rhetorical figures— that these patterns originate from elsewhere—the book has tried to dissuade you from the person and figure of the author as the source, the agent, and the proprietor of these figurative activities. In elaborating the nature of these literature texts as texts, as highly patterned and deeply rhetorical uses of language, the book has offered a counterweight to the content-driven and sociopolitical approaches that have defined Asian American literary scholarship since its emergence in the late 1960s. While it is true that this book has taken its theoretical energy from critical trends like deconstruction that are uncongenial, if not antagonistic, to the political commitments of Asian American studies, I would argue that it has been given warrant to do so by the texts themselves. In fact I would even say that the Asian

American texts under consideration ask us to think of them this way, as congeries of figurative activity and rhetorical behavior rather than merely or solely ethno- and psychobiographies.

Death of the Asian American Author

To begin, let us consider Maxine Hong Kingston's remarks disowning her authorship of *China Men* as an opening to the rhetorical absence of the Asian American author. How is the old paradigm of an Asian American literature secured by the intentions of the Asian American-identified author displaced by Kingston's recusal of her own authorship in "The Laws"? In that 1991 interview Kingston is reported as saying, "I didn't even write that part. My editor, who was a correspondent in Asia during World War II, wrote it to make it sound really legal, journalistic, and not my language."[1] Indeed, we might see this move as a rhetorical gesture quite typical of Kingston's literary signature. Christopher Lee, for example, characterizes her as the Asian American author who "illuminates the theoretical conundrum of post-identity Asian American studies. Ironically, her authorial agency is most evident not when she asserts an identity, but rather when she facilitates its dissolution."[2] In subsequent communications Kingston has clarified her earlier statement, explaining that her editor made alterations, as editors do, to her language to distance it from the "poetic" language elsewhere in *China Men*, but that she herself wrote the original drafts for the chapter and is its author. There is something more at stake, though, when an author—even an author well-known for her postidentity strategies—disclaims her own authorship, when she is reported as declaring, of her own writing that it's "not my language." Without adjudicating between her two statements, what can be said is that the predicament Kingston elucidates, of writing in or speaking with a language not our own, is that of rhetoric specifically and of language more generally. Language precedes us; for a brief moment we may speak and intend and deviate within it, but not without first being constituted in and by it. Kingston's "absence" from her text is, in itself, a rhetorical gesture. There is a name for it, and the rhetorical tradition calls it apophasis. When Kingston says then that "The Laws" is "not my language," she gives us, however unwittingly, a direction for charting Asian American literature anew, as the latest, and most unquiet, inheritor of rhetorical resources that stretch back to classical antiquity. These resources, however, are themselves changed and made new as they must accommodate the specifically racial concerns exhibited by these Asian American texts.

For an even earlier inkling of the rhetorically absented Asian American author, we may look to *No-No Boy*'s prefatory and postscript material, written by Lawson Fusao Inada and Frank Chin, respectively. In Inada's introduction, appended to the 1976 printing of the novel, he describes the failed effort to locate Okada and his family and the resolution—on the part of himself and members of the Combined Asian-American Resources Project (CARP)—to disseminate the book, sowing along the way the seeds of Asian American community and consciousness. What's remarkable and unexpected about Inada's essay and Chin's afterword is how these texts are acutely conscious of the author's material detachment from his text, what, after Barthes, we know as the death of the author. As Inada put it after Okada's widow, Dorothy, had been tracked down, "It hurt to have her tell us that 'you really didn't miss meeting him by very long.'" What the death of the author prompts, then, is the moving attempt to conjure up his presence, displaced now into other vessels: "So John was really there with us, all along. You could feel him in the presence of Dorothy. . . . You could feel him in the way she spoke of their children. . . . You can feel him as you read this book."[3] It would be all too convenient to extrapolate from this the inaugurating gesture of Asian American literary criticism, the binding of the race-identified author to his text and the text as the repository and final resting place of the author. Keeping in mind Jameson's directive to always historicize, we might historicize this opening Asian American critical gambit as specific to its distinct historical moment.

Inada's account, rich in historical detail, paints a portrait of a particular historical moment: in the mid-1970s Okada was unknown; Asian American studies programs had been newly established at UC Berkeley, San Francisco State University, and UCLA; and the founding of the Association for Asian American Studies itself was still a few years away, in 1979. Chin's afterword brings these circumstances into even sharper focus. What was known of Asian American culture, Chin writes, consisted of little more than Orientalized cookbooks and autobiographies: "I grew up told no one knew anything else about yellow writing because there was nothing else to know."[4] In this particular moment, in the opening pages of *No-No Boy*'s first reprinting by CARP in 1976, Inada commands us, regarding *No-No Boy*, "Take it, and give it, from John." And yet, while Inada and the members of CARP were instrumental to restoring *No-No Boy*'s visibility and availability, Inada's introduction persistently redirects our attention to the novel itself. "We were talking about the book," the introduction begins. "We had *been* talking about the book, it seemed, for a very long time."[5] While I do not want to simply dismiss the attempt to resurrect the author via his novel— "You can feel him as you read this book," Inada insists—I also want to emphasize the very real tension that these essays present between the author's death, his profound nonpresence, and the book as the author's residual and much diminished material trace. Chin puts this more bleakly: "This is all that's left of John Okada: his one novel, *No-No Boy*, Seattle, the few memories of him a few Seattleites still keep."[6]

My point is simply that even in these early Asian American materials, ones we perceive as robust advocates for treating literary texts as extensions of their author, what we are actually "seeing"—if such a metaphor applies—is the declaration of the author's death, and what we "witness" is the rhetorical and imaginary attempt to revive that author. Chin's last lines are poignant and illuminating as they are addressed directly to Okada: "John, I read your book. I like it a lot."[7] We would make a mistake were we to forget that it is the *book*, the novel *No-No Boy*, that is the focus of all this rhetorical and imaginative energy. Inada's introduction is quite clear on this point: "John Okada's *No-No Boy* is much more than a great and lasting work of art. It is a *living* force among us." It is *No-No Boy*, not Okada, that is the "living force among us." And its life force as Inada conceives it is animated by its nature as literature, as a written *text*, because it is brought to life in the act of reading: "Whoever reads this book will be a bigger person for it. Whoever reads this book will never be the same. Whoever reads this book will see, and be, with greater strength and clarity. And in this way does the world begin to change."[8] Inada's language here is typical of the Asian American literary agendas of the 1970s, all of which, as David Leiwei Li has observed, were committed to the "grand promise of literature as the vehicle of social change," but in the context of the 2000s it also invokes an ethical language of deconstructive reading, a point to which I will return.[9]

What referential reading does is ensure that the literature, framed by racial concerns and authored by racial minorities, can never amount to anything but social documents, forms of history. This was precisely the problem that *No-No Boy* encountered at its initial reception. As the editors of *Aiiieeeee!* inform us, "Some scholars of Asian American literature have said that *No-No Boy* has no literary value, but is worth reading as a fairly accurate representation of the emotional and psychological climate of Japanese Americans at a certain period in history. Okada is worth reading as a social history, not as literature, these critics say."[10] The formal turn that characterizes the previous decade of Asian American scholarship has begun to challenge this perception, but much work remains to be done. I want to be clear: I am not saying that the person or the figure of the author should be discarded entirely, nor am I saying that race, and the uneven relations of power it expresses, does not matter. What I am maintaining is that the author is neither the origin nor the architect of figurative activity; these rhetorical figures are not the property of individuals. In no way can we claim, for example, that Kingston invents apophasis, that *No-No Boy* is the first to use the rhetorical question, or that Yamanaka intends to structure *Blu's Hanging* around catachresis. To disclaim the authority of these individual authors over these rhetorical figures is not to deny their artfulness in using language in distinctive ways. To discuss authorial craft we have recourse to aesthetics, which involves, in Sue-Im Lee's words, the "examination of Asian American literary works as aesthetic objects—objects that are constituted by and through deliberate choices in form, genres, traditions, and conventions."[11] Any of these elements can be, and have been, manipulated by Asian American writers, as the recent anthologies *Form and Transformation in Asian American Literature* and *Literary Gestures: The Aesthetic in Asian American Writing* have attested and the work of scholars as varied as Patricia Chu, Josephine Park, Dorothy Wang, Timothy Yu, and Daniel Kim, among a host of others, have amply and extensively demonstrated.

This focus on authorial agency I take to be the primary difference between examining these texts under the aegis of aesthetics and investigating these texts as examples of rhetorical activity. No author has authority over these rhetorical figures, bearing in mind that *author* and *authority* share a root (Latin *augēre*, "to make to grow, originate, promote, increase").[12] From antiquity to the Renaissance, from rhetoric's banishment by the Enlightenment to its revival today, the figures of speech have withstood changes in classification, and occasionally terminology, but they have proven an extraordinarily durable twenty-first-century inheritance as we continue to use the terms invented by the ancients to describe the same distinctive verbal patterns and configurations. Contemplating the remarkable longevity of rhetoric, Roland Barthes considered it "a veritable empire, greater and more tenacious than any political empire in its dimensions and its duration." Above all Barthes reminds us that rhetoric is one of the few remaining ways "our society has recognized language's sovereignty."[13] Knowing the intimate history between language and Asian American identity, might we, following Barthes, regard the presence of these rhetorical patterns in Asian American writing as postcolonial iterations? As racialized examples of the "empire"—in Ashcroft, Griffiths, and Tiffin's memorable phrase—writing back?

If the popular rhetoric is to be believed, we are living in a postracial moment, one that has done away with race and its attendant legacies of disenfranchisement, exclusion, and inequality. About this so-called age of color blindness David L. Eng cautions us that "the formal legal institution of colorblindness has not led to a U.S. society free of racial conflict, discrimination, and contradiction, as millions of people continue to be affected by race and afflicted by racism." Restoring the proper historical perspective on such politics, he urges us "to consider how colorblindness after *Brown* and *Loving* is only the latest historical incarnation of what legal scholar Cheryl I. Harris has described as a long and enduring history in U.S. law of 'whiteness as property.'"[14] In terms of literary production and reception, of the material conditions that determine ease of access to representation, race continues to play a significant and indisputable role, but if the race-identified person of the author still plays a role in organizing a specific grouping of texts—as Asian American, for example—such a figure is less essential as the guarantor of the rhetorical activity at work in the text.[15] In this sense we do not require the person or figure of the race-identified author, if ever that was a reliable barometer of Asian American identity or sensibility, to make the connection between race and figurative activity, between race and literary form, because the texts themselves give us direct access to their concerns with race.

When we look at the rhetorical moves describing *No-No Boy*'s introduction and afterword or characterizing authors like Kingston, what we see in these Asian American texts is not the relinquishing of the author but the exploration of a more subtle move, based on what Derrida calls "citationality," referring to the graftable nature of the sign such that no single context can enclose it: "In such a typology, the category of intention will not disappear; it will have its place, but from that place it will no longer be able to govern the entire scene and system of utterance."[16]

Derrida's frame of reference here is the vast realm of marks, written or oral, from which the absence of the author (as originary context) is the condition of possibility for the sign. We, on the other hand, have been concerned with a highly specific set of writings called Asian American literature, but the texts themselves are what authorize our move away from the person and figure of the author and toward these figurative activities. They feature linguistic patterns "other" to Asian America; the tropes we have encountered come from elsewhere, from an ancient rhetorical tradition, and they precede Asian America by millennia. It is under these conditions that Thomas Keenan inquires, "who speaks, writes, and reads, then? Not simply humans—in spite of all the tired protests against deconstructive antihumanism or even inhumanity. . . . One name for that enigma within humanity is inhumanity, and it emerges in language, in the terrible way language dispropriates us, precedes and exceeds us, without in its turn offering or constituting itself as a reliable ground."[17] Kingston's disclosure that "The Laws" is "not my language" offers up an inadvertent and powerful Asian American example of this "inhumanity."

This book represents a first pass at restoring Asian American literature to its rightful place, as a heterogeneous set of complex and complicated figurative activities involved in the task of theorizing representation in relation to specific racial problematics. My efforts here have been circumspect; I have merely tried to illuminate the evidence of linguistic patterns from elsewhere than Asian America in the hope of revealing the rhetorical and linguistic densities of a literary tradition often perceived as lacking such figurative engagements. To a certain degree neither this book nor I have been able to free ourselves from holding onto the "fiction" of Asian America, as Susan Koshy terms it, even as we have sought to increase the distance between these texts and Asian America by bracketing the person or figure of the author and by envisioning the Asian American referent as a set of historical problematics figured into literary form. This book has not pursued the utmost consequences of its premise, given the infinite horizons of rhetorical activity. Conceivably the old national, periodizing, and disciplinary borders would no longer hold in the pursuit of a general rhetoricity that recognizes no such boundaries; the scholarship of the previous half century stands as proof of its immense reach as disciplines as varied as linguistics, cognitive science, philosophy, literary criticism, communications, and psychoanalysis have turned to the rhetorical tradition to explain their specific objects of analysis. The actual condition of textuality is a rather disquieting, if not terrifying, one of alienation, difference, and alterity. In their New Critic polemic against authorial intention, W. K. Wimsatt and M. C. Beardsley caution, "The poem is not the critic's own and not the author's (it is detached from the author at birth and goes about the world beyond his power to intend about it or control it)."[18] As writing these texts will, by their very nature, circulate in contexts quite alien and unfamiliar to their original ones, as we have seen in the Asian American emergence of these ancient rhetorical tropes.

In the contemporary world of a digital humanities—from blogs to Twitter to Google Books—the anchoring of these texts to a single or permanent address grows more and more unlikely. It is because of this radical textuality that, as Gayatri Chakravorty Spivak observes, the critic's work involves a double duty: "This *is* sometimes the task of the literary academic. To restore reference in order that intertextuality may function; and to create intertextuality as well."[19] Restoring reference, as Spivak puts it, has always been the strength of the ethnic literature disciplines, but it now must be supplemented by its other, that of creating intertextuality. There is of course a much broader range of figurative activity at work in these texts than the ones to which I have alluded. My concentration on these particular figures is intended not to limit the kind of figurative activity to be found in these texts but to serve as a heuristic device—an initial, slightly wild, and certain to be imprecise volley meant to clear some space for future theoretical or conceptual endeavors.

Ethics of Reading

In exploring these rhetorical figures as exemplars of literary language, as opacities within and deviations from proper usage, this book has been animated by a version of close reading routed through deconstruction and ethics. In Spivak's words, we ought to approach literature "not as anthropologist; we stand rather as reader with imagination ready for the effort of othering, however imperfectly, as an end in itself. [20] What is othered, however, is the self, who must learn to imagine through the eyes of the other. The language of othering and responsibility is derived from philosopher Emmanuel Levinas, for whom the Other is to be understood as absolute alterity. In positing ethics as the foundation of philosophy rather than ontology, Levinas seeks to check the egoism of the sovereign consciousness, which approaches the Other as a version of itself. Thus he declares, "A calling into question of the same—which cannot occur within the egoist spontaneity of the same—is brought about by the other. We name this calling into question of my spontaneity by the presence of the Other ethics."[21] We are accustomed to thinking of the other as a problem; in earlier centuries we worried about the Negro problem and the Oriental problem; today we worry about the Muslim problem. Crudely put, Levinas reverses the direction of the problem; it is the self who comes into being from the Other, the self who owes an infinite debt of responsibility to the Other.

Literary study takes up Levinasian ethics such that the literary text represents the Other before whom and to whom the literary critic is responsible. As Derek Attridge explains, "To respond fully to literature is to be responsively aware of that otherness, in the unique form that the text gives it, and of the demands it makes upon us."[22] If the text is an "other," it is close reading that can best respond to the singularity and the texture of literature, but doing so involves opening oneself up to that which one cannot control, to which the self must be responsible and cannot anticipate. Keenan, who derives his insights from careful readings of the contradictions embodied by the fable, explains the ethical condition of reading as "our exposure to something that breaks with the regimes of meaning and sense it purports to offer, to something irreducible to ourselves and what we already know how to do."[23] Close reading, Jane Gallop contends, "makes for more ethical reading" because it guards against our "projections," what we think the text is saying rather than what it is actually—literally, as Maureen Quilligan might remind us—saying. The ethical dimension of close reading, Gallop argues, involves "learning to hear what's really on the page, listening closely to the other, and being willing to catch what the other actually says, and able to hear what we didn't expect him to say. If we can learn to do that with books, we might learn to do that with people."[24] To put this in ruthlessly practical terms, close reading is an ethical exercise with potentially high yield and comparatively lower risk of collateral damage. With close reading, we learn—and earn—our encounter with the other. These are not readings that operate remotely, at a distance; nor do they presume the easy transparency of the text in question. In taking seriously the texture, the rhetoricity, and the opacity of language, such reading practices are perforce painstaking, meticulous, and patient, and they call, in Keenan's terms, for a "politics of difficulty."[25] Few of these deconstructive critics deal directly, as do these Asian American texts, with the material, psychic, and cultural consequences of race. It seems to me, then, that given their subject matter and their real material effects— *Blu's Hanging* comes to mind—these Asian American texts demand of us an even greater degree of scrupulousness.

I want to end, as this book began, with an insight from *Aiiieeeee!* However distasteful we might find the strident homophobia, sexism, and exclusionary cultural nationalist politics in its pages, it is for those vocal identity politics that the anthology is remembered today. What has been obscured in the clamor and the skirmishing over those same positions is that *Aiiieeeee!* never set out to elaborate a politics but an aesthetics. Mark Chiang remarks, "While almost every discussion of this anthology has accepted its polemic at face value, as typical of the politicization of culture in the 1960s, critics failed to recognize that the editors' main concern was less to prescribe a politics of Asian American culture than to devise a theory of cultural production that would provide 'serious art' with a political rationale."[26] The prefatory materials to *Aiiieeeee!*, however, go much further than this. In "An Introduction to Chinese and Japanese American Literature," the second essay in the trio of essays that serve as prefatory material, and the first essay of the introduction proper, subtitled "Fifty Years of Our Whole Voice," the editors use a distinctly literary and tropological language to describe the raison d'être of Asian American literature. As they excoriate the critics responsible for *No-No Boy*'s chilly reception, they contend, "In reading Okada or any other Asian American writer, the literary establishment has never considered the fact that a new folk in a strange land would experience the land and *develop new language out of old words*."[27] Here they are indicting the critical reaction to *No-No Boy* and other Asian American texts as versions of "bad English," but we might draw a thread between their allusion to "new language" and the poetic dictum "Make it new" made famous by Ezra Pound. Indeed, Josephine Park's meticulous study of the unacknowledged affiliations between Asian American poetry and the Orientalist imaginings of American modernism would help us make these connections, but we do not need to look to twentieth-century modernism to trace the kind of move that *Aiiieeeee!* makes here.

If, as *Aiiieeeee!* puts it, a "new folk in a strange land" take upon themselves the making of a "new language out of old words," the introduction calls distinctly on the traditional association of literary language with creativity, with the imagination, and with new and strange uses of everyday language. If we discern from this a certain formalist echo, an understanding that Asian American literature must "estrange" or "defamiliarize" the customary or familiar language of the Anglo literary establishment, we would not be far off the mark. The anthology's language here, however, reaches for an even older lineage. The ancients used the word *trope* (Greek, "a turn") to describe changes in meaning wrought by rhetoric, and while rhetoricians still argue over the exact scope of the term and its relationship to its companion term, *figure*, they nevertheless agree on its effect as a "turn" away from proper or normative usage. "For Quintilian," Richard Lanham explains of the famous Roman rhetorician and educator, "a figure is a form or pattern of speech or writing which differs from the ordinary."[28] In *Aiiieeeee!* then we find, quite unexpectedly, at the start and origin of Asian American literature a grasp of Asian American literature as a historical emergence bound up with figurative activity. In the dictum to make "new language out of old words" we discover an exhortation toward figuration and the imperative to turn ordinary language into figures strange and new.

The notion that the sign, racial or linguistic, can mean multiply is what grants it the possibility for new meanings. From *Aiiieeeee!* onward, that we can speak of Asian American literature(s) at all is surely a testament to this capacity for resignification. To the extent that we can reconceptualize the texts that constitute Asian American literature as language that exceeds its historical usage, as writing capable of strange and potentially unpredictable meaning, we participate in the political project of imagining this literature, and these peoples, as more than simply Asian American.

Notes

Introduction

1. Nguyen, *Race and Resistance*, 3.
2. Levinson, "What Is New Formalism?," 559. For a different approach to form, one aimed at rejuvenating cultural studies, see Levine, who argues that literary forms trouble and destabilize sociopolitical forms: "What follows is a broad redefinition of form and the outlines of a method for reading the social, which I call strategic formalism" ("Strategic Formalism," 627).
3. Cheryl Wall, "On Freedom and the Will to Adorn: Debating Aesthetics and/as Ideology in African American Literature," in Levine, *Aesthetics and Ideology*, 286–87.
4. Xiaojing Zhou, "Introduction: Critical Theories and Methodologies in Asian American Literary Studies," in Zhou and Najmi, *Form and Transformation*, 4.
5. Ibid., 5.
6. Both these characterizations belong to Mark Chiang, who discusses *No-No Boy* in "Autonomy and Representation: Aesthetics and the Crisis of Asian American Cultural Politics in the Controversy over *Blu's Hanging*," in Davis and Lee, *Literary Gestures*, 25, and *Aiiieeeee!* in chapter 4 of *Cultural Capital*, 146.
7. The introduction by Lawson Inada and the afterword by Frank Chin that accompany *No-No Boy*'s 1976 reprinting are exemplary in this respect. Both essays describe the attempt to locate Okada, the living author, but what they actually record is their recognition of his irrecuperable death and absence. Upon meeting Okada's widow, Dorothy, for example, Inada

laments, "It hurt to have her tell us that 'you really didn't miss meeting him by very long.' You could say that John was 'ahead of his time,' that he was born too early and died too young" (v). Chin's afterword echoes the bleak recognition of the author's death: "John died in February 1971 of a heart attack. He was 47. I'd missed meeting John by a few months. If only I'd read his book sooner, I might have gotten together with Lawson Inada, the Sansei poet, and gone driving down to L.A. looking for John sooner" (256).

8. Spivak, *Death of a Discipline*, 22, 34, 26, 13.

9. de Man, "Semiology and Rhetoric," in *Allegories of Reading*, 10.

10. Wiegman, *American Anatomies*, 22, 31.

11. Butler, *Gender Trouble*, 172–73.

12. In trying to come to terms with the complexities of resignification, Kent Ono in "Re/signing 'Asian American'" proposes that we engage in a constant questioning of the term and be prepared for "re/signing" it, both in the sense of "refiguring" it and "retiring" it altogether. Susan Koshy uses a more explicitly deconstructive language when she concludes, "'Asian American' offers us a rubric that we cannot not use. But our usage of the term should rehearse the catachrestic status of the formation" ("The Fiction of Asian American Literature," 342).

13. Chuh, *imagine otherwise*, 8, 9.

14. Ibid., 27, my emphasis.

15. Ibid..

16. Richard Lanham, *A Handlist of Rhetorical Terms*, 2nd ed. (Berkeley: University of California Press, 1991), s.v. "metaphor."

17. Okihiro, *Margins and Mainstreams*, 28–29.

18. Park, *Apparitions of Asia*, 19.

19. Mann, *Outlaw Rhetoric*, 9.

20. See Bender and Wellbery, "Rhetoricality: On the Modernist Return of Rhetoric," in *The Ends of Rhetoric*, 4. Bender and Wellbery point to the emergence of rhetoric in linguistics, cognitive science, psychoanalysis, communication or media studies, and literary criticism. Not every call to renew rhetoric is so catholic. Brian Vickers, for example, is disturbed by the tremendous "atrophy" of rhetoric to a handful of master tropes and singles out figures as varied as Vico, Jakobson, Eichenbaum, Burke, and White as responsible for this fragmentation. Vickers reserves particular excoriation for de Man's work, maintaining that "his actual knowledge of rhetoric as revealed in these essays is limited to a fundamentally misguided conception of the art, and to a few tropes, not always correctly understood" (*In Defence of Rhetoric*, 457). The difference between a literary orientation and one seeking to defend classical rhetoric might be measured in the distance between a Vickers, who complains that de Man is "making communication impossible" (464), and a de Man, who is "calling 'literary,' in the full sense of the term, any text that implicitly or explicitly signifies its own rhetorical mode" ("The Rhetoric of Blindness," in *Blindness and Insight*, 136).

21. The rhetorical figures, originally classified under "style," the third of the five traditional parts of rhetoric, constitute a mere fragment of the vast territory encompassed by the rhetorical tradition. The terms *trope* and *figure* have been used interchangeably throughout the ages, and I do so here, while acknowledging that, as Lanham points out, what little agreement there is tends to use *trope* to refer to changes in meaning and *figure* (or scheme) to refer to the rearrangement of words. See Lanham, *Handlist*, s.v. "trope."

22. This is Wayne Rebhorn's phrase from *The Emperor of Men's Minds*, 12. For similar work, see Adamson et al., *Renaissance Figures of Speech* and Mann, *Outlaw Rhetoric*.

23. As a place to begin, we might invert the order in David Lloyd's contention that in the modern era "every racial judgement is simultaneously an aesthetic, an ethical and a political one" to glimpse the immensity of the territory yet to be explored. Lloyd's starting point is the eighteenth century (Kant and Schiller), but he indicates the broad historical sweep of his argument in an earlier part of his essay, where he argues, "The discourse on culture that emerges in the 'modern era' of the West is itself structured at every level by this normative developmental schema: the racism of culture is not a question of certain contingent racist observations by its major theoreticians nor of the still incomplete dissemination of its goods, but an ineradicable effect of its fundamental structures. These structures, indeed, determine the forms, casual and institutional, that racism has taken in the post-enlightenment era" ("Race under Representation," 70, 63).

24. Lye, "Reading for Asian American Literature," 484.

25. Fahnestock, *The Rhetorical Style*, 7.

26. Leech, "Linguistics and the Figures of Rhetoric," 145.

27. Parker, *The Invention of Native American Literature*, 168, 171.

28. Sue-Im Lee, "Introduction: The Aesthetic in Asian American Discourse," in Davis and Lee, *Literary Gestures*, 2.

29. Fahnestock, *The Rhetorical Style*, 13.

30. Chow, *The Protestant Ethnic*, 107, 127.

31. Chow's point of departure is the Chinese ethnic and her primary examples are Chinese film and literature, so this may explain her confusion about ethnic studies in the United States as the "investigation of ethnicity" (ibid., 125) rather than the study of power relations articulated around ethnicity, race, nation. Furthermore Asian American studies began by rejecting the legacy of Orientalism, which meant an emphatic differentiation from Asian studies. For a well-known articulation, see Wong, "Denationalization Reconsidered."

32. Chow, *The Protestant Ethnic*, 125. Chow's intellectual lineage is quite different from the race-based paradigm of Asian American studies, as she draws on Wallerstein and Balibar for her understanding of ethnicity. She acknowledges as much in expressing her preference for trading on the "ambiguity" between the terms *ethnicity* and *race*. Howard Winant explains

that ethnicity- or class-based theories of race cannot account for the malleable new forms of racism that are "less visible" in the wake of political reforms that ended state-sponsored segregation: "In Western Europe, these theories take the form of 'differentialism,' which repudiates the racist cultural hierarchies of the past but affirms the exclusionist commitments of (French, German, British, etc.) 'national culture,' thus upholding barriers to immigration and racial pluralism, not to mention integration" (*The New Politics of Race*, 161). See also Omi and Winant, "Ethnicity," in their landmark *Racial Formation in the United States*, 14–23. In the crudest of formulas ethnicity is chosen, whereas race is imposed. The transnational adoption of Asian babies by white American families demonstrates these complexities. What is known as the "ethnicity school" in the United States, founded by the work of pioneering sociologist Robert E. Park and represented in literary study by figures like Werner Sollors, has been a poor barometer for the particularities of African Americans and Asian Americans since its model is the European immigrant. See Sollors, *Beyond Ethnicity* (New York: Oxford University Press, 1987). The other problem with an ethnicity-based paradigm, as many scholars have shown, is that in the case of white ethnics, such a paradigm cannot account for white privilege. For a historical account of ethnicity in relation to European immigrants, see Roediger, *Working toward Whiteness*.

33. Chow, *Protestant Ethnic*, 24.

34. Lowe, *Immigrant Acts*, 10.

35. *Silva Rhetoricae*, s.v. "metaphor," February 26, 2007, accessed June 15, 2014, http://rhetoric.byu.edu/.

36. Wong, *Reading Asian American Literature*, 14, my emphasis.

37. Ibid., 14, 13. Wong borrows "Necessity" and "Extravagance" from two well-known passages in Kingston's *Woman Warrior*. Necessity is explained by the narrator's mother: "My mother . . . will add nothing unless powered by Necessity. . . . She plants vegetables rather than lawns; she carries the odd-shaped tomatoes home from the fields and eats food left for the gods" (6). Extravagance is suggested by the no-name aunt's extramarital affair: "Adultery is extravagance. Could people who hatch their own chicks and eat the embryos and the heads for delicacies . . . eating even the gizzard, could such people engender a prodigal aunt?" (7).

38. Carby, "The Multicultural Wars," 13.

39. There are earlier antecedents for this approach. Shirley Geok-Lin Lim argues in 1993 that the works of Kingston, David Henry Hwang, and Amy Tan, among others, require us to look beyond Asian America: "These works already reflect non–Asian American values, and their narrative strategies, verbal resources, and postmodern stances say as much about mainstream American literary traditions and systems of values and interpretations as they do about Asian American identity" ("Assaying the Gold," 160–61). David Palumbo-Liu's 1999 *Asian/American* offers a magisterial study of the

role that Asia and Asian America have played in constructing American modernity.

40. Lye, "Reading for Asian American Literature," 492.

41. Lawson Inada, introduction to Okada, *No-No Boy*, iii.

42. Chin et al., *Aiiieeeee!*, xi. Subsequent references are cited parenthetically in the text.

43. Eng, *Racial Castration*, 210.

44. Lye, "Reading for Asian American Literature," 484.

45. Kim, *Writing Manhood*, 223.

46. Derrida, "Signature Event Context," in *Limited, Inc.*, 12, 7.

47. James Kim, "Theses on Asian American Anger," paper presented at Future Asian Americas: A Symposium on Asian American Studies, Fordham University, June 6–7, 2008.

48. Farnsworth, *Farnsworth's Classic English Rhetoric*, 3.

49. *Silva Rhetoricae*, s.v. "antanaclasis," February 26, 2007, accessed June 15, 2014, http://rhetoric.byu.edu/.

50. Puttenham, *The Art of English Poesy*, 3.19.292.

51. Lanham, *Handlist*, s.v. "antanaclasis."

52. We might relate this movement to the rhetoricity of other reclaimed terms, such as *nigger* and *queer*. The difference, I would say, lies in the fact that "AIIIEEEEE!!!" also seeks to inaugurate a literary tradition. Henry Louis Gates Jr. is the pioneering figure here, arguing in *The Signifying Monkey* for a distinctly African American tradition of "signifyin'," derived from the black vernacular tradition.

53. Frank Whigham and Wayne A. Rebhorn, introduction to Puttenham, *Art of English Poesy*, 59.

54. Mann, *Outlaw Rhetoric*, 24.

55. Ibid., 2.

56. Richard Sherry, *A Treatise of Schemes and Tropes* (1550), edited by H. W. Hildebrandt (Gainesville, FL: Scholars' Facsimiles & Reprints, 1961), 8, quoted in Mann, *Outlaw Rhetoric*, 2.

57. On mimesis otherwise, see Chow, "Sacrifice, Mimesis, and the Theorizing of Victimhood"; Esty and Lye, introduction to "Peripheral Realisms Now." By "peripheral realisms," Esty and Lye designate a critical use of realism in literary texts across the breadth of the "Third World" that question the account of reality and depart from the reference point of Europe in the form of the nation-state or the bourgeois subject. Chow reconceptualizes mimesis away from imitation and pursues it instead as the sign of sacrifice. Mimesis, she suggests, is "the sign that *remains* . . . in the aftermath of a process of sacrifice. . . . Mimesis is the (visibly or sensorially available) substitute that follows, that bears the effects of (an invisible or illegible) sacrifice" (137). Through the "twinned logics" of mimesis and sacrifice, Chow is able to explore a potential agency foreclosed in her earlier model of coercive mimeticism: "The very act of

imitating one's victimizer may yet be an aperture to a different kind of future" (140–41).

58. Gayatri Chakravorty Spivak, "In a Word: *Interview*," with Ellen Rooney, in Schor and Weed, *The Essential Difference*, 157, 158.

59. Here Spivak references Derrida's well-known reading of Plato's views on writing in *Phaedrus*. Plato describes writing as a *pharmakon* (drug), a term that is typically translated as "poison," initiating a cascade whereby the derivative and artificial qualities of writing are viewed as inferior to the presence and truth of speech. In the course of deconstructing the speech/writing binary, a principle that has shaped the fundamental values of Western thought, Derrida points out that *pharmakon* is also the word for "medicine." See Jacques Derrida, "Plato's Pharmacy," in *Dissemination*, translated by Barbara Johnson (Chicago: University of Chicago Press, 1981).

1 / Rhetorical Question

1. Okada, *No-No Boy*, 250–51. Subsequent references are cited parenthetically in the text.

2. Kim, *Asian American Literature*, 156; Lowe, *Immigrant Acts*, 50; Yeh, "To Belong or Not to Belong," 121; Sato, "Momotaro's Exile: John Okada's *No-No Boy*," in Lim and Ling, *Reading the Literatures of Asian America*, 241. Sato may unfavorably compare *No-No Boy*'s construction of the ethnic self to the "multi-tiered process" found in Ellison's *Invisible Man* and Kogawa's *Obasan*, but she attributes its one-dimensionality to the limitations of conceptualizing Japanese American identity in the postwar period beyond the binary of "Japanese" (disloyal) and "American" (loyal). Kim tacks in a similar direction when she argues, "The fragmentation and disintegrating influence of American racism on the Japanese American community and its members are depicted through the incompleteness of each individual character: Ichiro is filled out by Kenji, Taro, Freddie, and Bull."

3. Mark Chiang, "Autonomy and Representation: Aesthetics and the Crisis of Asian American Cultural Politics in the Controversy over *Blu's Hanging*," in Davis and Lee, *Literary Gestures*, 25, 29.

4. Leech, "Linguistics and the Figures of Rhetoric," 136.

5. Culler, *Literary Theory*, 3.

6. Chuh, *imagine otherwise*, 27.

7. See, for example, Berman, *Fiction Sets You Free*, 167: "Literature democratizes; autonomous literature elicits autonomous individuality. . . . Literature, as writing, contributes to the spread of literacy and the development of an increasingly inclusive public."

8. Chin et al., "An Introduction to Chinese and Japanese Literature," in *Aiiieeeee!*, 26, 20.

9. Ling, *Narrating Nationalisms*, 50.

10. Such a narrative also prevails in Stan Yogi's "Introduction to Japanese American Literature," in Cheung, *An Interethnic Companion to Asian*

American Literature, 137: "The book [*No-No Boy*] was rescued from obscurity by young Asian American writers and critics in the 1970s, and it has subsequently been canonized as a classic of Asian American literature." See also Inada's introduction and Chin's afterword to *No-No Boy*.

11. Even earlier exceptions are Stephen Sumida, who discusses the device of the unreliable narrator ("Japanese American Moral Dilemmas in John Okada's *No-No Boy* and Milton Murayama's *All I Asking for Is My Body*," in Nomura et al., *Frontiers of Asian American Studies*, 222–233); Sato, who analyzes the contradictory formal behavior of the Momotaro folktale ("Momotaro's Exile," in Lim and Ling, *Reading the Literatures of Asian America*); Patricia P. Chu, who discusses the family romance (*Assimilating Asians*, 27–63).

12. Ling, *Narrating Nationalisms*, 33.

13. *Silva Rhetoricae*, s.v. "rhetorical question," February 6, 2007, accessed May 8, 2014, http://rhetoric.byu.edu/.

14. Ngai, *Impossible Subjects*, 177. FDR's Executive Order 9066 of February 1942 authorized the mass removal and incarceration of Japanese Americans based on "military necessity," a sentiment notoriously embodied by General John DeWitt, the officer in charge, who insisted, as historian Sucheng Chan writes, that "the Japanese race were 'an enemy race' . . . whose 'racial affinities [were] not severed by migration' and whose 'racial strains' remained 'undiluted' even among members of the second and third generations" (Chan, *Asian Americans*, 125). Michi Weglyn observes indignantly, "One of the gross absurdities of the evacuation was that a preponderance of those herded into wartime exile represented babes-in-arms, school-age children, youths not yet of voting age, and an exhausted army of elderly men and women. . . . The average age of the Nisei was eighteen. The Issei's average age hovered around sixty" (*Years of Infamy*, 42). Ngai summarizes the scholarly consensus on internment: "We now know that investigations by the Federal Communications Commission (FCC) and FBI found the charge of signaling to be entirely without substantiation. . . . The Office of Naval Intelligence (ONI) had, in fact, conducted an investigation of Japanese Americans in the fall of 1941 and concluded categorically that both Issei and Nisei were loyal to America. The ONI report was circulated at the highest levels of government and was seen by President Roosevelt in November 1941" (*Impossible Subjects*, 176). The so-called racial pretext for internment was highly suspect, since, as historian Roger Daniels points out in *Concentration Camps USA*, 100–101, leave processing began almost immediately. By his calculations, in 1942 alone nearly ten thousand volunteers were granted temporary release as low-wage labor for growers on the West Coast, and approximately 4,300 college-age students were approved to leave camp and enter college as a tactic to promote long-term democracy. To further problematize the racial rationale, no mass incarceration was carried out in Hawaii, where Japanese Americans constituted the majority of the workforce; officials feared this

would cripple the economy. Approximately 110,000 Japanese Americans from the West Coast, two-thirds of them citizens, were imprisoned in concentration camps. Over 120,000 persons in total were interned (including transfers from other locations and those born in camp). Weglyn notes that relocation of Japanese was hemispheric in scope: "forced uprootings" (56) occurred in Alaska, Canada and Mexico, and more than 12 South American nations detained resident Japanese or deported them to the United States for incarceration. Ironically, as Ngai points out, the civilians appointed to lead the War Relocation Authority, the agency in charge of internment, were antiracists who envisioned the camps as "planned communities" and "Americanizing projects" that would teach democratic habits of mind to the Japanese (*Impossible Subjects*, 177).

15. When Lowe, *Immigrant Acts*, 48, argues that Japanese Americans of the period were confronted by an "impossibly binary demand" forcing them to either identify themselves with Japan, thus becoming enemies of the state, or to assimilate into white America, thus rejecting all cultural affiliation with Japan, she leaves implicit the referential abyss that is suddenly opened up at the site of the racialized body. Essentially the demand to "choose" their allegiance to Japan or the United States ushered in a whole set of anxieties regarding the verification of Japanese intention: now the "same" sign, the racialized body, can denote either Japaneseness or its opposite, Americanness.

16. Several factors made the questionnaire an unreliable barometer of Japanese intentions. Its title ("Application for Leave Clearance") was misleading and its original wording rendered it, in Daniels's words, "singularly inappropriate" (*Concentration Camps*, 113). Question 27 was initially intended for draft-age male nisei and so its query regarding "combat duty" was not appropriate for female nisei or issei (first-generation Japanese immigrants) of either sex. As for question 28, answering yes at one point would have turned the issei into stateless persons. Ngai observes, "Issei 'yes' answers improved when WRA reworded question 28: 'Will you swear to abide by the laws of the United States and to take no action which would in any way interfere with the war effort of the United States?'" (*Impossible Subjects*, 184). The subsequent protests over registration itself further demonstrated the diagnostic inadequacy of such instruments. At Tule Lake, the most troubled of the camps, over a third of the internees refused to register at all. A nisei boycott at Heart Mountain, a supposed "happy camp," resulted in the Army accepting conditional answers to questions 27 and 28.

17. For extended treatments of the loyalty questionnaire, see chapter 6 of Daniels, *Concentration Camps USA*; chapter 8 of Weglyn, *Years of Infamy*; chapter 5 of Ngai, *Impossible Subjects*.

18. Ngai, *Impossible Subjects*, 184.

19. Austin, *How to Do Things with Words*, 12.

20. Ngai, *Impossible Subjects*, 188.

21. Derrida, "Signature Event Context," in *Limited Inc.*, 3, 4.
22. Da Silva, *Toward a Global Idea of Race*, 6.
23. Rudanko, "On Some Aspects of Rhetorical Questions in English," 29.
24. DeWitt quoted in Eng, *Racial Castration*, 105; Chan, *Asian Americans*, 124, my emphasis.
25. Chan, *Asian Americans*, 124.
26. Farnsworth, *Farnsworth's Classical English Rhetoric*, 212.
27. Kertzer, "Rhetorical Questions," 242–43.
28. *Silva Rhetoricae*, s.v. "ratiocinatio."
29. *Silva Rhetoricae* categorizes *ratiocinatio* as a "related figure" to *erotesis*. Lanham, *Handlist*, xv, regards it as a "synonym." I have taken the liberty of treating *ratiocinatio* as a form of rhetorical question, with which the extensive classifications created by the classical sources may not agree. I take my cue from the general understanding among contemporary rhetoricians that these groupings were extremely variable. *Silva Rhetoricae* notes, for example, in "Overview" to "Figures of Speech," that "the number, names, and groupings of figures have been the most variable aspect of rhetoric over its history."
30. Grosz, *Volatile Bodies*, 4.
31. Lloyd, "Race under Representation," 64, 70.
32. Derrida, "Signature Event Context," in *Limited, Inc.*, 8.
33. Wiegman, *American Anatomies*, 6.
34. Warren quoted in Ngai, *Impossible Subjects*, 176.
35. Ngai, *Impossible Subjects*, 177. For a demonstration of Ngai's point, see Jorg Nagler, "Internment of German Enemy Aliens in the United States during the First and Second World Wars" and George E. Pozzetta, "Alien Enemies or Loyal Americans? The Internment of Italian Americans," both in Saunders and Daniels, *Alien Justice*.
36. Dyer, *White*, 1–2.
37. Sara Ahmed, "Declarations of Whiteness: The Non-Performativity of Anti-Racism," *borderlands e-journal* 3.2 (2004), accessed May 8, 2014, http://www.borderlands.net.au/vol3no2_2004/ahmed_declarations.htm.
38. Weglyn, *Years of Infamy*, 140.
39. Ngai, *Impossible Subjects*, 182.
40. Scobey quoted in ibid.
41. Masaoka quoted in ibid.
42. de Man, "Semiology and Rhetoric," in *Allegories of Reading*, 10.
43. Ibid.
44. This is the title of Renaissance rhetorician Henry Peacham's *The Garden of Eloquence* (1577). *Silva Rhetoricae* states that classical sources typically referred to the figures of speech as the "flowers of rhetoric."
45. de Man, "Semiology and Rhetoric," in *Allegories of Reading*, 10.
46. Chu, *Assimilating Asians*, 61, 42, 28.
47. Wiegman, *American Anatomies*, 41.

48. Ibid., 38.

49. Szikszai-Nagy, "On the Rhetoric and Stylistics of Interrogative Figures," 61. For a deconstructive version of this visual crisis as distinctly literary, see Barbara Johnson's brilliant reading of Poe's "Purloined Letter" in "The Frame of Reference: Poe, Lacan, Derrida," in Muller and Richardson, *The Purloined Poe*, 213–51.

50. Chu, *Assimilating Asians*, 59. See also Sato, "Momotaro's Exile," in Lim and Ling, *Reading the Literatures of Asian America*; Chuh, *imagine otherwise*.

51. Chu, *Assimilating Asians*, 59–60.

52. Ibid., 58.

53. Kim, "Once More, with Feeling," 69, takes a psychoanalytic approach to suggest that Ichiro is castrated. The "non-normative sexuality" that defines him is the result of the topsy-turvy gender relations that the novel attributes to his mother, whose "virile, fertilizing agency . . . is traditionally the prerogative of fathers." The novel does seem to support this Oedipalization, as it makes Ichiro berate himself for "the selfish bond that strapped a son to his mother" (31), which prevented him from saying yes. Kim goes on to suggest that by the end of the novel, Ichiro's masculinity has been transformed into a specifically maternal and affective one.

54. See, for example, Chuh, *imagine otherwise*, 72, considering the passage delineating Ichiro's reasons. For her the "disordered chaos" of the syntax is representative of Okada's attempt to convey Ichiro's experience of nullified citizenship. See her chapter 2.

55. Lowe, *Immigrant Acts*, 50, 51, 44.

56. Ling, *Narrating Nationalisms*, 36, 48, 43, 38, 37, 38, 44, 46, 50, 38.

57. See Eagleton, *The Ideology of the Aesthetic*, 9.

58. My assessment is unwontedly crude as this certainly depends on the intertextual company the novel is made to keep. Daniel Kim, for example, teaches *No-No Boy* as a modernist text by putting it in the company of Gertrude Stein and Ernest Hemingway.

59. Farnsworth, *Farnsworth's Classical English Rhetoric*, viii.

2 / Apophasis

1. Timothy Pfaff, "Talk with Mrs. Kingston," in Skenazy and Martin, *Conversations with Maxine Hong Kingston*, 15.

2. See Donna Perry, "Maxine Hong Kingston," in Skenazy and Martin, *Conversations with Maxine Hong Kingston*, 179. This collection is far from obscure. The sales department of the University of Mississippi Press confirms that 2,432 copies were sold (combined hardcover and paperback). In fact the Perry interview was originally published in Donna Perry, ed., *Backtalk: Women Writers Speak Out* (New Brunswick, NJ: Rutgers University Press, 1993), 171–93. The editor in question is Charles Elliott, who confirms,

"The fact of the matter is that I believe I did write a few pages (or paragraphs) of distinctly uncreative material about immigration law (I cannot remember the details and don't have a copy of the book to hand at the moment)," email message to author, March 7, 2014.

3. Lee, *The Semblance of Identity*, 8.

4. Lye, *America's Asia*, 1.

5. Lye, "Reading for Asian American Literature," 483, 490.

6. Sue-Im Lee, "Introduction: The Aesthetic in Asian American Literary Discourse," in Davis and Lee, *Literary Gestures*, 3. For a very dated version of this debate, see Barthes's provocatively titled "Death of the Author," and Foucault's rebuttal, "What Is an Author?"

7. Kingston, *China Men*, 14–15. Subsequent references are cited parenthetically in the text.

8. Pfaff, "Talk with Mrs. Kingston," 15.

9. Paula Rabinowitz, "Eccentric Memories: A Conversation with Maxine Hong Kingston," in Skenazy and Martin, *Conversations with Maxine Hong Kingston*, 69; Kim, *Asian American Literature*, 119.

10. Hsu, *Dreaming of Gold*, 67, 97.

11. Okihiro, *Margins and Mainstreams*, 151.

12. Takaki, *Strangers from a Different Shore*, 7.

13. Li, *Imagining the Nation*, 28.

14. Cheung, "Re-Viewing Asian American Literary Studies," in *An Interethnic Companion to Asian American Literature*, 17, suggests that its generic distinction as ethnic autobiography made *The Woman Warrior* more palatable for Anglo-American audiences and that the overt racial politics of the later books made them less so.

15. Li, "*China Men*," argues that *China Men* rewrites the American canon. Nishime, "Engendering Genre," explores its challenging of the traditional gender of genres like history or autobiography. Hattori, "China Man Autoeroticism," considers its queered masculinity.

16. Li, "*China Men*," 484.

17. Franke, "Preface: Apophasis as a Genre of Discourse," in *On What Cannot be Said*, 1, 4, 1.

18. Sells, *Mystical Languages of Unsaying*, 3, 9, 8.

19. Franke, "Preface," 2, 1.

20. Lanham, *Handlist*, s.vv. "apophasis," and "expeditio."

21. Gibbons, "On Apophatic Poetics," 19.

22. An exception is Cristy Beemer, "The Female Monarchy: A Rhetorical Strategy of Early Modern Rule," *Rhetoric Review* 30.3 (2011): 258–74. Sells, *Mystical Languages of Unsaying*, chapter 7, discusses the female mystic Marguerite Porete.

23. Eng, *Racial Castration*, 36–37, 51.

24. On intertextuality, see Shu Mei Shih, "Exile and Intertextuality in Maxine Hong Kingston's *China Men*" in *The Literature of Emigration and*

Exile, edited by James Whitlark and Wendell Aycock (Austin: University of Texas Press, 1992), 65–77.

25. See Lowe's introduction to *Immigrant Acts*; Yang, "Indispensable Labor."

26. Ty, *The Politics of the Visible*, 8.

27. Kawash, *Dislocating the Color Line*, 130.

28. See, for example, Lee, "Kingston's *China Men*."

29. Taking advantage of the Fourteenth Amendment, those Chinese returning to the United States would regularly declare the birth of male children born in China, whether or not a child was actually born. This practice created slots that were sold or used by immediate and extended family. In creating these paper slots the Chinese overwhelmingly claimed male over female children. Xiaojian Zhao reports that in 1925 the ratio stood at 13.7:1. From 1945 to 1952 the ratio was 4.9:1. Scholars tend to attribute the severe gender imbalance to the "sojourning" mind-set of early immigrants or to the patriarchal values of Chinese culture, but Zhao sees it differently. In *Remaking Chinese America*, 29, she argues that the preference for males served as "a means of maximizing the number of new entries to the country," a long-term strategy that "enabled more families to emigrate to the United States." Estelle Lau, *Paper Families*, discusses the complex networks in place to secure these transnational transactions.

30. Quoted in Hsu, *Dreaming of Gold*, 75. The very next chapter in *China Men*, "Father from China," features a paper son: "BaBa would go with two sets of papers: bought ones and his own, which were legal. . . . But his own papers were untried, whereas the fake set had accompanied its owners back and forth many times" (46–47).

31. Koshy, *Sexual Naturalization*, 13. Koshy's study of miscegenation offers a different route to thinking race when it is not explicitly present. As she puts it, these antimiscegenation laws "turned sex acts into race acts" (1).

32. Hortense Spillers makes a similar conceptual move regarding the normative subject of psychoanalysis. Using as her pivot the enslaved African American female, Spillers argues that this particular subject demonstrates the historical specificity of the psychoanalytic subject as a privileged (because liberated) one. African American history thus rethinks psychoanalysis and its normative notions of gender, sexuality, and kinship. "Mama's Baby, Papa's Maybe: An American Grammar Book," *Diacritics* 17.2 (1987): 64–81.

33. Lau, *Paper Families*, 2, 54.

34. Franke, "Preface," 111.

35. Exod. 33: 22–23, in *Exodus: The Traditional Hebrew Text*.

36. Childs, *Exodus*, 596.

37. *Exodus: The Traditional Hebrew Text*, 215.

38. I thank Manu Vimalassery for pointing out that the misrecognition of the stranger also means that any china man can be a father.

39. I am referring to the famous photographs taken by A. J. Russell (#227, *East and West*, Union Pacific Museum) and Charles R. Savage (*Meeting of Engines*, Central Pacific Railroad Museum). Several photographs of the ceremony were taken by Savage and Russell, both photographers for the Union Pacific Railroad. A painting later commissioned by the Central Pacific Railroad, Thomas Hill's *The Last Spike* (California State Railroad Museum), did include the Chinese. My contention here follows the general critical consensus by pursuing the symbolic absence of the Chinese from the official photograph, both in light of the photograph's "reality effect" in relation to history and in light of Chinese exclusion. On anti-Chinese racism in relation to labor history, see Alexander Saxton, *The Indispensable Enemy* (Berkeley: University of California Press, 1971). On Chinese and the railroad, see chapter 3 of David Roediger and Elizabeth Esch, *The Production of Difference: Race and the Management of Labor in U.S. History* (NY: Oxford University Press, 2012). For the Russell photograph, see Union Pacific, "A. J. Russell Views," accessed April 22, 2014, http://www.up.com/aboutup/history/photos/aj_russell/index.htm. For the Savage photograph, see Central Pacific Railroad Photographic History Museum, accessed April 22, 2014, http://cprr.org/Museum/Exhibit/_savage._meeting_engines_.html.

40. Sells, *Mystical Languages of Unsaying*, 8–9.

41. Franke, "Preface," 2.

42. Chan, *Asian Americans*, 48.

43. Lau, *Paper Families*, 37.

44. Takaki, *Strangers from a Different Shore*, 234.

45. Shan, "Law as Literature," 237; Sledge, "Maxine Hong Kingston's *China Men*," 5. Shan acknowledges that elsewhere *China Men*'s narrative strategies complicate ideas of history and literature by juxtaposing fact and fiction together. Sledge's comment about testimony indexes her larger argument, that *China Men* turns oral history into the literary form of epic. Kingston's narrative, however, is not always correct. Brook Thomas, "*China Men*," 714, remarks in a footnote that "Kingston's legal history is not always accurate. For instance, she lists the victory of *Yick Wo v. Hopkins* as 1896 instead of 1886, and her account of this case and of the 1879 constitution is a bit misleading."

46. Perry, "Maxine Hong Kingston," in Skenazy and Martin, *Conversations with Maxine Hong Kingston*, 179.

47. Goellnicht, "Tang Ao in America," 196.

48. Ling, *Narrating Nationalisms*, 120.

49. Chan, *Asian Americans*, 46.

50. Kingston writes that "Charles Elliott *edited* 'The Laws.' I did all the research and wrote the original half dozen drafts. When he read what I'd written, Chuck said that the style needed to sound more legalistic, not so poetic. He changed some words and phrasing, and rewrote some passages. His work is within the purview of editing, not writing." Maxine Hong Kingston, email to author, May 6, 2014.

51. Kocijančič, "Apophasis," 250.

52. Gibbons, "On Apophatic Poetics," 20, my emphasis. He cites Dick Davis, who argues that this foreign borrowing is responsible for "most of the innovation in the whole history of English poetry" (20).

3 / Catachresis

1. Nguyen, *Race and Resistance*, 157.

2. For critical analyses of the award controversy, see Nguyen's conclusion to *Race and Resistance*; Chuh's introduction to *imagine otherwise*; Chiang's chapter 5 of *Cultural Capital*. For the most cogent discussion of the novel as racist, see Fujikane, "Sweeping Racism under the Rug of 'Censorship.'" Fujikane's concern is the novel's reinforcement of local Japanese racism against Filipinos, but in making this argument she resorts to a mimetic view of literature: "Representing a racist stereotype does not in and of itself constitute a critique of that stereotype. Moreover, depicting a racial conflict does not in and of itself constitute a critique of power when the conflict is portrayed in ways that benefit the dominant group" (176).

3. On the petition, see chapter 5 of Chiang, *Cultural Capital*.

4. On queer critique see Wu, "Revisiting *Blu's Hanging*." On melancholia see Parikh, "Blue Hawaii"; Suzuki, "Consuming Desires."

5. Rocío G. Davis seems to be one of the few scholars interested in the generic qualities of Yamanaka's work. See Davis, "Short Story Cycle and Hawai'i Bildungsroman: Writing Self, Place, and Family in Lois-Ann Yamanaka's *Wild Meat and the Bully Burgers*," in Zhou and Najmi, *Form and Transformation*, 231–48.

6. Fujikane, "Sweeping Racism under the Rug of 'Censorship,'" 168, 169.

7. Chiang, *Cultural Capital*, 174, 207.

8. Ibid., 174, 175. Chiang's framework of cultural capital, borrowed from Bourdieu, consistently offers perceptive analyses of class as it intersects with gender, sexuality, and race, but is less able to explain the operations of the novel qua novel. In one illuminating instance he inquires whether Blu's rape should be understood as fiction or nonfiction, borrowing this language from a scene in the novel where Ivah reminds Blu that he is "nonfiction" and dismisses his car-washing scheme as "fiction" (since the scheme is inspired by a children's book). For Chiang the binary between fiction and nonfiction recalls the separation imposed by the controversy between "literary" (aesthetic) and "realist" (political) representation: "These are the same alternatives, we can now see, offered by the book itself. The antithesis of political representation and aesthetic representation is referenced in the division between fiction and nonfiction and figures directly in the book in the contrast between Ivah and the Reyes girls" (205). Chiang goes on to argue that the novel identifies Ivah with the disinterested autonomy of aesthetics, whereas the Reyes nieces are associated with politics (they are

self-interested; their sexual favors are strategies of winning consent). But when we consider that the scene between Blu and Ivah takes place within a greater frame of fiction, the novel itself, the binary of fiction/nonfiction that Chiang works within no longer holds. Recourse to figurative activity rather than the usual (and artificial) opposition between aesthetics and politics may have offered a different kind of leverage by troubling this boundary. For Chiang's first treatment of the division between aesthetics and politics, see "Autonomy and Representation: Aesthetics and the Crisis of Asian American Cultural Politics in the Controversy over *Blu's Hanging*," in Davis and Lee, *Literary Gestures*, 17–34.

9. Chiang, *Cultural Capital*, 206.

10. Brooks, "The Heresy of Paraphrase" in *The Well Wrought Urn*, 197.

11. OED Online, "trope, n.," accessed June 11, 2014, http://www.oed. com/view/Entry/206679?rskey=2icAfl&result=1.

12. Motooka, "Sentimentalism, Authenticity, and Hawai'i Literature," 27.

13. Okihiro, "The History of Ethnic Studies." For a sociological version of this understanding, see Jung, *Reworking Race*, 59, who suggests, "If race, nation, and class are 'largely empty receptacles' to be filled with live history, the receptacles themselves possess particular 'styles' that enable them to receive and carry certain matters of history, and not others, and that render them recognizable as themselves across different historical moments."

14. Chiang, *Cultural Capital*, 189.

15. Wu, "Revisiting *Blu's Hanging*," 34. After the U.S. annexation of Hawaii, the islands were dominated by a small group of haole (originally "foreigner" but now "white") elites who ruled the sugar industry and controlled a vast pool of labor comprised of Native Hawaiians and immigrants from Portugal, China, Japan, Korea, and the Philippines. Jung demonstrates how these groups of laborers were racialized differently in a climate of carefully cultivated ethnic antagonism. Filipino laborers were consistently assigned the most demeaning and underpaid work. See Jung, "Different Racisms."

16. Lanham, *Handlist*, s.v. "catachresis."

17. Quintilian, "*Institutio Oratoria*," 8.6.34.

18. Lanham, *Handlist*, s.v. "catachresis."

19. Spivak, "Translation as Culture," 14.

20. Koshy, "The Fiction of Asian American Literature," 342.

21. Nguyen, *Race and Resistance*, 157.

22. Yamanaka, *Blu's Hanging*, 95. Subsequent references are cited parenthetically in the text.

23. Freinkel, "The Use of the Fetish," 117.

24. Lee, "Menarche and the (Hetero) Sexualization of the Female Body."

25. Brumberg, "'Something Happens to Girls,'" 104, 121.

26. See Charlesworth, "Paradoxical Constructions of Self," on how corporations like Tambrands (manufacturers of Tampax) and Personal

Products Corporation (makers of Modess) have influenced health education in American public schools by also being the ones responsible for the pamphlets that explain menstruation. In the process these companies reproduce heteronormative and patriarchal attitudes about the female body as "aberrant" while ensuring future consumers for their products.

27. Patricia Parker, "Metaphor and Catachresis," in Bender and Wellbery, *The Ends of Rhetoric.*

28. Lee, "Menarche and the (Hetero) Sexualization of the Female Body," 360, my emphasis.

29. Grosz, *Volatile Bodies*, 189.

30. Chiang's reading of this scene, for example, reveals the racial hierarchy implicit in the protagonist's desire to acquire what he calls "middle-class respectability": "The Ogatas' aspiration to middle-class status is what separates them from the Reyes. Physical modesty and sexual abstinence, then, are coded as class markers, and the intense prohibitions against self-display and sexual activity that Ivah obeys indicate her desire to 'better' herself" (*Cultural Capital*, 198).

31. Stephen H. Sumida, "Postcolonialism, Nationalism, and the Emergence of Asian/Pacific American Literatures," in Cheung, *An Interethnic Companion to Asian American Literature*, 278.

32. Valerie Takahama, "Controversial Adventures in 'Paradise': Bully Burgers and Pidgin," *Orange County (CA) Register*, February 15, 1996, E1, accessed April 9, 2014, http://www.swarthmore.edu/Humanities/pschmid1/engl52a/engl52a.1999/yamanaka.html.

33. Susan Y. Najita, "Pleasure and Colonial Resistance: Translating the Politics of Pidgin in Milton Murayama's *All I Asking for Is My Body*," in Shukla and Tinsman, *Imagining Our Americas*, 112, 127, 133.

34. Freinkel, "The Use of the Fetish," 119.

35. Parker, "Metaphor and Catachresis," in Bender and Wellbery, *The Ends of Rhetoric*, 72, 70, 73, my emphasis. See also Derrida, "White Mythology," from which Parker borrows the deconstruction of metaphor as catachresis.

36. Early reviews of Yamanaka's use of pidgin portray it as an act of agency. A representative example is found in an article by Michael Tsai, "'Tita' Finds Her Voice: Lois-Ann Yamanaka Lays Her Words on the Line," *Hawaii Herald*, January 7, 1994, A22.

37. I wish to thank James Kim for the insightful observation that the novel identifies Uncle Paulo as Filipino by disavowal.

38. Kawash, *Dislocating the Color Line*, 125, 132.

39. See Stahl, "Authentic Boy Bands on TV?," 318, my emphasis. The producer in question is Berton Schneider. The television show featured a struggling rock band, but in reality The Monkees were a phenomenal commercial success. After the show went off the air, the band went on to produce hit records and to tour Europe, the United States, and Australia. Laura

Goostree focuses on the show's high degree of self-consciousness and the ways it utilized various devices to deconstruct the line between reality and television: "Rather than reality as television show, *The Monkees* gives its audience television show as reality" ("*The Monkees* and the Deconstruction of Television Realism," 52).

40. The Hekawi as imagined by *F Troop* were still stereotypes. Plains Indian culture was typically depicted as bloodthirsty; the Hekawi, however, were portrayed as too "cowardly" to fight. As the business partners of various members of F Troop, they manufactured "authentic" Indian artifacts to sell to tourists. Celeste C. Lacroix identifies them as examples of the "degraded Indian," the Native as corrupted by his encounter with white culture ("High Stakes Stereotypes," 3). Chief Wild Eagle was played by a veteran Italian American actor, Frank de Kova, whose sidekick, "Crazy Cat," was played by a Yiddish actor, Don Diamond. The name of the tribe itself was a running gag that mocked indigenous languages. In one episode the chief explains that the Hekawi got their name from an ancestor who got lost and asked, "Where the heck are we?" In 1991 *F Troop* was picked up for syndication by Nickelodeon/Nick at Nite. See the Internet Movie Database (IMDb), s.v. "F-Troop," accessed April 1, 2014, http://www.imdb.com/title/tt0058800/.

41. J. A. White's description of Davy Jones as "the teenage heartthrob; he was English, very tiny, cute, and vaguely feminine," productively connects his ambiguous sexuality to the potential queering of Uncle Paulo's sexuality ("The Monkees," 6).

42. Jung, "Racialization in the Age of Empire," 417, 418.

43. Slotkin, "Unit Pride," 472, 473.

44. Najita, "Pleasure and Colonial Resistance," in Shukla and Tinsman, *Imagining Our Americas*, 111.

45. Quoted in Fujikane, "Sweeping Racism under the Rug of 'Censorship,'" 164.

46. This is where an understanding of the novel's figurative activity might take us further than the concerns of several critics that no Native Hawaiians appear in *Blu's Hanging*.

47. Chiang, *Cultural Capital*, 177.

48. Kaplan, "Violent Belongings and the Question of Empire Today."

49. OED Online, "Filipino, n. and adj.," accessed June 11, 2014, http://www.oed.com/view/Entry/70211.

50. J. Hillis Miller, "Catachresis, Prosopopoeia, and the Pathetic Fallacy: The Rhetoric of Ruskin," in Hagenbuchle and Skandera, *Poetry and Epistemology*, 403, 406.

51. Sarah Harasym with Gayatri Chakravorty Spivak, "Practical Politics of the Open End," in Harasym, *The Post-Colonial Critic*, 108.

4 / Allegory

1. The term *Asian Donorgate* is William Safire's. In *Racial Politics* Michael Chang argues that "Donorgate" begins with the Democratic campaign finance scandal and culminates in the federal case against Wen Ho Lee.

2. Chen, *Double Agency*, 22.

3. Hsu, *Dreaming of Gold*, 56.

4. Chen, *Double Agency*, 23.

5. Puar, "Queer Times, Queer Assemblages," 132. Puar uses this phrase to describe a constellation of desires aimed at disciplining the terrorist body into "visibility," a desire she links to the banning of head scarves in France, the depilation of Guantánamo detainees before their incarceration, and the shaving of Saddam Hussein's beard directly after his capture.

6. This is a playful echo of Derrida on "white mythology," his critique of philosophical pretensions to truth that rest on a disavowed foundation of metaphor.

7. Okihiro, *Margins and Mainstreams*, 7.

8. David Cole, in his foreword to *Enemy Aliens*, xxii–xxiii, states that the 9/11 Commission "found that none of the government's immigration measures had netted any terrorists" and that Special Registration, which registered eighty thousand individuals, had similar results: "Not one has been charged with a terrorist crime. Nor has the government attributed a single terrorist prosecution to the roundup." His statistics present an eerie echo of Japanese mass removal and internment during World War II, which, despite allegations of a fifth column, also failed to discover any such proof. On Special Registration, see n26 below.

9. Lowe, *Immigrant Acts*, 5.

10. Chen, *Double Agency*, 18. See Chang, *Racial Politics*, for an extended analysis of this discourse in "Asian Donorgate."

11. Lye, *America's Asia*, 7.

12. Jeon, *Racial Things, Racial Forms*, xxxiv.

13. Abrams and Harpham, *A Glossary of Literary Terms*, 394.

14. de Man, *Allegories of Reading*, 205.

15. Whitman, *Allegory*, 2.

16. Kelley, *Reinventing Allegory*, 3, 5.

17. Puttenham, *The Art of English Poesy*, 271; Whigham and Rebhorn, introduction to Puttenham, *Art of English Poesy*, 55, 59. Puttenham's "Englishings," as his editors put it, of these figures of speech may offer an additional point of entry into the relationship between classical rhetoric and nationalism.

18. Fletcher, *Allegory*, 2, 3.

19. Cawelti and Rosenberg, *The Spy Story*, 55.

20. The antinomy between allegory and symbol can be traced to the Romantics, who devalued the former for its mechanical nature and limited

range of meaning and promoted the latter for its unity and organic form. According to Coleridge, a central figure here, the symbol is characterized by the "translucence" of the universal in the particular (Fletcher, *Allegory*, 16n29). An echo of this Coleridgean language for symbol and allegory finds its way into the novel when the terms *transparency* and *opacity* are used to describe the particular mode of ethnic espionage. Of course de Man's essay "Rhetoric of Temporality" is well-known for profoundly upsetting this traditional periodization with its argument that Romantic poets like Wordsworth demonstrated instead an allegorical sensibility. See de Man, *Blindness and Insight*.

21. For Asian American exceptions to the former trend, see Lye, "Reading for Asian American Literature," 493: "[The] problem of Asian American political representation is framed by the novel as one of aesthetic representation, in that the politician's story is the subject of the protagonist's secret reporting, whose writing style becomes more 'fanciful' as he tries to break free of his assignment." See also Daniel Kim, who examines the novel's representation of the vernacular in "Do I, Too, Sing America?" For the latter, Jonathan Arac invokes the human in "Violence and the Human Voice," and Paul Narkunas, capital in "Surfing the Long Waves of Global Capital." Reviewers Verlyn Klinkenborg, "Witness to Strangeness," and David Flusfeder, "Hungry for America," both employ "America" as the general category.

22. Winant, *The New Politics of Race*, 189.

23. Puttenham, *Art of English Poesy*, 271n5. As his editors explain, Puttenham's renaming of allegory refers to an allegorical figure, Faus-Semblant (False Semblance or Appearance), who appears in *The Romance of the Rose*, a well-known medieval allegory by Guillaume de Lorris and Jean de Meun.

24. Lee, *Native Speaker*, 6. Subsequent references are cited parenthetically in the text.

25. On allegory and enigma, see Dirk Obbink, "Early Greek Allegory," in Copeland and Struck, *The Cambridge Companion to Allegory*, 15–25. Northrop Frye makes a well-known argument in *Anatomy of Criticism* that all criticism, insofar as it seeks to interpret meaning, is essentially allegorical.

26. From 1882 to 1943, with exclusion acts restricting their entry, Chinese immigrants had to demonstrate their right to enter the United States by submitting to examinations before immigration officials. During World War II over 120,000 Japanese Americans were interned in concentration camps, and in 1943 internees over the age of seventeen were issued questionnaires to ascertain their loyalty to the United States. Under the 1956 Chinese Confession Program, Chinese who had entered illegally as "paper sons" could naturalize if they informed on others. From 2002 to 2011 Special Registration required noncitizen males over sixteen from predominantly Muslim nations in Asia and Africa to report to immigration offices, where they were fingerprinted, photographed, interviewed, and made to swear loyalty oaths. Registrants were not told that the process would result in deportation for

minor infractions. Those not deported were compelled to report annually to immigration offices; their movements inside and outside the United States were also tracked. The program was an initiative of the Department of Homeland Security; it was eventually revoked in April 2011. On Special Registration, see Sarkar and Ling, *Special Registration*. On Asian American impersonation, see Chen, *Double Agency*, 3–34, who suggests a linkage between Japanese picture brides and Chinese paper families, who had to practice impersonation to enter the United States because of immigration restrictions.

27. Chow, *The Protestant Ethnic*, 115.

28. The *OED* gives two definitions of *evidence*—"quality or condition of being evident," (def. I), "that which manifests or makes evident" (def. II)—and another possible meaning, "ground for belief; testimony" (def. II.5). See *OED Online*, "evidence, n.," accessed June 12, 2014, http://www.oed.com/view/Entry/65368?rskey=9icyoI&result=1.

29. Kelley, *Reinventing Allegory*, 86.

30. Quilligan, *The Language of Allegory*, 26, 68. Quilligan's principal quarrel lies with the confusion of allegory proper (allegorical composition) with allegoresis (allegorical interpretation), which involves imposing meanings not originally intended. The latter is also what gives rise to the association of allegory as saying one thing and meaning another, as it manufactures, in Quilligan's generic point of departure, a disjuncture between what a text says and means.

31. Butler, *The Psychic Life of Power*, 202n1.

32. Spivak, *Death of a Discipline*, 25.

33. Chen, *Double Agency*, 173.

34. Cawelti and Rosenberg, *Spy Story*, 13.

35. Chen, *Double Agency*, xvi, xix.

36. Butler, *Psychic Life of Power*, 3. Elsewhere (201n1) she cites Hayden White's genealogy. White, *Tropics of Discourse*, 2, explains that the word *trope* in early English is derived from *tropos* (Greek, "turn"), which is translated into Latin as *tropus*, which can mean both "metaphor" and "figure of speech." His point is that such language is designated as "style" today to distinguish it from what he calls "discourse," its more referential counterpart.

37. Butler, *Psychic Life of Power*, 4.

38. I thank Scott Combs for this important insight. Questions 27 and 28 of the loyalty questionnaire had to be answered by yes or no, and thus were particularly controversial. The first demanded an oath of allegiance disavowing Japan, and the second for military service as proof of loyalty. Leave processing from camp was keyed to interpreting "yes, yes" as loyal and "no, no" as disloyal. See Ngai, *Impossible Subjects*, 173–201, on the questionnaire's unintentional rhetorical consequences. Voluntary declaration of one's ethnicity during World War II was another version of subjection. Ronald Takaki, *Strangers from a Different Shore*, 364–66, 370–71, describes how Chinese

distributed buttons declaring "I am Chinese" and Koreans wore badges stating "I am Korean" to distinguish themselves from "enemy" Japanese.

39. Palumbo-Liu, *Asian/American*, 3.

40. Wu and Nicholson, "Have You No Decency?," 16.

41. Lye, "Reading for Asian American Literature," 485.

42. Quilligan, *Language of Allegory*, 27. Also see Fletcher, *Allegory*, 2.

43. Lye, *America's Asia*, 5.

44. Lee, *Orientals*, 181, 190.

45. Lye, *America's Asia*, 16, 17.

46. OED Online, "paper, n. and adj.," accessed June 12, 2014, http://www.oed.com/view/Entry/137122?redirectedFrom=on+paper.

47. The *OED* offers an additional note: "Now generally used of something represented, promised, planned, or forecast (not always actually in writing), with a suggestion that the reality may not match up to expectations."

48. Quilligan, *Language of Allegory*, 26, 25.

49. See Kim, "Do I, Too, Sing America?" for the vernacular as Korean folksong.

50. Edge, "Natives, Speakers, and Models," 155.

51. Rampton, "Displacing the 'Native Speaker,'" 98.

52. Corley, "'Just Another Ethnic Pol,'" 78.

53. Song, "A Diasporic Future?," 96.

54. See Lloyd, "Race under Representation."

55. Fiske, *Media Matters*, 42.

56. For a World War II example of this transparency, consider Earl Warren, who, according to Mae Ngai, averred that "'We believe that when we are dealing with the Caucasian race we have methods that will test the loyalty of them. . . . But when we deal with the Japanese we are in an entirely different field and cannot form any opinion that we believe to be sound." Ngai goes on to observe that "Warren's assumptions about the loyalty of 'Caucasians' elided the history of war-induced assimilation and the constructedness of Euro-Americans' ethno-racial identities" (*Impossible Subjects*, 176, 177).

57. Winant, *New Politics of Race*, 181.

58. Warner, introduction to *Fear of a Queer Planet*, xxvi.

59. Eng, "Out Here and over There," 40–41.

60. Kim, "Do I, Too, Sing America?," 249.

61. Lee, *Orientals*, 1.

62. Eng, *The Feeling of Kinship*, 3.

Conclusion

1. Perry, "Maxine Hong Kingston," in Skenazy and Martin, *Conversations with Maxine Hong Kingston*, 179.

2. Lee, *The Semblance of Identity*, 97.

3. Lawson Inada, introduction to Okada, *No-No Boy*, v, vi.

4. Frank Chin, afterword to Okada, *No-No Boy*, 254.

5. Inada, introduction to Okada, *No-No Boy*, vi, iii.

6. Chin, afterword to Okada, *No-No Boy*, 260.

7. Ibid.

8. Inada, introduction to Okada, *No-No Boy*, vi, vi.

9. Li, *Imagining the Nation*, 34.

10. Chin et al., "An Introduction to Chinese and Japanese American Literature," in *Aiiieeeee!*, 20.

11. Sue-Im Lee, "Introduction: The Aesthetic in Asian American Literary Discourse," in Davis and Lee, *Literary Gestures*, 2.

12. OED Online, "author, n.," accessed June 12, 2014, http://www.oed.com/view/Entry/13329.

13. Roland Barthes, *The Semiotic Challenge*, translated by Richard Howard (New York: Hill and Wang, 1988), 14, 15.

14. Eng, *The Feeling of Kinship*, 5. *Brown v. Board of Education* (1954) is the Supreme Court case that put a formal end to the "separate but equal" doctrine of legal segregation. *Loving v. Virginia* (1967), another Supreme Court case, ruled as unconstitutional Virginia's antimiscegenation law.

15. See, for example, the Association's decision in 2008 to award the fiction prize to James Janko, a white American. Jennifer Ann Ho, "The Place of Transgressive Texts in Asian American Epistemology," *Modern Fiction Studies* 56.1 (2010): 205–25, examines the award and its implications for Asian American literature.

16. Derrida, "Signature Event Context," in *Limited Inc.*, 18.

17. Keenan, *Fables of Responsibility*, 3–4.

18. Wimsatt and Beardsley, "The Intentional Fallacy," 470.

19. Gayatri Chakravorty Spivak, "Ethics and Politics in Tagore, Coetzee, and Certain Scenes of Teaching," in *Aesthetic Education in the Era of Globalization* (Cambridge, MA: Harvard University Press, 2012), 319.

20. Spivak, *Death of a Discipline*, 13.

21. Emmanuel Levinas, *Totality and Infinity*, translated by Alphonso Lingis (Pittsburgh: Duquesne University Press, 1990), 43.

22. Derek Attridge, "Literary Form and the Demands of Politics," in Levine, *Aesthetics and Ideology*, 248.

23. Keenan, *Fables of Responsibility*, 2.

24. Jane Gallop, "The Ethics of Reading: Close Encounters," *Journal of Curriculum Theorizing* (Fall 2000): 16–17.

25. Keenan, *Fables of Responsibility*, 2.

26. Chiang, *Cultural Capital*, 143.

27. Chin et al., *Aiiieeeee!*, 22, my emphasis.

28. Lanham, *Handlist*, s.v. "trope."

BIBLIOGRAPHY

Abrams, M. H., and Geoffrey Harpham, eds. *A Glossary of Literary Terms*, 10th ed. Boston: Wadsworth, Cengage Learning, 2012.

Adamson, Sylvia, Gavin Alexander, and Katrin Ettenhuber, eds. *Renaissance Figures of Speech*. Cambridge, UK: Cambridge University Press, 2007.

Arac, Jonathan. "Violence and the Human Voice: Critique and Hope in *Native Speaker*." *boundary 2* 36.3 (2009): 55–66.

Ashcroft, Bill, Gareth Griffiths, and Helen Tiffin. *The Empire Writes Back: Theory and Practice in Post-Colonial Literatures*. 2nd ed. New York: Routledge, 2002.

Austin, J. L. *How to Do Things with Words*. Edited by J. O. Urmson. New York: Galaxy Book, 1967.

Bal, Mieke. *Narratology: Introduction to the Theory of Narrative*. 2nd ed. Toronto: University of Toronto Press, 1997.

Bender, John, and David E. Wellbery, eds. *The Ends of Rhetoric: History, Theory, Practice*. Stanford: Stanford University Press, 1991.

Berman, Russell. *Fiction Sets You Free: Literature, Liberty, and Western Culture*. Iowa City: University of Iowa Press, 2007.

Brooks, Cleanth. *The Well Wrought Urn*. New York: Harcourt, 1975.

Brumberg, Joan Jacobs. "'Something Happens to Girls': Menarche and the Emergence of the Modern American Hygienic Imperative." *Journal of the History of Sexuality* 4.1 (1993): 99–127.

Butler, Judith. *Gender Trouble: Feminism and the Subversion of Identity.* New York: Routledge, 1999.

———. *The Psychic Life of Power.* Stanford: Stanford University Press, 1997.

Carby, Hazel. "The Multicultural Wars." *Radical History Review* 54 (1992): 7–18.

Cawelti, John, and Bruce Rosenberg. *The Spy Story.* Chicago: University of Chicago Press, 1987.

Chan, Sucheng. *Asian Americans: An Interpretive History.* New York: Twayne, 1991.

Chang, Michael. *Racial Politics in an Era of Transnational Citizenship.* Lanham, MD: Lexington, 2004.

Charlesworth, Dacia. "Paradoxical Constructions of Self: Educating Young Women about Menstruation." *Women and Language* 24.2 (2001): 13–20.

Chatman, Seymour. *Story and Discourse: Narrative Structure in Fiction and Film.* Ithaca: Cornell University Press, 1978.

Chen, Tina Y. *Double Agency: Acts of Impersonation in Asian American Literature and Culture.* Stanford: Stanford University Press, 2005.

Cheung, King-kok, ed. *An Interethnic Companion to Asian American Literature.* Cambridge, UK: Cambridge University Press, 1997.

Chiang, Mark. *The Cultural Capital of Asian American Studies.* New York: New York University Press, 2009.

Childs, Brevard. *Exodus: A Commentary.* London: SCM Press, 1974.

Chin, Frank, Jeffery Chan, Lawson Inada, and Shawn Wong, eds. *Aiiieeeee! An Anthology of Asian American Writers.* New York: Meridian, 1997.

Chow, Rey. *The Protestant Ethnic and the Spirit of Capitalism.* New York: Columbia University Press, 2003.

———. "Sacrifice, Mimesis, and the Theorizing of Victimhood (A Speculative Essay)." *Representations* 94 (Spring 2009): 131–49.

Chu, Patricia P. *Assimilating Asians: Gendered Strategies of Authorship in Asian America.* Durham, NC: Duke University Press, 2000.

Chuh, Kandice. *imagine otherwise: on asian americanist critique.* Durham, NC: Duke University Press, 2003.

Cole, David. *Enemy Aliens: Double Standards and Constitutional Freedoms in the War on Terrorism.* New York: New Press, 2005.

Copeland, Rita, and Peter Struck, eds. *The Cambridge Companion to Allegory.* Cambridge, UK: Cambridge University Press, 2010.

Corley, Liam. "'Just Another Ethnic Pol': Literary Citizenship in Chang-rae Lee's *Native Speaker.*" *Studies in the Literary Imagination* 37.1 (2004): 61–81.

Culler, Jonathan. *Literary Theory: A Very Short Introduction.* New York: Oxford University Press, 2000.

Da Silva, Denise Ferreira. *Toward a Global Idea of Race.* Minneapolis: University of Minnesota Press, 2007.

Daniels, Roger. *Concentration Camps USA: Japanese Americans and World War II.* New York: Holt, Rinehart and Winston, 1972.

Davis, Rocio G., and Sue-Im Lee, eds. *Literary Gestures: The Aesthetic in Asian American Writing.* Philadelphia: Temple University Press, 2006.

de Man, Paul. *Allegories of Reading: Figural Language in Rousseau, Nietzsche, Rilke, and Proust.* New Haven: Yale University Press, 1979.

———. *Blindness and Insight: Essays in the Rhetoric of Contemporary Criticism.* 2nd ed. revised. Minneapolis: University of Minnesota Press, 1983.

Derrida, Jacques. *Limited, Inc.* Edited by Gerald Graff. Translated by Samuel Weber and Jeffrey Mehlman. Evanston, IL: Northwestern University Press, 1995.

———. "White Mythology: Metaphor in the Text of Philosophy." Translated by F. C. T. Moore. *New Literary History* 6.1 (1974): 5–74.

Dyer, Richard. *White.* London: Routledge, 1997.

Eagleton, Terry. *The Ideology of the Aesthetic.* Malden, MA: Blackwell, 2007.

Edge, Julian. "Natives, Speakers, and Models." *JALT Journal* 9.2 (1988): 153–57.

Eng, David L. *The Feeling of Kinship: Queer Liberalism and the Racialization of Intimacy.* Durham, NC: Duke University Press, 2010.

———. "Out Here and over There: Queerness and Diaspora in Asian American Studies." *Social Text* 52–53 (Fall/Winter 1997): 31–52.

———. *Racial Castration: Managing Masculinity in Asian America.* Durham, NC: Duke University Press, 2001.

Esty, Jed, and Colleen Lye, eds. Introduction to "Peripheral Realisms Now." Special issue, *Modern Language Quarterly* 73.3 (2012): 269–88.

Exodus: The Traditional Hebrew Text with the New JPS Translation. Commentary by Nahum M. Sarna. New York: Jewish Publication Society, 1991.

Fahnestock, Jeanne. *The Rhetorical Style: The Uses of Language in Persuasion.* Oxford: Oxford University Press, 2011.

Farnsworth, Ward. *Farnsworth's Classical English Rhetoric.* Boston: David R. Godine, 2011.

Fiske, John. *Media Matters: Race and Gender in U.S. Politics.* Minneapolis: University of Minnesota Press, 1996.

Fletcher, Angus. *Allegory: The Theory of a Symbolic Mode.* Ithaca: Cornell University Press, 1964.

Flusfeder, David. "Hungry for America." *Times Literary Supplement,* October 27, 1995, 23.

Franke, William. *On What Cannot Be Said: Apophatic Discourses in Philosophy, Religion, Literature, and the Arts.* Vol. 1, *Classic Formulations.* Notre Dame, IN: University of Notre Dame Press, 2007.

Freinkel, Lisa. "The Use of the Fetish." *Shakespeare Studies* 33 (2005): 115–22.

Fujikane, Candace. "Sweeping Racism under the Rug of 'Censorship.'" *Amerasia* 26.2 (2000): 159–94.

Gibbons, Reginald. "On Apophatic Poetics." *American Poetry Review* (2007): 19–23. Online. Accessed September 12, 2012.

Goellnicht, Donald. "Tang Ao in America: Male Subject Positions in *China Men.*" In *Reading the Literatures of Asian America,* edited by Shirley Geok-lin Lim and Amy Ling. Philadelphia: Temple University Press, 1992.

Goostree, Laura. "*The Monkees* and the Deconstruction of Television Realism." *Journal of Popular Film & Television* 16.2 (1988): 50–58.

Grosz, Elizabeth. *Volatile Bodies: Toward a Corporeal Feminism.* Bloomington: Indiana University Press, 1994.

Harasym, Sarah, ed. *The Post-Colonial Critic: Interviews, Strategies, Dialogues.* London: Routledge, 1990.

Hattori, Tomo. "China Man Autoeroticism and the Remains of Asian America." *Novel: A Forum on Fiction* 31 (1998): 215–36.

Hillis Miller, J. "Catachresis, Prosopopoeia, and the Pathetic Fallacy: The Rhetoric of Ruskin." In *Poetry and Epistemology,* edited by Roland Hagenbuchle and Laura Skandera. Regensburg, Germany: Verlag-Friedrich Pustet, 1986.

Hsu, Madeline Yuan-yin. *Dreaming of Gold, Dreaming of Home: Transnationalism and Migration between the United States and South China, 1882–1943.* Stanford: Stanford University Press, 2000.

Jeon, Joseph Jonghyun. *Racial Things, Racial Forms: Objecthood in*

Avant-Garde Asian American Poetry. Iowa City: University of Iowa Press, 2012.

Jung, Moon-Kie. "Different Racisms and the Difference They Make: Race and 'Asian Workers' of Prewar Hawai'i." *Critical Sociology* 28 (January 2002): 77–100.

———. "Racialization in the Age of Empire: Japanese and Filipino Labor in Colonial Hawai'i." *Critical Sociology* 32.2–3 (2006): 403–24.

———. *Reworking Race: The Making of Hawai'i's Interracial Labor Movement.* New York: Columbia University Press, 2006.

Kaplan, Amy. "Violent Belongings and the Question of Empire Today: Presidential Address to the American Studies Association, Hartford, Connecticut, October 17, 2003." *American Quarterly* 56.1 (2004): 1–18.

Kawash, Samira. *Dislocating the Color Line: Identity, Hybridity, and Singularity in African-American Literature.* Stanford: Stanford University Press, 1997.

Keenan, Thomas. *Fables of Responsibility: Aberrations and Predicaments in Ethics and Politics.* Stanford: Stanford University Press, 1997.

Kelley, Theresa M. *Reinventing Allegory.* Cambridge, UK: Cambridge University Press, 1997.

Kertzer, Jonathan. "Rhetorical Questions: Consensus, Authority, Enigma." *Language and Style: An International Journal* 20.3 (1987): 242–56.

Kim, Daniel. "Do I, Too, Sing America? Vernacular Representations and Chang-rae Lee's *Native Speaker.*" *Journal of Asian American Studies* 6.3 (2003): 231–60.

———. "Once More, with Feeling: Cold War Masculinity and the Sentiment of Patriotism in John Okada's *No-No Boy.*" *Criticism* 47.1 (2005): 65–83.

———. *Writing Manhood in Black and Yellow: Ralph Ellison, Frank Chin, and the Literary Politics of Identity.* Stanford: Stanford University Press, 2005.

Kim, Elaine. *Asian American Literature: An Introduction to the Writings and Their Social Context.* Philadelphia: Temple University Press, 1982.

Kingston, Maxine Hong. *China Men.* New York: Vintage, 1989.

———. *The Woman Warrior.* New York: Vintage International, 1989.

Klinkenborg, Verlyn. "Witness to Strangeness." *New Yorker,* July 10, 1995, 76–77.

Kocijančič, Gorazd. "Apophasis: Uncertain Theses about the Knowledge of God." In *Rivelazione e conoscenza*, edited by Giovanni Grandi and Luca Grion. Soveria Mannelli, Italy: Rubbettino, 2007.

Koshy, Susan. "The Fiction of Asian American Literature." *Yale Journal of Criticism* 9.2 (1996): 315–46.

———. *Sexual Naturalization: Asian Americans and Miscegenation.* Stanford: Stanford University Press: 2004.

Lacroix, Celeste. "High Stakes Stereotypes: The Emergence of the 'Casino Indian' Trope in Television Depictions of Contemporary Native Americans." *Howard Journal of Communications* 22 (2011): 1–23.

Lau, Estelle T. *Paper Families: Identity, Immigration Administration, and Chinese Exclusion.* Durham, NC: Duke University Press, 2006.

Lee, Chang-rae. *Native Speaker.* New York: Riverhead Books, 1995.

Lee, Christopher. *The Semblance of Identity: Aesthetic Mediation in Asian American Literature.* Stanford: Stanford University Press, 2012.

Lee, Janet. "Menarche and the (Hetero) Sexualization of the Female Body." *Gender and Society* 8.3 (1994): 343–62.

Lee, Robert. *Orientals: Asian Americans in Popular Culture.* Philadelphia: Temple University Press, 1999.

Lee, Yoon Sun. "Kingston's *China Men*: Circumscribing the Romance of Deterritorialization." *Yale Journal of Criticism* 11.2 (1998): 465–84. doi: 10.1353/yale.1998.0036.

Leech, G. N. "Linguistics and the Figures of Rhetoric." In *Essays on Style and Language: Linguistic and Critical Approaches to Literary Style*, edited by Robert Fowler. London: Routledge, 1966.

Levine, Caroline. "Strategic Formalism: Toward a New Method in Cultural Studies." *Victorian Studies* 48.4 (2006): 625–57.

Levine, George, ed. *Aesthetics and Ideology.* New Brunswick, NJ: Rutgers University Press, 1994.

Levinson, Marjorie. "What Is New Formalism?" *PMLA* 122.2 (2007): 558–69.

Li, David Leiwei. "*China Men*: Maxine Hong Kingston and the American Canon." *American Literary History* 2.3 (1990): 482–502.

———. *Imagining the Nation: Asian American Literature and Cultural Consent.* Stanford: Stanford University Press, 1998.

Lim, Shirley Geok-Lin. "Assaying the Gold: Or, Contesting the Ground of Asian American Literature." *New Literary History* 24.1 (1993): 147–69.

Lim, Shirley Geok-Lin, and Amy Ling, eds. *Reading the Literatures of Asian America.* Philadelphia: Temple University Press, 1992.

Ling, Jinqi. *Narrating Nationalisms: Ideology and Form in Asian American Literature.* New York: Oxford University Press, 1998.

Lloyd, David. "Race under Representation." *Oxford Literary Review* 13.1–2 (1991): 62–94.

Lowe, Lisa. *Immigrant Acts: On Asian American Cultural Politics.* Durham, NC: Duke University Press, 1996.

Lye, Colleen. *America's Asia: Racial Form and American Literature, 1893–1945.* Princeton: Princeton University Press, 2005.

———. "Reading for Asian American Literature." In *A Companion to American Literary Studies,* edited by Caroline Levander and Robert Levine. Malden, MA: Wiley-Blackwell, 2011.

Mann, Jenny C. *Outlaw Rhetoric: Figuring Vernacular Eloquence in Shakespeare's England.* Ithaca: Cornell University Press, 2012.

Motooka, Wendy. "Sentimentalism, Authenticity, and Hawai'i Literature." *Bamboo Ridge* 73 (Spring 1998): 22–32.

Muller, John P., and William J. Richardson, eds. *The Purloined Poe: Lacan, Derrida, and Psychoanalytic Reading.* Baltimore: Johns Hopkins University Press, 1988.

Narkunas, Paul. "Surfing the Long Waves of Global Capital with Chang-rae Lee's *Native Speaker*: Ethnic Branding and the Humanization of Capital." *Modern Fiction Studies* 54.2 (2008): 327–52.

Ngai, Mae M. *Impossible Subjects: Illegal Aliens and the Making of Modern America.* Princeton: Princeton University Press, 2005.

Nguyen, Viet T. *Race and Resistance: Literature and Politics in Asian America.* New York: Oxford University Press, 2002.

Nishime, LeiLani. "Engendering Genre: Gender and Nationalism in *China Men* and *The Woman Warrior.*" *MELUS* 20.1 (1995): 67–83.

Nomura, Gail M., Russell Endo, Stephen H. Sumida, and Russell C. Leong, eds. *Frontiers of Asian American Studies.* Seattle: University of Washington Press, 1989.

Okada, John. *No-No Boy.* Seattle: University of Washington Press, 1979.

Okihiro, Gary Y. "The History of Ethnic Studies." *Columbia Spectator,* October 15, 2007. Accessed November 1, 2007. http://www.columbiaspectator.com/2007/10/15/history-ethnic-studies.

———. *Margins and Mainstreams: Asians in American History and Culture.* Seattle: University of Washington Press, 1994.

Omi, Michael, and Howard Winant. *Racial Formation in the United States From the 1960s to the 1990s.* 2nd ed. New York: Routledge, 1994.

Ono, Kent A. "Re/signing 'Asian American': Rhetorical Problematics of Nation." In "Thinking Theory in Asian American Studies." Special issue, *Amerasia Journal* 21.1–2 (1995): 67–78.

Palumbo-Liu, David. *Asian/American: Historical Crossings of a Racial Frontier.* Stanford: Stanford University Press, 1999.

Parikh, Crystal. "Blue Hawaii: Asian Hawaiian Cultural Production and Racial Melancholia." *Journal of Asian American Studies* 5.3 (2002): 199–216.

Park, Josephine Nock-Hee. *Apparitions of Asia: Modernist Form and Asian American Poetics.* Oxford: Oxford University Press, 2009.

Parker, Robert Dale. *The Invention of Native American Literature.* Ithaca: Cornell University Press, 2003.

Puar, Jasbir. "Queer Times, Queer Assemblages." *Social Text* 84–85, 23:3–4 (2005): 121–39.

Puttenham, George. *The Art of English Poesy. A Critical Edition.* Edited by Frank Whigham and Wayne A. Rebhorn. Ithaca: Cornell University Press, 2007.

Quilligan, Maureen. *The Language of Allegory: Defining the Genre.* Ithaca: Cornell University Press, 1992.

Quintilian, Marcus F. "*Institutio Oratoria.*" In *LacusCurtius.* Edited by William Thayer. Translated by Harold E. Butler. University of Chicago. Accessed January 24, 2014. http://penelope.uchicago.edu/Thayer/E/Roman/Texts/Quintilian/Institutio_Oratoria/home.html.

Rampton, M. B. H. "Displacing the 'Native Speaker': Expertise, Affiliation, and Inheritance." *ELT Journal* 44.2 (1990): 97–101.

Rebhorn, Wayne A. *The Emperor of Men's Minds: Literature and the Renaissance Discourse of Rhetoric.* Ithaca: Cornell University Press, 1995.

Roediger, David. *Working toward Whiteness.* New York: Basic Books, 2006.

Rudanko, Juhani. "On Some Aspects of Rhetorical Questions in English." *Studia Neophilologica* 65 (1993): 29–36.

Sarkar, Saurav, and Sin Yen Ling. *Special Registration: Discrimination and Xenophobia as Government Policy.* A Report from the Asian American Legal Defense and Education Fund. New York: Asian American Legal Defense and Education Fund, 2004. Accessed June 12, 2014. http://www.aaldef.org/docs/AALDEF-Special-Registration-2004.pdf.

Saunders, Kay, and Roger Daniels, eds. *Alien Justice: Wartime Internment in Australia and North America.* Queensland: University of Queensland Press, 2000.

Schor, Naomi, and Elizabeth Weed, eds. *The Essential Difference.* Bloomington: Indiana University Press, 1994.

Sells, Michael A. *Mystical Languages of Unsaying.* Chicago: University of Chicago Press, 1994.

Shan, Te-Hsing. "Law as Literature, Literature as Law: Articulating 'The Laws' in Maxine Hong Kingston's *China Men.*" *Tamkang Review* 26.1–2 (1995): 235–64.

Shukla, Sandhya, and Heidi Tinsman, eds. *Imagining Our Americas: Toward a Transnational Frame.* Durham, NC: Duke University Press, 2007.

Skenazy, Paul, and Tera Martin, eds. *Conversations with Maxine Hong Kingston.* Jackson: University of Mississippi Press, 1998.

Sledge, Linda. "Maxine Hong Kingston's *China Men*: The Family Historian as Epic Poet." *MELUS* 7.4 (1980): 3–22.

Slotkin, Richard. "Unit Pride: Ethnic Platoons and the Myths of American Nationality." *American Literary History* 13.3 (2001): 469–98.

Song, Min. "A Diasporic Future? *Native Speaker* and Historical Trauma." *LIT: Literature, Interpretation, Theory* 12 (2001): 79–98.

Spivak, Gayatri Chakravorty. *Death of a Discipline.* New York: Columbia University Press, 2003.

———. "Translation as Culture." *parallax* 6.1 (2000): 13–24.

Stahl, Matthew. "Authentic Boy Bands on TV? Performers and Impresarios in *The Monkees* and *Making the Band.*" *Popular Music* 21.3 (2002): 307–29.

Suzuki, Erin. "Consuming Desires: Melancholia and Consumption in *Blu's Hanging.*" *MELUS* 31.1 (2006): 35–52.

Szikszai-Nagy, Irma. "On the Rhetoric and Stylistics of Interrogative Figures." *Sprachtheorie und germanistische Linguistik* 19.1 (2009): 61–68.

Takaki, Ronald. *Strangers from a Different Shore: A History of Asian Americans.* Updated and revised ed. Boston: Back Bay Books, 1998.

Thomas, Brook. "*China Men*, *United States v. Wong Kim Ark*, and the Question of Citizenship." *American Quarterly* 50.4 (1998): 689–717.

Ty, Eleanor. *The Politics of the Visible in Asian North American Narratives.* Toronto: University of Toronto Press, 2004.

Vickers, Brian. *In Defence of Rhetoric.* 1988. Oxford: Oxford University Press, 1990.

Warner, Michael, ed. *Fear of a Queer Planet: Queer Politics and Social Theory.* Minneapolis: University of Minnesota Press, 1993.

Weglyn, Michi. *Years of Infamy: The Untold Story of America's Concentration Camps*. 1976. Seattle: University of Washington Press, 1996.

White, Hayden. *Tropics of Discourse*. Baltimore: Johns Hopkins University Press, 1985.

White, J. A. "The Monkees: A Happily but Safely Diverse Portrait for a New America." *Popular Culture Review* 21.1 (2010): 5–10.

Whitman, Jon. *Allegory: The Dynamics of an Ancient and Medieval Technique*. Cambridge, MA: Harvard University Press, 1987.

Wiegman, Robyn. *American Anatomies: Theorizing Race and Gender*. Durham, NC: Duke University Press, 1995.

Wimsatt, W. K., Jr., and M. C. Beardsley. "The Intentional Fallacy." *Sewanee Review* 54.3 (1946): 468–88.

Winant, Howard. *The New Politics of Race: Globalism, Difference, Justice*. Minneapolis: University of Minnesota Press, 2004.

Wong, Sau-ling Cynthia. "Denationalization Reconsidered: Asian American Cultural Criticism at a Theoretical Crossroads." *Amerasia Journal* 21.1–2 (1995): 1–27.

———. *Reading Asian American Literature: From Necessity to Extravagance*. Princeton: Princeton University Press, 1993.

Wu, Cynthia. "Revisiting *Blu's Hanging*: A Critique of Queer Transgression in the Lois-Ann Yamanaka Controversy." *Meridians* 10.1 (2010): 32–53.

Wu, Frank, and Nicholson, May. "Have You No Decency? An Analysis of Racial Aspects of Media Coverage on the John Huang Matter." *Asian American Policy Review* 7 (1997): 1–37.

Yamanaka, Lois-Ann. *Blu's Hanging*. New York: Farrar, Straus and Giroux, 1997.

Yang, Caroline. "Indispensable Labor: The Worker as a Category of Critique in *China Men*." *Modern Fiction Studies* 56.1 (2010): 63–89.

Yeh, William. "To Belong or Not to Belong: The Liminality of John Okada's *No-No Boy*." *Amerasia Journal* 19.1 (1993): 121–33.

Zhao, Xiaojian. *Remaking Chinese America: Immigration, Family, and Community, 1940–1965*. New Brunswick, NJ: Rutgers University Press, 2002.

Zhou, Xiaojing, and Samina Najmi, eds. *Form and Transformation in Asian American Literature*. Seattle: University of Washington Press, 2005.

Index

aesthetics, 2–6, 23, 65–66, 156, 166, 175n3; in *Aiiieeeee!*, 171; Asian American, 21, 63, 68, 69; in *Blu's Hanging* award controversy, 100–103, 126, 188n8; in *No-No Boy*, 34–38

Ahmed, Sara, 48

Aiiieeeee! An Anthology of Asian American Writers (ed. Chin, et al.), 4, 19, 33, 37, 165, 171–73; preface of, 23–32; repetition in, 26–28

allegory, 20, 134–35, 139, 140, 153, 160, 192n20, 193n25; as allegoresis, 131, 194n30; in *China Men*, 78; as deconstruction, 149; in *Native Speaker*, 22, 130–31, 133, 137, 147, 149–53, 155; in Puttenham, 135, 137, 193n23

antanaclasis, 5, 29, 130. *See also* Rebound

apophasis, 5, 20–21, 69, 74–75, 90, 98, 105, 130; in *China Men*, 70–72, 76, 84, 86, 88, 91, 93, 98–99, 163, 165

Asian American literature: and aesthetics, 166; classical rhetorical tropes in, 5–6, 13; critical tendencies in study of, 2, 12, 18,

33, 35; deconstructive tendencies of, 16–17; figurative behavior of, 14, 19, 140, 173; racial concerns of, 3, 17; redefining, 68–69, 143, 146, 161–63, 168; referential aberration in, 7–8; reterritorializing, 10–11, 41; and social change, 165

Asian American studies, 3, 8, 26, 35, 73, 107, 161–62, 164, 177nn31,32; Association for, 1, 100–101

Asian Donorgate, 128–29, 148, 192n1. *See also* Chang, Michael

Asiatic racial form, 133, 152, 154

Austin, J. L., 40, 89, 91, 151

author: absence of, 68, 97–99, 146–47; agency of, 70, 162, 166; death of, 163–64, 167–68, 185n6; deconstruction of, 43, 46; intentions of, 64–65; limitations of, 13, 114, 161; race-identified, 4, 12, 69; racialized anxiety of, 55–56

Barthes, Roland, 163, 166, 185n6

Bender, John and David Wellbery, 11, 176n20

Blu's Hanging (Yamanaka), 2, 19, 21, 112; award controversy, 1, 18,

About the Author

Elda E. Tsou is Associate Professor of English at St. John's University in New York.

Teresa Williams-León and Cynthia Nakashima, eds., *The Sum of Our Parts: Mixed-Heritage Asian Americans*

Tung Pok Chin with Winifred C. Chin, *Paper Son: One Man's Story*

Amy Ling, ed., *Yellow Light: The Flowering of Asian American Arts*

Rick Bonus, *Locating Filipino Americans: Ethnicity and the Cultural Politics of Space*

Darrell Y. Hamamoto and Sandra Liu, eds., *Countervisions: Asian American Film Criticism*

Martin F. Manalansan IV, ed., *Cultural Compass: Ethnographic Explorations of Asian America*

Ko-lin Chin, *Smuggled Chinese: Clandestine Immigration to the United States*

Evelyn Hu-DeHart, ed., *Across the Pacific: Asian Americans and Globalization*

Soo-Young Chin, *Doing What Had to Be Done: The Life Narrative of Dora Yum Kim*

Robert G. Lee, *Orientals: Asian Americans in Popular Culture*

David L. Eng and Alice Y. Hom, eds., *Q & A: Queer in Asian America*

K. Scott Wong and Sucheng Chan, eds., *Claiming America: Constructing Chinese American Identities during the Exclusion Era*

Lavina Dhingra Shankar and Rajini Srikanth, eds., *A Part, Yet Apart: South Asians in Asian America*

Jere Takahashi, *Nisei/Sansei: Shifting Japanese American Identities and Politics*

Velina Hasu Houston, ed., *But Still, Like Air, I'll Rise: New Asian American Plays*

Josephine Lee, *Performing Asian America: Race and Ethnicity on the Contemporary Stage*

Deepika Bahri and Mary Vasudeva, eds., *Between the Lines: South Asians and Postcoloniality*

E. San Juan Jr., *The Philippine Temptation: Dialectics of Philippines–U.S. Literary Relations*

Carlos Bulosan and E. San Juan Jr., eds., *The Cry and the Dedication*

Carlos Bulosan and E. San Juan Jr., eds., *On Becoming Filipino: Selected Writings of Carlos Bulosan*

Vicente L. Rafael, ed., *Discrepant Histories: Translocal Essays on Filipino Cultures*

Yen Le Espiritu, *Filipino American Lives*

Paul Ong, Edna Bonacich, and Lucie Cheng, eds., *The New Asian Immigration in Los Angeles and Global Restructuring*

Chris Friday, *Organizing Asian American Labor: The Pacific Coast Canned-Salmon Industry, 1870–1942*

Sucheng Chan, ed., *Hmong Means Free: Life in Laos and America*

Timothy P. Fong, *The First Suburban Chinatown: The Remaking of Monterey Park, California*

William Wei, *The Asian American Movement*

Yen Le Espiritu, *Asian American Panethnicity*

Velina Hasu Houston, ed., *The Politics of Life*

Renqiu Yu, *To Save China, To Save Ourselves: The Chinese Hand Laundry Alliance of New York*

Shirley Geok-lin Lim and Amy Ling, eds., *Reading the Literatures of Asian America*

Karen Isaksen Leonard, *Making Ethnic Choices: California's Punjabi Mexican Americans*

Gary Y. Okihiro, *Cane Fires: The Anti-Japanese Movement in Hawaii, 1865–1945*

Sucheng Chan, *Entry Denied: Exclusion and the Chinese Community in America, 1882–1943*